Library of
Davidson College

Defoe and
Fictional Time

Defoe and Fictional Time

PAUL K. ALKON

The University of Georgia Press
Athens

Copyright © 1979 by the University of Georgia Press
Athens 30602

All rights reserved

Set in 12 on 14 point Garamond No. 3 type
Printed in the United States of America

Library of Congress Cataloging in Publication Data

Alkon, Paul Kent.
　Defoe and fictional time.
　Includes index.
　1.　Defoe, Daniel, 1661?–1731—Criticism and interpretation.　2.　Time in literature.　I.　Title.
PR3408.T54A5　　　　823'.5　　　　78–6021
　　　　ISBN 0–8203–0548–1

To
ELLEN, KATHERINE, CYNTHIA,
and
MARGARET

This eternal time-question is accordingly, for the novelist, always there and always formidable; always insisting on the *effect* of the great lapse and passage, of the "dark backward and abysm," by the terms of truth, and on the effect of compression, of composition and form, by the terms of literary arrangement. It is really a business to terrify all but stout hearts into abject omission and mutilation, though the terror would indeed be more general were the general consciousness of the difficulty greater.

Henry James,
preface to *Roderick Hudson* (1907)

Contents

	Acknowledgments	ix
	References and Abbreviations	xi
1	Fictional Time and Real Time	1
2	Setting and Chronology	23
3	Time-Consciousness	81
4	The Reader's Memory	105
5	Tempo	168
6	Implications	232
	Notes	257
	Index	271

Acknowledgments

University of Minnesota Faculty Research Grants were helpful to me. So was cooperation from the staff of the Bell Library and the Rare Books Division of Wilson Library at the University of Minnesota. For opportunities to learn something of scientific time-concepts at the Minnesota Chronobiology Laboratory, I am grateful to Franz and Irma Halberg. Parts of chapter one are adapted from my essay "Historical Development of the Concept of Time," published in *Biorhythms and Human Reproduction*, ed. Michel Ferin et al. (New York: John Wiley and Sons, 1974), and appear here with the permission of the publisher. Paula R. Backscheider, O. M. Brack, Jr., Franz Halberg, Oliver F. Sigworth, and Anthony Zahareas invited me to speak about problems of fictional time at academic meetings. It would have been harder to write this book without those occasions. It would have been harder, too, without the chance to exchange ideas at the Indiana meeting of the Comparative East Asian Literature Committee and at conferences of the American Society for Eighteenth-Century Studies. Suggestions which I much appreciate have come from J. Douglas Canfield, Thomas Clayton, Tyna T. Orren, Ronald C. Rosbottom, Sheldon Sacks, Ely Tabachnick, and Howard D. Weinbrot. To Robert Buffington of the University of Georgia Press I owe special thanks for his encouragement of this project. And for assistance with its final stages I am most grateful to Ben Gurion University of the Negev.

References & Abbreviations

RC	Daniel Defoe, *Robinson Crusoe*, ed. J. Donald Crowley (London: Oxford University Press, 1972).
MC	Daniel Defoe, *Memoirs of a Cavalier*, ed. James T. Boulton (London: Oxford University Press, 1972).
CS	Daniel Defoe, *Captain Singleton*, ed. Shiv K. Kumar (London: Oxford University Press, 1973).
SRRC	Daniel Defoe, *Serious Reflections During the Life and Strange Adventures of Robinson Crusoe with his Vision of the Angelic World*, introduction by G. H. Maynadier (Boston: Dana Estes & Co., 1903).
MF	Daniel Defoe, *Moll Flanders*, ed. J. Paul Hunter (New York: Thomas Y. Crowell Co., 1970).
JPY	Daniel Defoe, *A Journal of the Plague Year*, ed. Louis Landa (London: Oxford University Press, 1969).
CJ	Daniel Defoe, *Colonel Jack*, ed. Samuel Holt Monk (London: Oxford University Press, 1970).
R	Daniel Defoe, *Roxana*, ed. Jane Jack (London: Oxford University Press, 1964).
Bailey	Nathan Bailey, *Dictionarium Britannicum* (London, 1730).
Bailey (1736)	Nathan Bailey, *Dictionarium Britannicum*, 2nd ed. (London, 1736).
Johnson	Samuel Johnson, *A Dictionary of the English Language*, 4th ed. (London, 1773).

1
Fictional Time & Real Time

Defoe often mentions time. He makes the reader's hours interesting. He found different ways to organize reading-time and allude to clock-time even in narratives that are similar in theme. *The King of the Pirates, Captain Singleton*, and *A General History of the Pyrates* do not much resemble one another in temporal structure or in their manner of suggesting chronology. Nor do *A Journal of the Plague Year, Due Preparations for the Plague*, and *The Storm*, although they might have been closer in form despite their differences in purpose. Crusoe's account of conversion is similar to Colonel Jack's, but their stories hardly impose the same demands upon the reader's memory or, as a consequence, upon his moral imagination. In *Roxana* Defoe avoids duplicating *Moll Flanders*. Where there are such dissimilar treatments of parallel themes that might have been handled in the same way more easily, I infer different intentions and will argue that the resulting variations in effect are significant. This book is partly designed to show how extensively, and how successfully, Defoe's narratives dealt with time immediately prior to those innovations which are usually taken as the transition to distinctively modern forms of the novel.

Without denying the importance of Richardson and Sterne, I also argue that Defoe is among the early writers whose treatment of time deserves attention as much because it points forward as because it marks the end of an older tradition. There are continuities which extend from Defoe to the twentieth century. And for that reason his narratives are also useful test cases for critical theory. They invite exploration of three issues that are now central to the problem of fictional time: the question of how temporal settings within narratives may be related to the outside world of clock- and calendar-time, the question of how time-concepts shared within a culture may influence expectations about the writing and reading of fiction, and above all the question of how narratives shape the phenomenal time experienced by their readers.

These are my topics, although my subject is Defoe. My discussion is largely confined to him for the sake of doing justice to the range of his experiments, but I suggest applications elsewhere. To pursue every implication, however, is beyond the scope of one book and, for that matter, beyond the reach of present theories of fictional time. The most general purpose of this study, therefore, is to suggest through Defoe's example some ways of extending current theories, especially those aimed at better understanding of temporal settings, memory, and tempo. To show the contexts which focus attention on these topics, and which also make it possible to see Defoe's relevance to them, I want to single out some recent developments in literature and criticism, and then remark how Fielding brought the issue of tempo to prominence in a way not yet entirely explained.

1

Consider first Nabokov's achievement in *Ada.* The temporal location of its world is obscured in ways that prevent readers from easily relating themselves to the time within which its fictional events unfold. From scattered allusions and partial explanations we gradually infer that Van and Ada live on a twin to our earth in a parallel universe where the years almost correspond to our own without being exactly synchronized to them, but where events have taken a happier turn. The cultures of England, France, and prerevolutionary Russia have blended on the North American continent. England had annexed France in 1815. The development of electricity has been forbidden, although amusing substitutes have been permitted. What results is a world reminiscent of our pre–1914 era, with beautiful estates sprinkled over prosperous countrysides. The disasters that characterize our twentieth century are known only through the garbled reports of a few individuals claiming visions of a twin world known to them as Terra. The reports are so filled with horrors that the visionaries are dismissed as lunatics. Finally a shrewd film director garbles the accounts still further in turning them into a science-fiction movie.

Ada thus portrays two times at once: an implausible alternative past *and* a present that might have occurred if some crucial events in our world's history had worked out differently. Nabokov's readers are cut adrift, but not wholly adrift, from familiar time and projected imaginatively into an era that did not, could not, and will not ever exist except in the mind—where, as Augustine was the first to argue persuasively, all times exist for us in any case. Similar experiences have always been available in literature. Mythological pasts like those found in the *Aeneid* and Arthurian legends are still familiar. So, to a lesser degree, are the largely fictive pasts that serve as settings for plays like *King Lear* and *Macbeth*. Also familiar are the dreamlike temporal environments in works like *Pilgrim's Progress* or any fable beginning with some variant of "once upon a time" to signal that the ensuing narrative takes place apart from the time occupied by real people. Other conventional devices such as the presence of supernatural beings serve to remove epics and romances from historical time.

But in such works there is no confusion. The reader knows where he stands with respect to the depicted time: it may be either totally unrelated to that of his own world, as in most fairy tales, fables, and dream visions; or it may be connected to the reader's historical moment as Troy's destruction is linked in the *Aeneid* to the Roman empire of Augustus. Even mythologized history of a more explicit kind, as in *Henry V* or *Richard III*, creates no uncertainty: readers may accept, reject, or debate the versions of real events so presented, but there is no problem deciding which part of historical time is to be compared with that depicted by the writer. So too most eighteenth- and nineteenth-century novels clearly locate their temporal setting with respect to the reader's sense of historical time. Tom Jones encounters soldiers going to fight Prince Charles, thus locating events around 1745.[1] Despite the prophetic distortions of narrative chronology in *Tristram Shandy*, Toby's participation in the siege of Namur puts him in unequivocal relationship to every reader's historical moment. Fabrice experiences his famous confusion as he wanders over the field of Waterloo.

What sets fiction like *Ada* decisively apart from earlier traditions of temporal representation are the extreme difficulties created for any reader who tries to relate the depicted time to his own time. Nabokov avoids conventional means of establishing that relationship while also inducing attempts to locate *Ada*'s action with respect to the sequence of events in the reader's world. By calling Van Veen's planet Antiterra, Nabokov even turns his novel into a temporal mirror-image of our world. *Ada*'s setting is therefore both an alternate past and a puzzling time-reversed reflection of the present in which imaginary poets like John Shade are real and real authors like Martin Gardner become imaginary. *Ada*'s first sentence reverses the opening of *Anna Karenina* although the statement is nevertheless attributed to Tolstoy. Within the narration of events leading to Lucinda's suicide toward the end of the novel is the curious observation that she is only five hours old if one reverses the human time-current. By such invitations to consider his Antiterra as a place where time may be running backward, or at least differently from that experienced in our world, Nabokov induces another level of temporal uncertainty. Actions are thus placed in a kind of temporal limbo which is neither affiliated to historical time in any precisely definable way, nor altogether consistent, nor yet entirely removed to the fabulous regions of once upon a time which never induce anyone to wonder about calendric relationships between the depicted time and that occupied by themselves. These inconsistencies of temporal setting and chronology support complex artistic ends.[2]

Works like *Ada* do not resort to unstable temporal settings primarily to show us what may happen if, what might have happened if, or what should or should not happen, although such intentions may be achieved as subordinate goals. Instead, by nagging at us to locate their action temporally without allowing us to do so, such works create heightened awareness of our situation in time by wrenching us uncomfortably away from the usual possibilities of getting our temporal bearings. They make us think about where (and how) we are located in time. To the categories of past, present, and future first rendered suspect by Augustine's argument that in fact we only experience a present of things past, a present of things present, and a present of things future, recent developments in fiction have added another category which is neither past, present, nor future; nor is it even a realm of timelessness like that envisioned in traditional concepts of eternity or like that embodied in fables set in an order of mythic time. The new modes of unlocatable time are distantly related to those categories of fictional time designed, as Sir Philip Sidney remarked, to show what may be or should be. Only science fiction and similar modes of satiric fantasy are still defined by their attempts to serve these purposes. Disorientation in time has supplanted location in past, future, or mythic time as well as displacement in space as a technique for inviting attention to our own situation.

Swift's invitation to consider modern society took the form of keeping Gulliver in the eighteenth century but sending him to imaginary places. Orwell locates Winston Smith in 1984. The rising popularity of time-travel and future-located stories is also reflected in such transitional figures as Bellamy, Wells, and Huxley. But the very specificity of fiction like *Nineteen Eighty-Four* makes it akin to *Gulliver's Travels*. Readers can easily follow the chronology of events within Orwell's narrative, and they can measure their temporal distance from Oceania as a first step to thinking about their ethical distance from it. The first sentence focuses on Winston Smith during a bright cold day in April as the clocks are striking thirteen. As calendar years go by for the book and its readers, 1984 will approach, arrive, and recede into the past. Clock-time, with its fixed categories of past, present, and future, is still the most conspicuous temporal dimension. The author of *Nineteen Eighty-Four* does not seek for its satiric purposes the dislocations of time that are a distinctive feature of more recent works whose temporal settings and chronology remain intentionally uncertain, or paradoxical.

Alain Robbe-Grillet's novels are among the most extreme examples of this tendency. They also show what can be achieved by sustained use of various techniques that disorder the reader's subjective time-sense. *In The Labyrinth*, for example, refers to hours, days, minutes, and weeks within a context which challenges readers to locate events in time while also denying them the information essential for doing so. At the outset Robbe-Grillet establishes uncertainty about the historical setting while nevertheless insisting that readers are to relate its events nonallegorically to their own lives: "This narrative is not a true account, but fiction. It describes a reality not necessarily the same as the one the reader has experienced: for example, in the French army, infantrymen do not wear their serial numbers on their coat collars. Similarly, the recent history of Western Europe has not recorded an important battle at Reichenfels or in the vicinity. Yet the reality in question . . . is subject to no allegorical interpretation. The reader is therefore requested to see in it only objects, actions, words, and events which are described, without attempting to give them either more or less meaning than in his own life, or his own death."[3] Recurring conversations between a boy and a lost soldier trying to deliver a package after the battle of Reichenfels seem very much alike, because whenever these characters meet similar dialogue takes place. Dates are not provided. The temporal settings for the conversations are so vague—during the day, at night, when it is snowing, when it is not snowing—that, just as when minutes, hours, and days are mentioned, the only purpose served by the text's time-signals is to arouse insatiable temporal curiosity.

It is never possible to work out a satisfactory ordering of episodes with respect to one another within the chronology of a coherent plot because Robbe-Grillet omits that dimension of fictional time. He thereby reduces the reader's time-frame to one order of real time: the clock-time and phenomenal time of his encounter with the book. Yet without the stable reference-points usually provided by a fictional chronology of relationships along the time-line of a story whose events are sequential even if the order of their narration is not, readers cannot very well keep in mind even the sequence of narrated episodes as they have been experienced in clock-time from the moment of starting the first sentence to the moment of finishing the last page. Memory is short-circuited by the piling up of similar incidents and the suppression of temporal clues.

Robbe-Grillet's novel affects its reader's time-perception by impeding the formation of memories. They cannot be altogether abolished, but the reader nonetheless finds himself in a labyrinth as he loses the ability to remember exactly where he has been, and consequently cannot say, even during subsequent readings, just where, at any particular moment, while reading any particular sentence, he is going next. For him time is abolished insofar as it no longer seems a framework within which events—in his case the reading of narrated episodes—flow measurably from one to another. As perceived distinctions between past and present moments of reading-time collapse, however, the impulse to make such distinctions remains. Habit and, arguably, the psychological necessity for temporal orientation establish expectations which impel readers to keep searching for some way out of their confusion. So does prior experience of more conventional novels. From this search for temporal order (even where it does not exist) come a variety of pleasures appealing to the twentieth-century mentality. Much recent fiction provides similar though less extreme evidence of the advantages of unstable temporal settings. Alteration of the reader's phenomenal time often replaces imitation of events in some real or fictional time as a primary aesthetic intention.

2

Criticism should account for the role of those temporal structures that narratives call into being within the reader's mind. Attention to the phenomenology of reading has clarified distinctions between texts and their realization.[4] Critical focus has shifted from analyzing textual patterns to recording experiential structures. There has been more awareness that such structures may differ significantly from narrative sequence on the printed pages just as narrative sequence may, and indeed usually does, vary from the chronological order of the events being narrated.[5] There nevertheless remains a methodological dispute between what might be called the spatial and the temporal modes of criticism. Those who describe patterns visible only after a book has been completed and can be regarded as a whole "object" (as if it were available in space for contemplation like a painting) are at odds with critics who charge that procedure with falsifying the experience which unfolds during reading-time. They insist that criticism must describe the moment-by-moment dynamics of each encounter with a text. This view encourages a valuable approach to the temporal structures of literature, although at risk of tipping the balance too much against concern with those memories that accumulate during as well as after reading. And such memories, in the case of Defoe or any writer, are a crucial aspect of form.

Roman Ingarden's discussion of the role of memory in apprehending literary works remains the best consideration of this neglected issue.[6] For one thing Ingarden stresses the distinction between first reading of any text, recollections of it afterward, and subsequent readings during which memories of the entire text (that is to say, of the narrative future) will contribute to the cognition of each part within its unfolding narrative sequence. He argues that "the first reading has the advantage over all following readings that it decides in large measure whether one will succeed in a correct apprehension of the work at all" (p. 145). He also dismisses as an illusion "the opinion that it is better or easier to apprehend a work from all sides after the reading" (p. 143). But Ingarden nevertheless insists that criticism will be inadequate if it avoids consideration of what happens during all three phases: the initial reading, the remembrance afterward, and the return to the text. He recognizes that "the aspect of the work which we have, or at least can have, after finishing our reading plays for various reasons an important role for the cognition of the work, not merely because we have already become acquainted with all parts of the work in the direct experience of reading, but also because we now have within our field of experience the definitive ordering of the objects portrayed in the work and of the sequence of parts in the mode of portrayal" (p. 144). Memory is thus given its proper status as an aspect of cognition.

In this theory remembering does not have to be distinguished in all cases from perceiving. Looking back at a text can thus be accepted as a valid part of any complete reading, although without downgrading prior stages of the process. It follows from Ingarden's position, and others like it which place equal stress on memory as cognition, that to explain the ending of any book adequately involves far more than merely describing closed, open-ended, or other plot structures. The final shape of memories induced by a text would have to be accepted as one of its formal attributes.

So too, according to Ingarden, would those memories of previous passages which affect response to subsequent passages while they are being read, whether for the first time or upon rereading a text with memories of its outcome. He distinguishes between recollections which are so general as to be almost "purely intuitive apprehension" on the one hand, and, at the opposite extreme, those localized recollections of particular episodes or even particular sentences verbatim (p. 398). The difference, which psychology has not yet fully clarified, is between largely unconscious awareness of any prior experience and specific conscious recollection of it. The difference is between what we "know" in the sense of traces from prior experience which determine some aspect of response to later events without, however, evoking awareness of the connection, and fully conscious juxtaposition of a past moment with a present one so that both are in mind simultaneously.

Ingarden understood, moreover, that "the literary work can be brought to appearance only in a multiplicity of successive aspects which flow into one another and cannot be apprehended all at once, in a single act" (p. 145). One consequence (whose implication for practical criticism I shall discuss in chapter 4) is that Joseph Frank's useful concept *spatial form* requires (as he too recognized) modification even though some texts do invite apprehension all at once. And while that is in fact seldom possible, it remains true that a passage may enforce conscious recollection of previous parts of the text to produce a kind of doubling in which the later words are accompanied in the reader's mind either by earlier phrases or by more general but conscious awareness of previous episodes. What results is a significant degree of experiential simultaneity for readers although the text itself, and usually the ordering of its episodes in the chronology of fictional time, will remain sequential. This phenomenon is to some extent understood in principle, but seldom attended to sufficiently in critical practice, and certainly not often enough remarked by Defoe's critics.

Ingarden also notes that to explain how readers retain passages either in general outline or in the form of specific memories, it is necessary to account for the fact that "in moving along with the new phases of the work which are revealing themselves to us, we 'see' previous parts of the work under constantly new phenomena of temporal perspective, usually in a selection which is at least partly determined by the content of the part of the work we are just reading" (p. 142). As corollary to this altering perception of previous passages, memories of them may also change. Indeed the reshaping of memories should be regarded as a major part of the mental mechanism by which prior events are seen differently as time passes. Foreshortening is always at work when reading just as it is in other activities when things drop out of mind, leaving a compressed recollection of events focusing on their highlights at the expense of details which in retrospect seem less significant. Sometimes, however, there may be expansion as partial memories lead to more nearly complete recall. And events may be rearranged to acquire different juxtapositions within the retrospect of memory than they had in the linear chronology of clock-time—whether real or imagined.

Sterne's application of this fact of mental life as a narrative principle is well understood. Defoe's application of the phenomenon to *A Journal of the Plague Year* is not sufficiently appreciated. Even for *Tristram Shandy*, however, there has not been much attention to the ways in which its reader's experiential sequences may and often must diverge from even the narrative sequence of episodes and ideas on the printed pages. These divergences which Sterne induces between Tristram's mental leaps and those which his readers must be taking would have to be accounted for in any complete formal description of *Tristram Shandy:* no easy task, although necessary. In this book I take up similar problems in Defoe to suggest approaches to this aspect of temporal structure.

On the related question of memory gaps left after completion of a work, Ingarden's view is more problematic. He remarks that upon reading a text through to its end it is necessary, for cognition of it as an aesthetic object, to perform those "analytical and synthetic acts of apprehension, on which a deeper knowledge of the work depends." This is to be done by (among other things) going back to fill in blank spots: "It is necessary to return again and again to the results of the reading, especially when some details of the work are forgotten or were never clearly apprehended in the first reading" (p. 144). Ingarden explains that it is only the cognitive process which takes place after reading that allows us to perceive such gaps, and which therefore refers us back to the text: "Without this return to the work and without rereading it, one cannot progress in the effort to understand the work in its own peculiar construction and in its specific details and to apprehend it synthetically" (pp. 144–45). Insofar as this only recommends rereading together with attention to one's developing response in order to arrive at reconstruction for critical purposes of the actual "results of the reading," there cannot be much ground for disagreement.

Most criticism, including much of what follows in this book, depends upon such reconstruction. To some extent Ingarden is mainly urging what anyone concerned with describing the phenomenology of reading must in any case do. Insofar as Ingarden's approach or any similar one imposes pressure for total recall of textual details as the precondition for correct apprehension of the work, however, it may lead to falsification of the very responses which are the object of synthetic construction or analytic retrieval. And usually in critical practice if not theory, there does appear even among those not concerned with phenomenology an assumption like Ingarden's that such total recall is desirable. It may even seem more necessary and it may be more often pursued where it is unobtainable during an ordinary reading or rereading. But this is to discount the possibility that texts may achieve their proper effects by sometimes impeding as well as creating memories of themselves. I also use Defoe's example to explore the role of those memory gaps which should be left alone and regarded as a valid part of a narrative's temporal structure.

Another consequence of remembering was suggested by Ingarden when he noted that surveying a work after reading it, although necessary, always converts the dynamics of its temporal structure (as experienced while reading) into the stasis of retrospect. What gets lost is tempo. Changes of tempo are especially hard to recapture. Of tempo itself, and the role of its changes or their causes, however, Ingarden says little. Nor has this issue been so much considered as the related matters pointed to by Ingarden and others concerned with the phenomenology of reading. Mendilow's four pages on tempo are still the best available theoretical treatment of that topic.[7] He argues that one of the ways in which any novelist displays his greatest skill is in variations of speed. But except for comments on the uses of acceleration to keep readers moving along, and comments on adjustments in the scale of narration like those which Fielding makes to show what is important in *Tom Jones*, and like those which Richardson makes to slow down *Clarissa*, neither Mendilow nor his successors have very often dealt with this issue at the level of practical criticism. An exception, pointing, I hope, to future trends, is J. Paul Hunter's discussion of motion and pause in *Joseph Andrews* and *Tom Jones*.[8] Certainly tempo—and even, I shall argue, the tempo of remembering—should claim greater attention as much on historical as on theoretical grounds.

3

Fielding associated variation of tempo with his initiation of a new province of writing. It is a puzzling claim. But there is no mistaking the importance given to the question of pace when Fielding discusses it early in *Tom Jones*. At the start of book 2 readers are invited to consider the difference between Fielding's method and that of "the painful and voluminous Historian" (no one is named, but Richardson is usually understood as well as Cibber) whose narratives resemble newspapers with a fixed number of pages that must be filled whether or not there is anything really newsworthy to report. Such historians think themselves "obliged to keep even Pace with Time" and travel "as slowly through Centuries of monkish Dulness" as through busier periods. Fielding cautions his reader "not to be surprized, if . . . he shall find some Chapters very short, and others altogether as long; some that contain only the Time of a single Day, and others that comprise Years; in a Word, if my History sometimes seems to stand still, and sometimes to fly."[9] But who would have been surprised?

There is little novelty in skipping over periods when nothing much happened in favor of concentrating narrative attention on crucial years, months, or single days. Defoe did that. So did his predecessors, with varying success. Even Richardson's journalistic technique of writing to so many moments assumes selection of what in *Pamela* and *Clarissa* can hardly be dismissed as an insignificant year. Richardson also concentrates on important days to the exclusion of "empty" intervals: Clarissa's year is not told in 365 letters, much less in letters giving equal space to each day of her last year. Pamela's diary, although divided into entries that follow days of the week, does not give the same space to each day: some are more important than others, and Richardson varies his speed accordingly as measured by the ratio of pages, and thus reading-time, to narrated time.

It is, nevertheless, in the sentence after preparing readers for whatever surprise there might be in discovering variations of chapter length and scope that Fielding justifies his method in *Tom Jones* by insisting that he is "in reality, the Founder of a new Province of Writing," and therefore "at liberty to make what Laws" he pleases therein. Critics have accepted this claim on various grounds without dwelling on its placement as a non sequitur in the essay introducing book 2 of *Tom Jones*. Variation of tempo away from a monotonous "even pace" was not Fielding's distinctive innovation, however justified he was in drawing attention to his skillful control of pace. Yet Fielding was not setting up a straw man; nor was he being ironic to no purpose. Among the strategies that *are* new in *Tom Jones* is the way its readers are alerted by Fielding's claim and by other devices to the role of reading-time as an index of importance, and thus made aware that the duration of reading is a significant dimension of the encounter with any book.

Although Defoe, Richardson, and even Boswell (as he adapted novelistic techniques to his new mode of biography later in the century) controlled the duration of reading for similar purposes, their readers were not invited to stand back and take conscious note of correspondences between how time passes while reading, and how it passed during the narrated events. Quite the contrary. The less conscious attention to the duration of *A Journal of the Plague Year*, *Clarissa*, and *The Life of Samuel Johnson*, for example, the better. During an ordinary reading even the effects which result from protraction of reading-time are not enhanced by noting (as I or any critic must) all the machinery that is at work. But only by vastly increasing the usual ratio of reading-time to read-about time, and thus decelerating objective as well as subjective pace could Richardson have achieved in *Clarissa* so powerful a representation of how personal time seems to flow. Boswell, as I have shown elsewhere, made that ratio very high for related purposes, thereby enhancing the *Life*'s verisimilitude.[10] He avoided discussion of this achievement, however. And in the preface and postscript to *Clarissa* Richardson is defensive about its length, even trying so far as possible to deflect attention from that essential aspect of its mimetic power. He wanted to create the illusion of involvement in Clarissa's daily existence, just as Boswell tried by related means to bring readers close to Johnson. These experiments in the manipulation of pace to enhance representational power, like those by Defoe which I shall discuss, were not announced as artistry to be admired or otherwise reckoned with consciously by readers.

Fielding, however, insists upon the importance of reading-time from the outset of *Tom Jones*. In the introduction to book 1 he provides comic assurance that "our Reader may be rendered desirous to read on for ever." This invites attention to the fact that *Tom Jones* will certainly take a long time to get through. Its table of contents implicitly makes the point soon rendered explicit by Fielding's discussion of tempo at the beginning of book 2. After allusions to books as containers of "Scenes" and "memorable Transactions," headings for each book throughout the table of contents switch to descriptions that stress the varying amounts of time that will be dealt with: "Containing the Time of a Year.... Containing a Portion of Time, somewhat longer than Half a Year.... Containing about three Weeks," and so on through the final book "Containing about Six Days." Readers are thus alerted to reading-time as the "container" of narrated time.

Fictional Time & Real Time

Fielding's statement that *Tom Jones* has been "some Thousands of Hours in the composing" is, among other things, a reminder that it cannot be read quickly, although it might take fewer hours to read than were necessary for its writing (p. 435). Fielding thus places value on both the author's and the reader's investment of time. "A Farewel to the Reader" at the start of book 18 announces arrival of readers and author "at the last Stage of our long Journey." This metaphor is then elaborated in a way that is not altogether metaphoric: "As we have therefore travelled together through so many Pages, let us behave to one another like Fellow-Travellers in a Stage-Coach, who have passed several Days in the Company of each other" (p. 706). This conceit is another reminder that readers have indeed been in company with *Tom Jones* for "several Days" of their time—real time.

Together with such explicit references to reading-time, Fielding's other editorial reflections and comments on the unfolding story also maintain awareness of the reader's encounter with the book as well as with its narrated events. This double focus is sustained until the chapters after Fielding's "Farewell," when he minimizes authorial comment. Even then, however, chapter headings invite awareness of how rapidly the book is coming to its end: "Continuation of the History.... Farther Continuation.... A further Continuation.... Wherein the History begins to draw towards a Conclusion.... The History draws nearer to a Conclusion.... Approaching still nearer to the End.... In which the History is concluded." *Tom Jones* thus sustains attention to the progress of reading-time as well as narrated time. By doing so, Fielding played a role in the articulation of modern time-consciousness.

Fielding did not go as far as Sterne. Recent criticism has

clarified not only Sterne's mastery of time as an explicit theme but his achievement in developing those structures best described as variations of spatial form. A partial grammar of spatial forms, at least as they evolved in the eighteenth century, might be outlined by recollecting what Sterne does in *Tristram Shandy:* (1) narrative sequence determined by association and other nonchronological orderings takes precedence over those meanings inherent in the linear chains of causation displayed by the arrangement of narrated events in calendar time; (2) readers are constantly invited to make some effort at apprehending many parts of the book at once; (3) largely owing to these structures, characters unequivocally located in calendar time are nevertheless also detached from their connections with the dates of battles and births to achieve the timeless existence of those who reside in the ideal world of myth; (4) the resulting myth subsumes and takes its departure from the world of history instead of ignoring it altogether or applying to it only allegorically; (5) attention is directed to the book as object and to reading-time as such; and (6) *Tristram Shandy* is therefore among those novels which provide a temporal experience claiming validity in its own right instead of by virtue of being a mirror to some other time.

Seen from this perspective, Fielding's most interesting innovation in the fictional treatment of time is not an attempt to avoid inconsistencies by recourse to an almanac.[11] Nor can Defoe's chronologies be examined solely with an eye to their consistency and consequent effects on verisimilitude. Like *Tristram Shandy*, but to a lesser extent, *Tom Jones* points to the ascendancy of spatial forms. Wayne Booth implies as much by remarking that "in *Tom Jones*, the 'plot' of our relationship with Fielding-as-narrator has no similarity to the story of Tom. There is no complication, not even any sequence except for the gradually increasing familiarity and intimacy leading to farewell."[12] No sequence that matters much as sequence, that is. All writing displays sequence that generates some meaning.[13] For the relationship of readers to Fielding as narrator, however, sequence —and consequently the order of reading-time—is not paramount. But the story of Tom and Sophia derives part of its meaning from the linear structures of both narrated time and the reader's order of involvement with narrated events. Fielding accordingly achieves a balance of plot and plotless revelation of character: of temporal and spatial forms.

The implications of that balance for *Tom Jones* must be pursued elsewhere. I mention it at the outset of this study together with a few key issues in twentieth-century literature and criticism to make explicit the vantage-points which allow sharper definition of Defoe's narrative techniques and their historical significance. The entire context which now invites reconsideration of Defoe can only be seen here in a note listing many of the surveys of recent work on time in philosophy, psychology, physics, and biology as well as literature and the performing arts.[14] One result of such interdisciplinary study as this is appreciation of continuities between our own time-consciousness and that of earlier writers. Attention to Sterne is only the most conspicuous example. Recent investigations of Defoe have suggested that his fiction too has affinities to twentieth- as well as eighteenth-century views of how the self acquires identity and exists through time.[15]

In stressing throughout this book the many additional ways in which Defoe's handling of fictional time links him with the newer provinces of writing established by Richardson, Fielding, and their successors, I do not mean to deny Defoe's roots in those earlier traditions that have been more often studied and to which he has been persuasively connected by many critics during the past few decades. I take their studies for granted as providing another necessary perspective on Defoe by placing him into relationship with his own past and present. We are also separated from him by some crucial discontinuities. Indeed it is only by turning next to eighteenth-century contexts that I can suggest how Defoe came to foreshadow those writers who use temporal settings and chronology to convey meaning instead of as devices for enhancing verisimilitude.

2
Setting & Chronology

Problems of intention and meaning arise almost equally when Defoe mentions time and when he avoids allusions to it that we might expect. Part of the difficulty is that we do not always know what to expect. Take the small but typical question of why Captain Singleton does not fly the Jolly Roger. Defoe's own work is sufficiently varied to provide a context within which to start defining the interpretive issues involved in this and similar omissions that seem strange. The 1728 edition of *A General History of the Pyrates*, for example, contains a letter telling how the *Greyhound* was captured in 1716 by John Martel, who flew one flag "in Which was the Figure of a Man, with a Sword in his Hand, and an Hour-Glass before him, with a Death's Head and Bones." In two other flags "were only the Head and Cross Bones."[1] Martel's main battle flag is a modified Jolly Roger. Nobody knows where the term came from, although it first meant a flag showing a skeleton with an hourglass in one hand—and a lance pointing to a heart beneath which there were three drops of blood in the other. Nor is it known when Defoe or his readers came to expect that pirates would fly some form of the Jolly Roger. The first recorded use of the black flag was in 1700 when during a battle off Santiago the French pirate Emmanuel Wynne flew "a sable ensign with cross-bones, a death's head, and an hourglass." In 1703 John Quelch was reported off Brazil flying the "old Roger," described as "an anatomy with an hourglass in one hand and a dart in the heart with three drops of blood proceeding from it in the other."[2]

The particular sources of this emblem are obscure, although clear enough in general. The hourglass is borrowed from traditional pictures of Time and put into the hands of the skeleton which represents Death. Emblematic conflation of Time and Death was not invented by pirates. Some plague broadsides show a skeleton brandishing a large arrow in one hand while holding an hourglass in the other, with skulls and crossbones appearing around the margins. Similar decorations were used on tombstones and funeral invitations. European armies sometimes adopted the skull and crossbones as a uniform insignia. More relevant than questions of origin, however, is the fact that pirates and authors had several options when they chose flags. A black ensign displaying only a skull with crossbones was the eventual favorite. Hollywood has ratified that choice so fully that other possibilities are often forgotten. But there were several, differing mainly in the extent to which they allude to time.

The skull with crossbones, the plain black flag, and the red flag signifying "no quarter" all threaten death, and thus imply that time is running out for any ship that will not surrender. An hourglass, however, makes explicit the allusion to time. The purpose of all pirate flags was to avoid battle, for which most pirates showed little inclination, by frightening opponents. The *Greyhound*'s surrender measures the success of Martel's choice. Bartholomew Roberts exploited similar associations of time with death during his most famous exploit, as recorded by Defoe in 1724: "They came to *Whydah* with a St. George's Ensign, a black

Silk Flag flying at their Mizen-Peek, and a Jack and Pendant of the same: The Flag had a Death's Head on it, with an Hour-Glass in one Hand, and cross Bones in the other, a Dart by it, and underneath a Heart dropping three Drops of Blood.—The Jack had a Man pourtray'd in it, with a flaming Sword in his Hand, and standing on two Skulls, subscribed A.B.H. and A.M.H. *i.e.*, a Barbadian's and a Martinican's Head."[3] The importance of these flags in Defoe's text is highlighted by their illustration in one of three engravings made by Cole for the 1724 edition of the *History of the Pyrates*. The frontispiece to its Dutch translation shows a flag with similar emblems of piracy: a skeleton, an hourglass, and skulls with crossbones.

Defoe makes the choice of a flag figure even more conspicuously in his chapter on the fictional Captain Misson, whose story of establishing a utopian society is told as though it were true in the 1728 volume of *A General History of the Pyrates*. After Misson is elected captain, his crew reject the black flag of piracy in favor of "*a white Ensign, with Liberty painted in the Fly, and . . . the Motto*, A Deo a Libertate, *For God and Liberty*, as an Emblem of our Uprightness and Resolution."[4] No skulls, no hourglass. Misson's purpose in choosing this flag is clear, although Defoe's intentions are more complicated because he neither endorses nor altogether repudiates Misson's revolutionary social goals, and is writing as usual under a penname: Captain Charles Johnson. There is no question, however, that Defoe intends readers to notice Misson's flag and decide what it tells about those who fly it.

Nor is there any doubt that by 1724, when he described Bartholomew Roberts's flags, Defoe knew the conventional emblems of piracy. Yet Henry Avery flies no distinctive flag in the account of his adventures written by Defoe and published on December 10, 1719, over Avery's signature, as *The King of the Pirates*. In this trial run for publication of *Captain Singleton* on June 4, 1720, Avery prefers to sail under British colors until his ship is close enough to attack. So, for the most part, does Singleton, although at one encounter he flies a "black Flag or Ancient . . . and the Bloody Flag at the Top-mast Head" (*CS*, p. 216). At sight of these flags Singleton's opponent surrenders. In another encounter, with three ships which he does not want to engage, Singleton first displays an English flag but then "hoisted a black Flag with two cross Daggers in it . . . which let them see what they were to expect" (p. 186). Singleton's black flag tells his purpose so clearly that all three ships sail away without firing a shot. Here too, however, it is not easy to be sure of Defoe's intentions. He has avoided the options of providing Singleton with either the white ensign of liberty or the most savage emblems of piracy. Crossed daggers appear instead of sword and crossbones. There is no skull, no skeleton, no hourglass. In the accounts of real pirates that I have seen, the crossed daggers have no precedent.

Perhaps Defoe wrote *Captain Singleton* before learning as much about pirate flags as he knew four years later. In that case Singleton's flags have only the explicit meaning (understood well enough by his enemies) that he is indeed a pirate. And yet Defoe's avoidance of the skeletons and hourglasses favored by real pirates is entirely in keeping with those other deviations from verisimilitude which lead Manuel Schonhorn to argue that "*Captain Singleton* bears little similarity to those piratical records it was intended to resemble."[5] Or intended not to resemble. Far from imitating his sources as closely as possible, Defoe modified them to create his portrait of Singleton.

The major departures from true narratives like those of Esquemelin and Dampier are avoidance of vividly depicted physical violence; avoidance of ritual actions centered around observance at sea of Christmas, New Year's, and other holidays composing the religious and social calendar; avoidance of allusions to wars and other political events marking the flow of historical time; and avoidance of frequent references to specific dates: "The sources and analogues behind *Captain Singleton* are anchored in time; jottings and log entries are given conscientiously, sometimes with precise daily notations." Whatever Defoe's intentions, Schonhorn rightly concludes that "the peculiar nature of Defoe's omissions and modifications would seem to make *Captain Singleton* an unfaithful reflection of the actualities of ocean life."[6] Even the real pirates took more note of passing time, and men like Quelch, Wynne, Martel and Roberts were certainly quicker than Singleton (or Defoe) to adapt to their purposes the traditional emblems of death and time.

It is nevertheless hard to credit Quelch either with greater knowledge of those familiar traditions than Defoe or with more imagination. Nor can the possibility be excluded that Defoe knew about every variety of pirate flag while writing *Captain Singleton*. It is thus tempting to suppose that although Singleton's flags do not call attention to themselves as Misson's white flag does, they are designed to contribute some share to the reader's impression of Singleton as a man at once less bloodthirsty than many pirates and yet disinclined to keep in sight any conventional *memento mori*, no matter how twisted away from its religious meanings. But until more evidence is at hand, this suggestion only deserves mention by way of establishing one end of a spectrum ranging from barely possible meanings through more probable meanings to, at the other end of the spectrum, unmistakable meanings created by Defoe's allusions—or avoidance of allusions—to time. It is the latter on which of course I will concentrate. Some of Defoe's most clearly intended meanings, however, like those of most other novelists worth reading, operate at levels of response less obtrusive in the reader's consciousness than those considerations invited by Misson's choice of a flag. I shall argue that many, though far from all, of Defoe's temporal allusions do their work most effectively at the periphery of the reader's awareness even though their effects are available to introspection and analysis for purposes of literary criticism.

1

There is no mistaking Defoe's symbolism, although it is neither easy nor necessary for appreciation of it to pin down *all* the meanings that echo in the passage where Robinson Crusoe tells of making a calendar in the shape of a cross: "It came into my Thoughts, that I should lose my Reckoning of Time . . . and should even forget the Sabbath Days from the working Days; but to prevent this I cut it with my Knife upon a large Post, in Capital Letters, and making it into a great Cross I set it up on the Shore where I first landed, viz. *I came on Shore here on the 30th of* Sept. 1659. Upon the Sides of this square Post I cut every Day a Notch with my Knife, and every seventh Notch was as long again as the rest, and every first Day of the Month as long again as that long one, and thus I kept my Kalander, or weekly, monthly, and yearly reckoning of Time" (p. 64). The connotations of reckoning his time on a cross underscore the spiritual significance of Crusoe's years on the island. The meaning of this passage is altogether different from the one in which Woodes Rogers tells how Alexander Selkirk "diverted himself sometimes by cutting his Name on the Trees, and the Time of his being left and Continuance there."[7] This tells nothing beyond the facts it reports.

Nor does the sentence from *The King of the Pirates* where Avery describes a message left for colleagues who have missed a rendezvous:

At parting we set up a post with this inscription, done on a plate of lead, with our names upon the lead, and these words:—
"*Gone to Madagascar, December 10, 1692;*"
(being in that latitude the longest day in the year;) and I doubt not but the post may stand there still.

Twenty pages later Avery mentions the discovery of "the post or cross erected by us."[8] Avery (or Defoe) seems unsure whether it was a post or a cross. But in *The King of the Pirates* it does not matter so far as readers are concerned. There is no ambiguity in Defoe's account of a similar incident in *Captain Singleton*: "Captain *Wilmot* . . . went away for the Rendezvous before us, and arrived there the Middle of *December*; but not liking the Port, he left a great Cross on Shore, with Directions written on a Plate of Lead fixt to it, for us to come after him" (*CS*, pp. 176–77). Rather than a precise date as in the passage from *The King of the Pirates*, there is only a reference to the middle of December of an unspecified year. There is no mention of how long the days are at that time in those waters. Wilmot's message is nailed to a cross not a post. The secular time told by months, years, and hours of daylight is less conspicuous than the cross which alludes to sacred time, or at least *may* do so in a way that cannot be achieved by Avery's description of a post, or the account of Selkirk cutting his name and some dates on the trees.

If the religious connotations of Wilmot's "great Cross" are in any way noticed by readers, the passage becomes an implicit comment on the spiritual poverty of men who are wasting their time on earth and have no better use for a cross than as a message post for pirates. This implicit meaning is suggested—although not made necessary—by an earlier episode in which Singleton's group does show some religious awareness: "our Artist, of whom I have spoken so often, set up a great Cross of Wood on the Hill . . . with these Words, but in the *Portuguese* Language, *Point Desperation. Jesus have Mercy!*" (p. 33). Whether this passage transforms the later one into a symbolic statement depends to some extent on the reader's memory.

By such phrases as "of whom I have spoken so often" the text encourages readers to remember (and apply) what they have read. If, when doing so, the first "great Cross" with its prayer is contrasted with the next "great Cross" giving only sailing directions, the comparison will suggest a falling off from what was at least a rudimentary spiritual impulse. That suggestion, however, only partly depends on the reader's strength of memory and the novel's encouragements to remember its text. Here again I do not wish to press a symbolic view of Wilmot's "great Cross" so much as to use that possibility to illustrate the consequences for my topic of yet another interpretive issue that cannot be avoided when dealing with texts like Defoe's—or Hemingway's, or Chaucer's—that allow but do not always compel a symbolic view of details. The account of Wilmot's message may certainly be regarded most easily as nothing more than one of

Setting & Chronology 31

those descriptions adding to *Captain Singleton*'s verisimilitude.

The question of Defoe's "realism" is being reconsidered.[9] To say that Wilmot's "great Cross," along with the vague specification "arrived there the Middle of *December*," conveys the impression of something that "really" happened is correct. The date, although imprecise when compared to that given in *The King of the Pirates*, is nevertheless more specific than (say) "arrived late in the year." There is no difficulty in visualizing Wilmot's cross or believing that pirates might leave such a message. Compared to *The King of the Pirates*, however, Defoe shifts in *Captain Singleton* from temporal to spatial verisimilitude.

The visual detail of Wilmot's cross stands out more sharply than the date, whereas in the earlier book "December 10, 1692, being in that latitude the longest day in the year" stands out more conspicuously than the meager description of "a post with ... a plate of lead, with our names [how many? what were they?] upon the lead." Avery's post is difficult to envision because nothing is said about its size or color. Its shape is also less determinate than that of a cross. Elsewhere in *The King of the Pirates*, however, there are visually specific scenes. Defoe does not avoid concrete details altogether.

But in *The King of the Pirates* he establishes verisimilitude primarily by sprinkling exact (and consistent) dates throughout the narrative. The reader often encounters such statements as "The wind presenting fair (February 2, 1692–3), we set sail, and ... doubled the Cape the 13th of March and ... made directly to the island of Madagascar, where we arrived the 7th of April." A few paragraphs later Avery explains that "we set sail the 3rd of January 1694, for the Cape of Good Hope."[10] Frequent references of this kind to the year, month and even day of events sustain plausibility: whatever has a date seems to have happened.

Spatial particulars are explicitly omitted, however, on the fictive grounds given by Avery, Defoe's narrator: "In things so modern, it is no way convenient to write to you particular circumstances and names of person, ships, or places, because those things, being in themselves criminal, may be called up in question in a judicial way; and therefore I warn the reader to observe that not only all the names are omitted, but even the scene of action in this criminal part is not laid exactly as things were acted, lest I should give justice a clue to unravel my story by, which nobody will blame me for avoiding."[11] After this remark even the absence of "particular circumstances" lends an air of truth to a narrative whose vagueness or occasional inaccuracies may be viewed as projections of Avery's dread of the law.

Because Singleton writes his story while living disguised to avoid capture in England after his retirement, he might have made similar excuses. But he does not. There is only a hint that some of his crimes have been omitted altogether from the narration: "Not in *England* only, but in *France* and *Spain*, Accounts have been made publick of our Adventures, and many Stories told how we murthered the People in cold Blood, tying them Back to Back, and throwing them into the Sea; one Half of which however was not true, tho' more was done than it is fit to speak of here" (p. 144). Singleton implies that whatever *is* included will be accurately described. Defoe thus warns readers against taking Singleton's narrative as the entire truth upon which to form their moral judgment of him: half the charges that he prefers not to discuss are true. Unlike Avery, however, Singleton gives

Setting & Chronology 33

no reason to doubt the spatial verisimilitude of his account. Details supplied by him about the geographical scenes of his actions may be supposed reliable, whereas only Avery's temporal references can be taken at face value. Except within the interpolated tale of Knox's captivity in Ceylon, Singleton avoids mentioning or is vague and inconsistent about calendar years, but often supplies the exact latitude and longitude of events.

Unlike Robinson Crusoe, who starts by saying "I was born in the Year 1632," Singleton does not even tell when he was born. Nor is he sure exactly how old he was when first taken to sea: "a Master of a Ship . . . took a Fancy to me . . . and . . . tho' I was not above Twelve Years old, he carried me to Sea with him, on a Voyage to *Newfoundland*." Where they went is clear. When they sailed is not. After "three or four Voyages" of unspecified duration, Singleton reports, he "grew a great sturdy Boy, when coming Home again . . . we were taken by an *Algerine* Rover . . . which, if my Account stands right, was about the Year 1695, for you may be sure I kept no Journal" (p. 3). Singleton then stresses again his failure to record adventures as they occurred so as to preserve an accurate chronological record: "I was too young in the Trade to keep any Journal of this Voyage, tho' my Master . . . prompted me to it" (p. 5). At almost every opportunity Singleton avoids taking, or blaming himself for not taking, those steps that might have put him into a proper relationship to time by making him notice the spiritual or even practical significance of its passage. Even when he first takes command, he keeps "no Journal of this Voyage" (p. 39). His apologies for not doing so are all placed before mentioning his first religious thoughts. These never prompt him to start a spiritual diary. And if a navigator's journal may be assumed for Singleton's later years of command at sea, it is never mentioned to corroborate his memory as narrator.

In *A Journal of the Plague Year* H.F. refers to the journals and memoranda which he has kept and which he subsequently uses to stimulate as well as confirm his recollections while writing his memories of the plague. His topic is of course more concerned with the real time of historical events than is Defoe's fiction of Singleton, and it benefits accordingly from allusions to journals whose presumed existence works along with the printed tables of mortality to establish verisimilitude. But Robinson Crusoe, equally fictitious and closer than H.F. to Singleton's profession before an illegal slaving voyage winds up in shipwreck, is careful to provide readers with "the Copy" of a journal which he kept on his island until his ink ran out (p. 69). Defoe's insistence on the absence of any journal from Singleton's hand thus has an effect beyond symbolizing, as Everett Zimmerman notes, how little "any spiritual order" extended to Singleton's youth.[12] By excusing his narrator from dating episodes, Defoe deflects attention from questions about how the events of Singleton's life are related to *each other* in calendar-time. Consequently the dates which Singleton does provide do something other than contribute to that air of verisimilitude that can be established by a coherent chronology of the kind that Defoe includes in *The King of the Pirates* (this demonstrates that he could do so when he chose), but withholds in *Captain Singleton* for reasons that are made to seem plausible.

After telling how he was captured by an Algerian pirate "about the Year 1695," Singleton describes without dating the events leading to his journey across Africa, his return to

Setting & Chronology   35

England, and his subsequent piracies up to the moment of joining with Captain Avery "at *Madagascar* in the Year 1699, or thereabouts" (p. 181). The interval between these two vaguely ("about. . . . or thereabouts") dated events is too short to accommodate the intervening action. But Singleton's reference to "the Year 1699, or thereabouts" is placed too far away from the first date to invite attention to the contradiction, and there is no trail of dates through the text encouraging readers to locate events with respect to one another in calendar time. Instead the second date achieves the more local effect of placing one phase of Singleton's life within the period of Avery's most famous exploits. For readers perusing *Captain Singleton* in 1720, Avery's well-known domination of Madagascar around the turn of the century may have seemed more like the past than part of their present.

The sense of decade and era during Defoe's lifetime has not been much discussed. But the start of a new century was regarded as a major turning-point. Defoe's choice of 1699 for the meeting with Avery locates that action in a preceding era, and thus puts Singleton at a distance. As in so many other matters, however, Defoe manages to have it both ways. The real Avery (Henry Every) was still alive in 1720. According to the novel Singleton is too. Crusoe would have been eighty-seven in 1719 when *Robinson Crusoe* was published. Moll Flanders, who is "almost seventy Years of Age" (p. 267) at her last return to England, would have been almost 109 years old when *Moll Flanders* was published in 1722 according to the novel's concluding statement that her memoirs were "Written in the Year 1683": a different situation with at least one obvious implication. Singleton, however, need not even be regarded as an old man in 1720. If he was "a great sturdy Boy... about 1695," he might be under, or certainly not much over, forty when he returns to England and starts writing.

Singleton does not date that return, however, only remarking in the book's last paragraph:

> And now, having so plainly told you, that I am come to *England*, after I have so boldly own'd what Life I have led abroad, 'tis Time to leave off, and say no more for the present, lest some should be willing to inquire too nicely after
>
>
>
> *Your Old Friend,*
>
> CAPTAIN BOB.
>
> FINIS
>
>

This open-ended conclusion transforms *Captain Singleton* into an undated letter which may remind readers of the two letters supposedly from Avery that compose *The King of the Pirates*. For Defoe's initial audience the "now" of Singleton's last sentence merged with their own "now" of 1720. For subsequent readers the effect remains similar despite the widening interval between their "now" and Singleton's. He will be imagined as living on into a still extant present into which readers have sufficiently projected themselves to enjoy the novel. Yet in 1720 there was also another kind of immediacy: piracy was still a major problem. Defoe thus exploits topicality while also retaining any advantages created by the distance between "now" and events taking place around the turn of the century.

The strategy is characteristic, and it deserves consideration. Even *A Journal of the Plague Year*, whose action is fixed in a more distant and particular past, had topicality in its favor because in the year of its publication there were fears of another outbreak of the plague. As Schonhorn points out, even within a work so bound to one historical

Setting & Chronology 37

moment, "more than a dozen times, Defoe's narrator, by his arguments for civic reform and better plague-control, deduced from lessons of the past in language appropriate to the present, shows his public concern and narrows the gap between his time and the reader's."[13] To Defoe the past was of interest primarily for exemplary purposes. Any such exploration of the past for help in solving present problems transforms history into a variety of deliberative rhetoric.

Its underlying assumption must be that the past does not differ essentially from the present or future.[14] The narrative consequences are most obvious in *Due Preparations for the Plague*, where Defoe provides a story from 1665 almost as vivid as anything in *A Journal of the Plague Year*, but with a prefatory explanation that "in order to direct any particular family who have substance to enable them to shut themselves up in so strict a manner as would be absolutely necessary for preserving them from contagion . . . I shall here describe a family shut up, with the precautions they used, how they maintained an absolute retreat from the world, and how far they provided for it, it being partly historical and partly for direction; by which pattern, if any family upon the like occasion thinks fit to act, they may, I doubt not, with the concurrence of Providence, hope to be preserved."[15] Defoe later explains that "the history I have given of a family preserved by retiring from conversation is really the history of several families rather than of one, and is a perfect model for future practice."[16] Model futures are most efficiently constructed by combining past particulars into a typical narrative. Several stories are summed up as one story. Many narrative times are conflated in one narration in which particular times are absorbed into a representative sequence of time. History is thus detemporalized, but it retains its claim to historical validity and exemplary truth. Particular dates cease to matter, however.

Similar assumptions about potential resemblances between past, present, and future govern Defoe's *History of the Union of Great Britain*, although without anything like so much detachment of its narrative from concern with dates and chronology. It has the twofold purpose of recording for posterity events leading to the union of England with Scotland while also persuading contemporaries that the union is a good thing for both countries and should therefore be supported against opposition still powerful in 1709. Defoe starts with "A General History of Unions in Britain" in order to show, among other things, that far from being a new idea, proposals for a union can be found as early as the reign of Edward I. His negotiations, "even in so remote a Time," are "the most exact Pattern of the Present Treaty." Defoe argues that the eighteenth-century union has the advantage of being "Formed upon the Foot of all the most Politick schemes of former Times; and all the Miscarriages of former Treaties have been as Warnings to furnish the Experience of these Times to make them wary, and instruct them how to avoid the Rocks that others Split on." Wars and bloodshed attributed by Defoe to the lack of a union are narrated because they provide "a good Lookingglass for those Gentlemen (*who have openly wished these Nations might make a Breach either on one Side or another*) to look into, and for them to see, if their Designs had succeeded, what their Posterity might have had cause to thank them for."[17] Here—and also in several other passages in the *History of the Union*—Defoe presents the past as a mirror of possible (and disastrous) alternative futures. For such purposes, no less than those of *Due Preparations for the Plague*, the fact of pastness matters more than particular dates.

Temporal settings, whether past, present, or future, become more important than chronology within the depicted eras. In the *History of the Union* as well as a fiction based on real history like *The King of the Pirates* Defoe provides an explicit and coherent chronological ordering of events with respect to each other in calendar time. There is attention to chronology in *A Journal of the Plague Year*, where H.F. tells how the plague spread from month to month but does not follow that order in his narrative sequence. It is in the *History of the Union* and *Due Preparations*, however, that Defoe most conspicuously invites readers to project into the future a past detemporalized because wrenched away from the chronology of specific dates and imagined apart from those dates as a typical sequence. What results are narratives—of previous attempts at union and wars fought because there was no union, or of a family that survived the plague—which must be regarded by readers as to a significant degree taking place in the past yet *also* as depicting a possible future (their own). By making such narratives "partly historical and partly for direction," Defoe manages one of the few possible ways of setting actions in two times at once.

Like others in the eighteenth century Defoe was still writing under the shadow of a longstanding conviction that, as Aristotle put it when defining deliberative rhetoric as the species of persuasion most concerned with the future, "nobody can 'narrate' what has not yet happened. If there is narration at all, it will be of past events, the recollection of which is to help the hearers to make better plans for the future."[18] Although the weight of such conventional wisdom argued against narratives set in the future except by implication, there was of course ample precedent for Defoe's inclination to argue that one period might include events that were "the most exact Pattern" of another. He never assumes that all eras are alike in major respects from creation to doomsday, and thus that history displays only essentially identical cycles, although such nonprogressive patterns are regarded as an unfortunate local possibility. Instead, Defoe adopts the more linear Christian view of historical time that went along with typological arguments that one period may resemble another while also prefiguring changes.

Defoe shared with the majority of his readers the typological habit of mind involved not only in the assumption that Old Testament events prefigure those of the New Testament but, more generally, that the past offers archetypes of the present and future. The implications for his narrative strategies are even more far-reaching than those which Paul Hunter and other critics have insisted upon in connection with *Robinson Crusoe*.[19] In order to understand the present or view the future by using the past as a guide and source of archetypes, distinctions between eras must often be collapsed or attention at least deflected from chronology, which of itself always defines differences between months, years, and centuries.

This background of typological thinking may offer the best clue to what has remained a major puzzle in Defoe's fiction: his avoidance of the (now) most usual varieties of chronological "placing" of events—and his frequent resort to anachronisms. Except for *A Journal of the Plague Year* and *Memoirs of a Cavalier* there are no sustained attempts in Defoe's most famous works to locate action within *one* moment of historical time. George Starr finds this a problem in *Moll Flanders*, but he provides a solution: "Some events and practices to which Defoe alludes were so recent that we should have to judge Moll's retrospective mention of them anachronistic, if ordinary chronology were at all crucial to her narrative. But it is not. The only past that concerns her is her own; the passage of time may furnish the chief organizing principle of her recollections, but the tale she tells ultimately eludes calendars and clocks, and hovers in a timeless fictional once-upon-a-time."[20] Certainly insofar as Defoe provides an exemplary tale whose lessons will always apply, or creates a powerful myth as he does in *Robinson Crusoe*, the absence of explicit connection with historical time has advantages.

Myths depend on some detachment from ordinary chronology, of which there is indeed a minimal amount in *Moll Flanders*, where Defoe provides only one date. It is a measure of his skill that he does succeed brilliantly in taking Roxana, Singleton, Moll, and especially Crusoe outside their own periods to coexist in that timeless realm of the imagination where they may easily be regarded as one of us. For this achievement ordinary chronology is not crucial, and it had to be transcended. Yet Defoe's mythic power is not grounded in those methods which altogether displace narratives from the flow of historical time.

Starr has chosen the right phrase in saying that in *Moll Flanders* Defoe *ultimately* eludes the world of calendars and clocks. There is no obvious plunge into once-upon-a-time as at the start of an apologue like *Rasselas*, which is so distanced in both space and cultural time as to have only the most tenuous connections to the eighteenth-century world where its action is placed but not located by means of a date. Nor does Defoe adopt a plan like Richardson's strategy for emphasizing the centrality of personal time as he does in *Clarissa* by omitting *any* complete dates in favor of providing a relative chronology whereby events can be located with respect to one another within the months of an unspecified year in a century which is clearly the eighteenth, but within which the time is never localized by year. Letter 1 is dated January 10, letter 2 is from "Harlow-Place, January 13," and so through the final letter from De la Tour dated December 18, n.s. Even Clarissa's will is only dated "This second day of September in the year of our Lord ———," for which Richardson provides a footnote, saying merely that "The date of the year is left blank for particular reasons."[21] Richardson's strategy prevents the action of *Clarissa* from being placed within the calendar of any real year and related to its historical events, as, for example, the story of *Tom Jones* must be located with respect to the year 1745.

Like Fielding, Defoe connects to specific years those fictive situations that also extend outside the flow of historical time and break away from its boundaries to achieve mythic power. His fiction often dramatizes the interaction of the timeless (whether of the Christian eternity or of archetypal situations and personalities) with events located within time. For this reason, perhaps, even though Defoe's work often displays spatial form with consequences that I discuss in chapter 4, his fiction has not come under the attacks levelled by Frank Kermode and others at twentieth-century literature that strives to place narrative actions altogether outside the confines of historicity and to create literary forms that seem to deny "our vital interest in the structure of time, in the concords books arrange between beginning, middle and end."[22] Defoe is much concerned with the structure of both narrative and historical time.

Robinson Crusoe, in which Defoe invents a central myth of modern civilization, connects its action to historical time at the outset by mentioning the year of Crusoe's birth, but then it deals mainly with interactions between personal time and eternity. And, to the bewilderment of critics, Defoe *returns* Moll Flanders to the world of calendars and clocks just at that point on the novel's last page where there was no obvious need to do so, and where it might seem that detemporalization of the kind that enhances mythic force might better have been achieved by avoiding any date. Starr also notes that "some investigators of the sources of *Moll Flanders* have been led astray by its last five words, 'Written in the Year 1683.'"[23] Granted that ordinary chronology is not crucial to this narrative, there still remains the problem of why its only date is placed where it cannot be missed and must be considered.

What is the meaning of that date? What is its intended effect? If it were always the case that Defoe avoided allusions to calendar time in his fiction, a convenient answer to both questions might be that he meant to do so throughout *Moll Flanders,* but at last forgot his plan. It would follow that the date is nothing more than a careless gesture at realism which fails because it does not square with previous allusions to customs—such as widespread ownership of small watches like those which Moll steals—which postdate 1683.[24] The assumption of this explanation and others like it is that whatever appears anomalous when seen by twentieth-century eyes can be charged to Defoe's hasty writing and is on that or some other ground best ignored.

To *judge* references anachronistic, moreover, is to regard them only as embarrassments while ruling out the possibility that they serve useful purposes. I want next to suggest that in the light of eighteenth-century attitudes toward anachronism as well as the more frequently discussed typological concepts which encouraged conflation of different eras and the setting aside of chronological orderings as the least significant temporal relationships, Defoe's major anachronisms are best regarded as intentional, not accidental, strategies. They reinforce the effects of his fiction. I also want to suggest that his achievement (and perhaps that of some later writers as well) is best understood when we can put aside the pejorative (and therefore question-begging) connotations of *anachronism* while using the concepts underlying that term—I wish there was some more neutral word—in a more precise fashion than anyone yet has as an instrument of critical analysis. Not all anachronisms are mistakes, as a play like Shaw's *Saint Joan* may remind us. Nor do all anachronisms take the same form. The kinds of anachronism in Defoe's fiction are as important to notice as the fact of their occurrence.

2

Defoe's objections to *Paradise Lost* are a clue to his thinking on the subject of anachronism. In *The Political History of the Devil* he criticizes Milton for making Christ refer to saints when "it is certain there were no Saints at all in *Heaven* or *Earth* at that Time." And "just such another Mistake ... he makes about *Hell*, which he not only makes *local*, but gives it a Being before the Fall of the Angels, and brings it in opening its Mouth to receive them. This is so contrary to the Nature of the Thing, and so great an Absurdity, that no Poetic Licence can account for it; for though

Poesy may form Stories, as Idea and Fancy may furnish Materials, yet Poesy must not break in upon Chronology, and make Things which in Time were to Exist, Act before they Existed."[25] This complaint does not seem to square with Defoe's own previous use of anachronism. But he is considering the special case of *Paradise Lost*, not prose fiction; and he is concerned with theological issues of a kind that always weigh heavily upon Milton's critics. Defoe is also discussing real, not imaginary, characters whose time is defined by history in a way that is altogether different from that of Crusoe, Moll Flanders, and Roxana, although like that of Avery and very close to that of H.F. and the Cavalier.

The comments on *Paradise Lost* illustrate Defoe's attention to the problem of temporal settings, but they cannot be taken as an entire statement of the theory which governed his earlier practice in the major fiction. Yet even in his criticism of *Paradise Lost* there is some backing away from total rejection of anachronism when Defoe lightens the gravity of his charge by summing up with the remark that "in a Word, Mr. *Milton* has indeed made a fine Poem, but it is *the Devil of a History*."[26] This concession implies that Milton's anachronisms are only liabilities to the extent that *Paradise Lost* is taken for true history, not poetic fiction.

Given Milton's subject and Defoe's beliefs, however, there was no way for him to avoid judging the poem by the standards of historiography. For narratives that claim historical truth, anachronism is a major fault that cannot be excused on the grounds of "poetic licence." But, as Dryden explained when taking Virgil's side by coming "to the defence of the Famous *Anachronism,* in making *Aeneas* and *Dido* Contemporaries," it is possible (especially where, as

Dryden also explains, the poet's intention is to draw some order of "Truth out of Fiction") that "a Man may be an admirable Poet, without being an exact Chronologer."[27] Dryden assumes that anachronisms will be regarded as mistakes that need some defense. But the thrust of his argument is toward classifying them as trivial mistakes that, on closer consideration, may turn out to have so many advantages as not really to be artistic mistakes at all.

He places the requirement for accurate chronology among "the mechanick Rules of Poetry" and calls it one of "those Laws" which "are not altogether fundamental." According to Dryden "Chronology at best is but a Cobweb-Law." The only occasions where it *must* be observed are those where a poem—that is to say a work primarily fictitious—includes events that are both real *and* familiar to every reader: " 'Tis not lawful indeed, to contradict a Point of History, which is known to all the World; as for Example, to make *Hannibal* and *Scipio* Contemporaries with *Alexander;* but in the dark Recesses of Antiquity, a great Poet may and ought to feign such things as he finds not there, if they can be brought to embelish that Subject which he treats."[28] It is only for historical contradictions in depicting a period not exactly among the "dark Recesses of Antiquity" that Defoe blames *Paradise Lost*. His remarks are therefore within the main stream of critical comment on anachronism.

Dryden even recommends Virgil's precedent as a model for imitation, although not by everybody: "They who will imitate him wisely, must choose as he did, an obscure and a remote *Aera*, where they may invent at pleasure, and not be easily contradicted." It is crucial only to avoid mistakes in chronology that readers may *easily* notice. It is not the presence but the visibility of anachronism which creates problems. Anachronism itself might, as in Virgil's hands, lead to what Dryden calls "the greatest Beauties." If this could be done without choosing a remote era for the action, so much the better, presumably, although Dryden does not envision the possibility. In principle, however, what he calls "a Fiction against the order of time" was in Dryden's opinion no different from an Ovidian metamorphosis or any other "Fictions against the Order of Nature": a device that might be used well or poorly, but which was not in itself invariably an artistic mistake.[29]

Whether or not Dryden's defense of anachronism was familiar to Defoe, his practice is in keeping with the conventional attitude that only for history, and fiction primarily intended to portray real events (in the manner of *Memoirs of a Cavalier* or *A Journal of the Plague Year*) was anachronism an inexcusable error. For other genres dealing mainly with imaginary events, it was among the devices available for employment, although regarded as a strategy that was difficult to use "wisely"—which is to say unobtrusively—and mainly on that ground to be avoided by all but the most skillful. For them the received views as articulated by Dryden might well offer strong encouragement to further experimentation with anachronism, perhaps even in settings that were not so remote. Only one kind of anachronism—misplacement of famous historical events and persons—was proscribed.

Seventeenth- and eighteenth-century definitions of anachronism reveal two distinct though related categories. Phillips blurs the distinction by defining *anachronism* as "An Errour in Chronology or in the Computation of Time; a false Chronicling."[30] Bailey defines it as "a Fault or Error in

Chronology, or a Computation of Time, when an Event is placed earlier than it really was." Ephraim Chambers explains anachronism as "in matters of chronology, an error in computation of time; whereby an event is placed earlier than it really happened. . . . Such is that of Virgil, who placed Dido in Africa at the time of Aeneas; though, in reality, she did not come there till 300 years after the taking of Troy.—An error on the other side, whereby a fact is placed later and lower than it should be, is called a *parachronism*."[31] These definitions all involve an absolute division between correct and mistaken references to time. But Samuel Johnson's definition is (as one might expect) more relativistic: "An errour in computing time, by which events are misplaced with regard to each other." As a concession to the most common usage, however, Johnson adds that "it seems properly to signify an errour by which an event is placed too early; but is generally used for any errour in chronology."

Nowhere in Defoe's major fiction is an important historical event ("known to all the world") placed either "earlier than it really was" or "later . . . than it should be." Although a very few small mistakes can be found in his placement of minor historical events, Defoe was scrupulous about historical accuracy. He avoided both parachronism and prochronism. The concept of anachronism as (to quote from two recent dictionaries of literary terms which are in the tradition of Bailey and Ephraim Chambers rather than Johnson) "something out of its proper time" or "something placed in an inappropriate time" assumes that it is possible to know the right time for whatever is misplaced.[32] This definition cannot be applied to a situation such as that in *Roxana*, however, where the protagonist is fictional and therefore has no "right" time except as specified by the author, and where it is impossible to say whether her involvement with the Restoration period, or the reference to her arrival in England as a child in 1683, is the mistake (if indeed there is a mistake) except by arbitrarily choosing one period (and one set of the novel's temporal allusions) as the correct reference point.

The chronological inconsistencies in *Roxana, Moll Flanders, Colonel Jack,* and *Captain Singleton* are best described by a relativistic concept like Johnson's definition of *anachronism* as "an errour in computing time, by which events are misplaced with regard to each other." But even this definition does not altogether fit these works because their chronological misplacements are not errors.

After a detailed study of topographical allusions in *A Journal of the Plague Year*, Manuel Schonhorn reports that of almost ninety references to buildings and locations "in nearly every instance... Defoe has concentrated upon landmarks and conspicuous objects of the London scene of 1665, all therefore chronologically relevant to the *Plague Year;* at the same time, these locations and structures were still part of the London scene of 1720." There is "no reminder ... of the thirty-three churches destroyed in the Great Fire and never rebuilt."[33] By mentioning instead only what survived or was reconstructed (under the same name), Defoe avoids prochronism while nevertheless allowing his eighteenth-century readers to experience the topographical references as simultaneous allusions to the past and to aspects of their own present. These references are not anachronisms in the sense of objects placed erroneously with respect to time or each other. Nor are they exactly anachronisms in the sense of something surviving beyond the period of its usefulness.

Defoe took care, however, to provide a background of

buildings and places that belong to more than one instead of only one temporal setting. By doing so, as well as by capitalizing on the topical interest of his subject, he wrote *A Journal of the Plague Year* in the way most calculated to diminish his readers' sense of distance between themselves and 1665, thus enhancing the possibility of emotional response to a narrative whose events are by many other means also brought as close as possible for the sake of making a greater impact. Defoe's related strategy of double temporal setting in *Moll Flanders* may be appreciated by answering Paul Hunter's question: "Why does a writer as political as Defoe assiduously avoid mentioning historical events, even though Moll lived through one of the most turbulent periods in English history?"[34]

One kind of answer is that proposed by David Higdon, who shows more clearly than anyone has the importance of this issue by working out for the first time (and necessarily by inference from the one date and Moll's references to elapsed months and years) an accurate chronology of Moll's life in relation to historical events. He then suggests that she omits mention of the civil war because during it she is in Virginia, and "when Moll is present during significant events such as the Restoration, the Plague, and the Great Fire, egocentricity keeps her unaware of their magnitude. She never develops an awareness of historical events except as they threaten her own existence. She fails to see that . . . the burning house she pillages may be part of a much larger fire."[35] It is hard to imagine that Moll would not regard the plague as threatening her own existence, however, and harder to believe that she could fail to notice that hundreds of other houses were burning simultaneously if they were.

Setting & Chronology 51

Had Defoe included references to the Restoration, the plague and the fire (points of history known to all the world), the action of *Moll Flanders* would be exclusively located in one era. He includes allusions to less conspicuous events and customs that only become anachronisms when readers arrive at the last five words: "Written in the Year 1683." Even then, anachronisms are only apparent if readers make an effort, which the text does not encourage, to think back over earlier passages and to notice contradictions. They *may* do so, and Samuel Macy may thus be right to suggest that the two references to the Bank of England are not only anachronistic, but "must have been patently so to the original readers of the work."[36] On encountering these allusions, however, readers are proceeding through a text which has not mentioned any dates at all.

There is no reminder from Defoe that the bank was founded in 1694. Readers might know that date, but they are only encouraged to regard the bank as an institution of indeterminate date: recent enough to be a part of their own time, while also old enough to form a link with the last years of the seventeenth century. When Moll mentions the bank, as much as when she steals watches, she will be regarded as the eighteenth-century reader's contemporary, but she cannot be placed in any particular year. Her time and the reader's imaginatively fuse. And so for the other allusions that may correctly be called anachronistic according to the final date—but only in retrospect, after the novel has been completed.

As *Moll Flanders* is read through from its beginning, it creates an impression that Moll is the eighteenth-century reader's contemporary, with whom it is therefore easiest to identify oneself and to sympathize. This effect works best for readers whose time-locus was in fact or is by imaginative projection the year when *Moll Flanders* was published—or shortly thereafter. Only at the end of the last page, just when readers are about to close the book and to pronounce their final judgment on Moll, does the one date in *Moll Flanders* intrude on their awareness. Its placement can no more be regarded as unintentional than the omission of references to the fire and plague. Its effect for eighteenth-century readers—which is to say the effect that Defoe intended—was not inescapably to create worries about anachronisms of setting, which might indeed be discovered, but which remain unobtrusive because they do not involve allusions to specific years or to "a Point of History which is known to all the world."

The date conveys an unequivocal meaning for those reading (in fact or by effort of historical imagination) in 1722: Moll, who in the previous paragraph mentions being "almost seventy Years of Age" at her last return to England, is dead and gone to a judgment more important than any which the reader can pronounce. Because of the first-person narrative, as well as her resilience, and all the references which bring her forward in time, Moll has seemed very much alive and close to readers. Suddenly she is removed to the past and (by inescapable implication) to the grave. This distancing inclines readers to suspend their impulses to condemn Moll in favor of emotions more closely approaching pity and terror.

In *Roxana* Defoe goes beyond this more local effect by creating anachronisms at the outset. David Blewett has shown how Roxana's masquerades at the court of Charles II become an allusion to similar masquerades during the reign of George I. What results is a novel whose central episode—the masked ball at which Roxana dances—exists for readers simultaneously as an historical and contemporary allusion. *Roxana*'s setting becomes both the Restoration *and* the early eighteenth century, as Blewett has the courage to point out: "The masquerades in *Roxana* take place in the reigns of Charles II and George I *at the same time*, as the double time-scheme of the novel makes clear. Ostensibly the novel is set in the seventeenth century. The title refers to 'the Person known by the Name of the Lady Roxana in the time of Charles II'; Roxana invites the reader to confuse her with Nell Gwyn by calling herself a 'Protestant Whore'; and her often-mentioned financial adviser, Sir Robert Clayton, prominent in the reigns of Charles II and James II, died in 1707. But the title-page is in conflict with the first page of the novel where we learn that Roxana, born in France, was brought to England at an early age . . . by her parents in 1683."[37] Defoe's use of anachronism to create a double temporal setting in *Roxana* has been hard for modern readers to accept.

Rodney Baine tries to resolve the paradox by arguing that "Roxana's Turkish costume . . . suggests clearly that Defoe wished the reader to visualize present time, in the courts of George I and the Prince of Wales." But for Baine's view (or any like it) that *only* present time was intended, "the anachronistic appearance of Sir Robert in a Georgian setting creates problems," as do references to the Duke of Monmouth. Therefore Baine retrenches the argument for an exclusively Georgian setting by regarding these references as "protective ambiguity" to guard against action for libel.[38] This is to accept a Georgian setting as the reference point against which Restoration allusions become the *only* anachronisms, and therefore mainly problems, whereas Defoe's text makes it impossible to decide on one reference point. His anachronisms in *Roxana* are "events ... misplaced with regard to each other," not with respect to calendar time outside the novel.

On that misplacement depends Defoe's formal intention of satirizing eighteenth-century society by showing ways in which it is no better than the court of Charles II. If the scene is put entirely in the eighteenth century, the satiric force of comparisons with a notoriously dissolute period vanish, although *Roxana* would still be a devastating picture of eighteenth-century high life. Conversely the implicit satirical meanings would either vanish or diminish in power if *Roxana* had been set entirely in the seventeenth century. Readers would in that case be less inclined to connect her depravity with eighteenth-century manners. However much it grates on modern sensibilities, Blewett is right to describe *Roxana* as set in two periods "at the same time." Conventions of formal realism established later in the century undermined Defoe's strategy. But it may seem less strange if compared to a work like *Absalom and Achitophel*, whose readers are invited to see that David is also Charles and who can easily follow a poem whose meaning depends upon locating the same narrative events in two periods.

Dryden's allegorical mode allows the problem of anachronism to be avoided. Defoe never built an entire narrative upon sustained metaphoric conflation of different temporal settings, although anachronism is employed in *Roxana* to create similar effects. Its readers are allowed to imagine events as taking place in either—or both—of two periods whose distinctions are blurred but not altogether collapsed. The strategy is rare. Mendilow, for example, lists only four novels "written simultaneously on historical and contemporary planes, or ... future and contemporary planes, requiring divided attention together with simultaneous apprehension": Cabell's *Jurgen*, Woolf's *Orlando*, James's *Sense of the Past*, and Morley's *Thunder on the Left*.[39] Yet I do not find in any of these works the pattern employed by Defoe. Nor, it well might be argued, do they require very much simultaneous apprehension of two different time-planes.

In *The Sense of the Past* and *Thunder on the Left* the reader must usually switch back and forth—without being troubled by any narrative superimposition of past on present or present on future. The time-travellers are mostly in one period or another, but not both at once. And so for Orlando's progress, except insofar as Woolf succeeds in compelling readers to accept an allegorical application of her tale. Only in a work like *The Faerie Queene* must events be regarded as occupying two periods simultaneously: Gloriana is part of the Arthurian past while also remaining Queen Elizabeth. Yet even such historical allegory is not constant. Sustained temporal doublings that are possible in fantasy and allegory, moreover, cannot easily be achieved in other modes. Mendilow is right to stress differences even between the effects he claims for his short list of novels with double temporal settings and works like Joyce's *Ulysses*, in which events do not take place in two times at once but derive significance from "being projected step by step against an ancient theme, itself not treated but constantly implied."[40] The methods are close but are not the same. Even in *The Faerie Queene* events at the narrative level remain confined to their Arthurian period. Of all English fiction it is *Roxana* that most fully exploits a double temporal setting.

It remains hard to appreciate in the twentieth century,

however, because we have come to want time-machines, a bash on the skull like that received by the Connecticut Yankee, or vague psychological hints like those supplied by James to account for Ralph Pendrel's journey before we can accept time-switches no more plausible than Roxana's quiet departure from the eighteenth century to the court of Charles II. The difference is between a convention that requires acknowledgment of time-travel or anachronism as something for which "explanations" must be provided, and a convention that did not. The difference is no greater than that between the appearance of verisimilitude required of a play with claims to strict historical accuracy, and the liberty easily granted to a work like Shaw's *Saint Joan*, which includes anachronistic conversations about ideas that interest the playwright and his audience but which could not have been discussed by people living in the represented era. Defoe was equally free to include anachronisms or otherwise mingle times without providing either announcement or "explanation."

Johnson's premise remains valid: "Time is, of all modes of existence, most obsequious to the imagination."[41] This not only explains why it was unnecessary for Shakespeare or his critics to worry about the unity of time. It also suggests why there will be no inherent difficulty in responding to the conflation of different times in works like *Absalom and Achitophel* or *Roxana*, although, as the dispute over Shakespeare's temporal settings shows, accepted critical conventions may prevent acknowledgment of such response.

Except on arbitrary grounds (that may, however, apply to other works in different traditions), we never have to choose between regarding Roxana's adventures as taking place in the seventeenth century or the eighteenth century:

the settings may simply fuse in the reader's memory as he proceeds through the book, just as throughout *Absalom and Achitophel* there will be some awareness of both David's time and Charles's time. This possibility allowed Defoe one advantage even greater than the satiric thrusts which Blewett has identified.

Without any change in the narrative point of view—which is always first-person retrospective—Defoe could provide a close view of his characters while also, as at the end of *Moll Flanders*, distancing them. The effect is clear even in *Captain Singleton*, where the pattern of a double temporal setting is least conspicuous. Because Singleton, unlike Moll, writes in the same time occupied by the novel's initial audience, readers were encouraged to imagine him as their exact contemporary while also travelling backward to "1699 or thereabouts" to enjoy the bad old days when Avery flourished on Madagascar. Singleton's crimes are put into a past that is within living memory but nevertheless remote for Defoe's first readers as well as later ones—and always receding further away in time. That temporal distance, in turn, contributes to the blunting of moral judgment which always increases the aesthetic pleasure derived from accounts of vicious conduct.

Defoe combines many ways of softening our condemnation of Singleton as well as Moll and Roxana. George Starr has suggested the role of casuistical thinking in Defoe's achievement of a complicated moral vision that allows readers to grapple with difficult ethical questions, pronounce judgments where appropriate, and yet sympathize with dubious protagonists.[42] A first-person narration also makes it harder to judge adversely. Even Singleton's admission that more was done than he thinks fit to write about reveals some degree of moral awareness and possible regret that inclines readers to view him more sympathetically. He is also portrayed (by himself) as far less violent than most of his crew. Toward the end he even makes some gestures in the direction of repentance. There nevertheless remain disturbing questions created by the stolen money which he retains to support his retirement.

Finally deciding what to make of Singleton would have been easier—and the novel less interesting—had Defoe not taken all the steps, including those which result in temporal distancing, that incline readers to sympathize with Singleton, or at least regard him with detachment. And so for the parallel cases of Moll and Roxana. Insofar as they are perceived as having lived a long time ago, the impulse to condemn them is weakened. There is a kind of putative statute of limitations that comes into force. But there is a danger in going too far into the past, as Johnson points out in noting that "distance . . . from the present time seems to preclude the mind from contact or sympathy."[43] For this reason among others, anachronistic contemporary costumes were favored for historical plays on the eighteenth-century stage, and they are often used in twentieth-century Shakespearian productions.

Everything which pulls the temporal settings forward may also work to enhance sympathy. There is no calculus for describing these effects; nor are they mutually exclusive. They are complementary. Moreover, insofar as the crimes described by Moll, Roxana, and Singleton are perceived as contemporary possibilities, the novels more powerfully enforce their moral lessons. Immediacy heightens exemplary force, for reasons which Johnson has also suggested: "Events long past . . . are not considered. We read with as little emotion the violence of Knox and his followers, as the irruptions of Alaric and the Goths."[44] First-person narratives may diminish such distance, even when set in a remote past. To go too far backward is nevertheless to risk losing contact. The question of temporal settings is most important in Defoe's fiction because it is involved in the larger problem of portraying ethically deficient characters without losing either human sympathy or moral perspective. And among Defoe's successful efforts to find effective solutions to that problem may be included his experiments with a double temporal setting.

3

There is another advantage to Defoe's freedom from the requirements of temporal verisimilitude: references to time may readily become symbolic. Dates and settings can thus convey meanings instead of primarily serving as a background of authenticating detail. They might anyway, of course: symbolism is not incompatible with various degrees of realism, as Chaucer, Hemingway, and other writers including Defoe amply demonstrate. But where verisimilitude must be sustained—or discovered—as the groundwork for different orders of symbolism and where verisimilitude is a basic requirement of readers no less than writers, it will be harder to use—or perceive—dates as an allusion to the moral significance of time. Defoe's steps toward the achievement of what might be called emblematic time can be seen most clearly by considering the varieties of time alluded to in *Colonel Jack*.

There are several, and their arrangement has been problematic in the twentieth century, although no evidence suggests that it was for Defoe's eighteenth-century readers. While noting that in *Moll Flanders* "there is no calendar time at all," whereas in *Robinson Crusoe* "calendar time is important, and the hero carefully observes it," Samuel Monk finds that "calendar time is a real problem in *Colonel Jack*." The difficulty is that "the title-page of the novel ties Jack to calendar time, and as the action develops, the Colonel becomes increasingly involved in actual, contemporary history. . . . But an editor remains utterly baffled if he sits down and as a simple-minded arithmetician tries to make sense of Defoe's reference to the passage of time in Jack's private life." Hence for modern readers with expectations set by later novels, there seems to be "a curious misuse of calender time in *Colonel Jack*."[45] These difficulties, however, are only a more extreme form of problems—or options—that occur in the other works as well.

Moll is also tied to calendar-time at the end in a way that clashes with other temporal references, although dates do not figure throughout her narration as they do in parts—but only in parts—of *Colonel Jack*. In *Robinson Crusoe* Defoe not only makes Crusoe observe time by constructing a calendar, but the author takes equal pains to make readers notice that Crusoe loses a day in the midst of his repentance. As Crusoe starts to read the Bible, he is also suffering from a tropical fever which, like the shipwreck, is part of the adversity that prompts serious reflection. On the evening when Crusoe prays for the first time in his life, he also tries to deal with the fever by a dose of rum and tobacco:

It flew up in my Head violently, but I fell into a sound Sleep, and wak'd no more 'till by the Sun it must necessarily be near Three a-Clock in the Afternoon the next Day; nay, to this Hour, I'm partly of the Opinion, that I slept all the next Day and Night, and 'till almost Three that Day after; for otherwise I knew not how I should lose a Day out of my Reckoning in the Days of the Week, as it appear'd some Years after I had done: for if I had lost it by crossing and re-crossing the Line, I should have lost more than one Day: But certainly I lost a Day in my Accompt, and never knew which Way. (p. 94)

No other explanation is offered, so for readers this passage settles the matter. Thus in the midst of awakening to God, who dwells in eternity, Crusoe is wrenched outside time in the only way possible apart from death, which his sleep simulates. Later when he realizes how he lost consciousness of twenty-four hours, he also appreciates and (as retrospective narrator) conveys the significance of those events which changed his spiritual relationship to the days which he records by cutting notches on "a great Cross." Defoe makes Crusoe's lost day as well as his calendar emblematic of relationships between ordinary time and sacred time.

To appreciate the related symbolism toward which Defoe moves in *Colonel Jack*, it is necessary to start by recognizing as Monk does the existence in it of two chronologies—public and private—whose relationship is indeed inconsistent but not incoherent. While they are not made congruent in clock-time, Defoe uses each one for thematic purposes that depend on the presence of both chronologies, and on relationships between them. The relationships are moral, not temporal. To realize these formal intentions inconsistency was not necessary, and inconsistency accomplishes nothing to enhance the themes involved. But for an audience that did not look for temporal realism, however willing readers were to accept it in works like *The King of the Pirates*, failure to make all the dates in *Colonel Jack* square with one another was not a deficiency that would turn attention away from the purposes that *are* served by including two chronologies. Such readers could respond to Defoe's intentions.

Throughout the parts of *Colonel Jack* where dates are conspicuous, Jack is bothered by even the thought of being cut off from public time. During the European adventures of his adult years he considers returning to Virginia: "But ... I could not prevail with my self to live a private Life. ... tho' I had nothing to do in the armies or in the War ... nor could I think of living in *Virginia,* where I was to hear my News twice a Year, and read the publick Accounts, of what was just then upon the Stocks, as the History of things past" (p. 233). Defoe's redefinition of private life in the modern world is one that Orwell might have envied. Jack does not regard a private life merely as one disengaged from active participation in public history but as one beyond the reach of "publick Accounts." Where newspapers may be read when published, there is involvement (or the illusion of involvement) every bit as satisfying as actual engagement in affairs of state. To be deprived of such vicarious participation in current events while they are current is to lapse into "a private Life." This is to be out of phase with public time and to be forced to view contemporary politics with the temporal detachment of an historian contemplating the past.

To anyone of Jack's disposition, disengagement from public time and retreat into a private life where there is only history may seem as unpleasant as it does to him. But Defoe repudiates Jack's craving for involvement with public time. *Colonel Jack* ends with Jack accepting the advantages of a "comfortable Retreat" where he finally learns to employ his time properly as a penitent looking "back upon a long ill-spent Life," not reading newspapers (p. 307).

In *Roxana* the use of anachronisms to create a double temporal setting also involves relationships between private and public chronologies. Roxana arrives in England as a child "about the Year 1683," leaves for the continent as a grown woman early in the eighteenth century, and then returns to seventeenth-century England where she dances with "the D——— of M———th" and becomes the mistress of Charles II (pp. 5, 181). Defoe uses the moral tone of the Restoration era as commentary on Roxana's hardening heart. The allusions to public history serve as revelations of private morality. Her involvement with the court of Charles II is one measure of Roxana's depravity. Defoe invokes the connotations of a particular historical era to help establish the controlling moral vision of *Roxana* as well as for the satirical purposes that Blewett has identified.

Because Defoe chose a period with such clear connotations, there have never been any difficulties over the general meaning of Roxana's encounter with the figures of public life. And because she plays no backstairs role in shaping political events, there are no allusions to particular episodes in the lives of Charles or Monmouth; and therefore no exact location of her affairs with respect to the calendar of public time exists. Nor do the private and public chronologies have a coordinate relationship: private time is more important throughout *Roxana*, and for this reason also the absence of references to particular years or public events during the Restoration episodes is not problematic. Nothing hinges on whether readers can find out (they cannot) when Roxana spent her "Time of Retreat" of "three Years and about a Month" living with the king (p. 181).

The balance between private and public chronology was also partly a matter of genre. As Maximillian Novak observes, for Defoe "a memoir was the study of a man in relation to his time," whereas the term *history* was often applied to biography or autobiography.⁴⁶ Thus, compared to *Roxana*, there is a reverse subordination of private to public chronology in *Memoirs Of A Cavalier: Or A Military Journal Of The Wars in Germany, And the Wars in England; From the Year 1632, to the Year 1648. Written Threescore Years ago by an English Gentleman, who served first in the Army of Gustavus Adolphus, the glorious King of Sweden, till his Death; and after that, in the Royal Army of King Charles the First, from the Beginning of the Rebellion, to the End of that War.* Here the temporal setting is single, not double. Action remains located as advertized, in the period from 1632 to 1648. Wars and battles follow in their chronological order. The Cavalier's private chronology dovetails with public chronology. There are no troublesome inconsistencies to cast doubt on Defoe's ability to handle time "correctly" when he wanted to.

By starting *Robinson Crusoe* with a sentence stating that its protagonist was born in 1632, Defoe initiates a structure that differs from that established by *Colonel Jack*'s avoidance of calendar dates throughout the part describing Jack's early life. Crusoe's life is perceived as a movement away from historical time toward the encounter with private and sacred time on his island, followed by a return to participation in the era which he left. At the end of the novel Crusoe sets out toward farther adventures "in the Year 1694" (p. 305). But Crusoe never mentions any curiosity about the public events that took place during his isolation, nor does anyone in the novel tell what happened by way of providing a public chronology to run parallel in the reader's mind with what Defoe in *Robinson Crusoe*'s preface calls the story of a "private Man's Adventures." Jack moves from vaguely specified beginnings toward increasingly well defined relationships with historical events and with calendar-time.

His birth is not dated by mentioning a year, as in *Robinson Crusoe*, but instead by a more complicated strategy of allusion to a famous public event brought into relationship to Jack's private chronology: "I WAS almost 10 Year old... when... my Nurse died; her Husband was a Seaman, and had been drown'd a little before in the *Gloucester* Frigat, one of the King's Ships which was Cast away going to *Scotland* with the Duke of *York*, in the Time of King Charles II" (*CJ*, p. 8). Monk correctly observes that "the sinking of the ship bearing the Duke of York to Scotland in 1682 irrevocably fixes Jack in 'real' time, for it gives the approximate date of his birth."[47] Readers familiar with history could remember that the *Gloucester* was lost in May 1682 and therefore could infer that Jack was born about 1672. But even while providing the information allowing that inference, Defoe shifts attention away from particular dates by the double vagueness of "almost 10" and "a little before." Jack may have been anywhere in his ninth year when his nurse died, while the "little before" does not pinpoint any particular time-span between her death and that of her husband. Defoe carefully prevents readers from locating Jack's birth precisely in the real time of calendars.

Even those who do remember the *Gloucester* are encouraged by Defoe's sentence to associate it and Jack with "the Time of King Charles II" rather than a particular date. That would be the inclination of most readers in any event, just as a majority of modern readers would be unable to supply exact dates but nevertheless able to grasp the political and moral associations of any reference to the *Titanic* or the *Maine*.

Jack's colonial experiences are to some extent anachronistic because they may be regarded as conforming to conditions prior to laws passed in 1670 forbidding the transportation of convicts to Virginia. But apart from this ambiguity of temporal setting which, if noticed, will create local effects like those which I have described above, time's arrow does not change its direction in *Colonel Jack* as it does in *Roxana*. Jack's birth is located "in the Time of King Charles II," and public events are disclosed to readers in a linear progression winding up with two conspicuous references to Jack's inclusion in a general pardon signed by "King GEORGE" (p. 276). The sequence of Jack's private chronology is equally clear, and nothing invites attempts to correlate it with the historical events that are mentioned. Discrepancies will only be noticed by making an unusual effort to remember passing references to the lapse of months that would not be totalled up in an ordinary reading. What stands out and may easily be remembered are the places where Defoe does such work and sums up with figures: "14 Year old.... now about 18 ... now above 30 Year old.... Now more than Thirty Year old.... I was, *I say*, above 30 Year old" (pp. 11, 62, 157, 169, 170). Defoe specifies that Jack has gone through childhood, youth, manhood, and into old age.

Dates do not attract attention—there are none—until Jack returns to Europe from Virginia as a man "above 30 Year old." But again Defoe stresses the nature of Jack's relationship to public time rather than the chronology of his experiences. He reports that his ship "left the Capes of *Virginia*, on the first of August ———" (p. 174). Omission of the year focuses attention on the fact of Jack's involvement with years rather than on a particular year: on temporality rather than on a specific time. Defoe employs a similar strategy in Jack's next mention of a date: "I came to *Ghent*, in *April* ———, just as the Armies were going to take the Field" (p. 183). Here too the kind of involvement with historical events rather than the year of involvement stands out.

In the next paragraph Jack describes his political and moral naiveté: "As to the Merit of the Cause on either side, I knew nothing of it.... The Prince of *Orange* had been made King of *England*, and the *English* Troops were all on his Side, and I heard a great deal of Swearing and Damming for King *William* among the Soldiers" (p. 183). Although Defoe's hero was William, he is certainly not Jack's. Any reader sharing Defoe's high regard for William would find Jack's attitude even more deficient than it is on account of his moral indifference to the issues at stake. Dates are implied, but they are omitted in favor of a more general reference to the period of a particular king.

After narrating his first military adventures and telling of an unsatisfactory marriage, Jack describes his next engagement with political time: "I came to *Dunkirk* in the Year ——— and here I fell into Company with some *Irish* Officers of the Regiment of *Dillon*" (p. 207). Here, too, the year is concealed, although Jack mentions an actual regiment and goes on to describe participation in "the Famous Attack upon *Cremona*" (p. 207). This dates events exactly—but again without explicit mention of a calendar year. Of Defoe's attention to accuracy throughout this episode, Samuel Monk remarks: "As usual Defoe follows history with great care. All the principal leaders mentioned actually served in the campaign. The account of the attack on Cremona is accurate" (*CJ*, p. 315, n. 2). It is therefore unlikely (although possible) that Defoe omits the date because he had no account mentioning it available to him, or because he was unconcerned with verisimilitude.

Whatever the reason, such passages show that "real time" may be alluded to in different ways and with different effects. By leaving out dates, Defoe shifts attention away from the particularity of Jack's involvement with specific years and toward the more general and symbolic meanings for him or anyone of participation in historical events. The device is reminiscent of that suppression of names in satiric poetry, which is one way of converting topical allusions into more general statements. Such conversion of history into poetry is a familiar eighteenth-century tactic. In passages such as these from *Colonel Jack* the deflection of attention is small, but that deflection does push the narration in the direction of transforming historical particulars into concrete universals that will have for readers lessons wider than Jack's own conclusion that "Courage is acquir'd by time, and Experience of things" (p. 208).

Jack finally mentions a particular year when he reports that "We had a Severe Campaign, *Anno* 1701. . . . The *Germans* push'd on their Design with great Success as the Histories of those Times more fully relate" (pp. 210–11). This is an invitation to remember (or read) those histories for a more complete picture of the events in which he took part. It is also a reminder that Jack was involved in "those Times"—an era with its own identity—not just 1701 or a series of years associated with it only chronologically. To some extent this inference could be made by readers in any case, but Defoe's narrative strategy here ensures that it will be. Jack's next sentence again mentions a date: "I was at the Action at *Carpi, July* 1701" (p. 211). The last two dates which Jack provides are also connected with campaigns at the turn of the century. Narration of increasingly unsatisfactory private affairs centering around his Italian wife then serve as transition away from the public time marked by political events. After two more marriages Jack leaves again for Virginia "in the Year ————" (p. 250). Jack's disengagement from public time, like his embarkation toward it from "*Virginia,* on the first of August ————," is thus located with respect to time itself instead of a particular moment. Defoe makes these temporal references emblematic of what Jack is doing rather than mere specifications of when the actions occurred. Verisimilitude, had that been the primary intention of such phrases, would have been served better by the fabrication of any plausible dates. It would have been easy enough to accomplish.

Even inconsistent dates would have been accepted more readily than the dashes as authenticating details, especially by an audience not disposed to check for chronological coherence where nothing depends upon it. The usual response to a date is to accept it as evidence, by its very presence, that there *is* a correct time-scheme. Unless something else in the text invites or compels readers to stop for the mental arithmetic of checking out time-references, dates forestall questions about chronology. For eighteenth-century readers of Defoe, in any case, they apparently did so. Even Gildon, who was looking for mistakes, did not include in his catalogue of implausibilities the question of whether Crusoe spent twenty-seven or twenty-eight years on the island: an unresolved issue which Dewey Ganzel has persuasively shown to be of small concern in itself but excellent evidence of how Defoe probably revised his first draft of *Robinson Crusoe* to focus greater attention on Friday's arrival and conversion.[48]

Dates suggest that an author has attended to chronology so that readers may concentrate on more important matters. The dashes do not quite convey this. Nor, however, do they serve as conspicuous signals. They convey the meanings that I have suggested without attracting notice unless put under the critical microscope for a purpose like mine. They do their work at the periphery of the reader's awareness, and they hardly need explaining during an ordinary reading in ways that are called for by issues like Crusoe's solitude or Misson's flag.

Allusions to time during Jack's European adventures are at the covert end of a spectrum whose opposite extreme contains symbols which demand conscious explication. The allusions are examples of that reciprocal process by which details acquire meaning from their thematic context, and thereby in turn contribute toward enforcement of the larger meanings they reflect. What allows the temporal allusions in *Colonel Jack* to reflect and amplify the meaning of his encounters with time is their clustering in parts of the text dealing with Jack's military years; the avoidance of specificity in those allusions even though it is not complete avoidance; and the fact that Defoe does not use dates elsewhere in the novel as a background of authenticating detail. There is also, of course, the fact that appropriate themes are in other ways introduced to provide the semantic framework allowing dates and dashes to acquire their resonances of meaning.

In the allusions which I have just traced Defoe is moving toward emblematic temporal references without taking the steps that make it necessary for readers to notice the symbolism as such in order for the passages to make their contribution toward reinforcing larger themes. But nothing is

Setting & Chronology

lost if readers do stop to notice. In Defoe's use of double temporal settings, the advantages diminish if his procedure is noticed (as critics often do) for the purpose of trying to resolve contradictions which admit no resolution, rather than simply by way of registering the temporal settings in passing, responding to each one locally, and then to their fusion in memory. Modern readers have to make a choice that was not thrust upon Defoe's initial audience. Readers who choose to impose (or who cannot help imposing) expectations of temporal consistency upon texts not designed to admit them may lose almost as much as those who do not try to find overt symbolism in episodes where it is meant to be discovered.

At the borderline between meanings conveyed without calling attention to their vehicle and those which do lie Defoe's summary statements about the relationship between Jack's involvement with public time and his more private years. After concealing the date of his return just as he concealed the date of his departure, Jack says that he came back to his Virginia plantation "after a Ramble of four and Twenty Years" (p. 251). To ramble, according to Bailey, is "to go to and fro, up and down, or astray." There is no question that Jack's European ramble has led him astray. Six paragraphs from the end of his account, Jack remarks that if he had "sincerely repented of what was pass'd" instead of leaving the colonies to become a soldier, he "had not for 24 Year together liv'd a Life of levity, and profligate Wickedness" (p. 308). Defoe therefore by reiteration invites readers to notice that Jack spent twenty-four years abroad.

Which years they were according to the calendar does not matter. Readers have no way of knowing exactly. Defoe specifies the amount of time to emphasize the folly of wasted years, not for purposes of chronological consistency that would enhance the verisimilitude of Jack's narration. The statements about levity, profligate wickedness, and rambling make explicit the moral framework within which readers are to judge the value of Jack's encounter with history. This reconciles public and private chronologies sufficiently because it shows their moral relationship. Nothing hinges upon whether they can be exactly correlated with reference to a calendar. Moreover Defoe's meaning would remain the same if he had made Jack stay in Europe twenty-three years, or twenty-five, or thirty.

Nothing in the text beyond Defoe's reiteration that it was in fact twenty-four years encourages readers to attach particular significance to that interval. But they *may* remember that it is the most famous period of misspent time:

> Go beare these tydings to great *Lucifer*,
> Seeing *Faustus* hath incur'd eternall death,
> By desperate thoughts against *Joves* Diety:
> Say he surrenders up to him his soule,
> So he will spare him foure and twenty years,
> Letting him live in all voluptuousnesse.[49]

If this association comes to mind, the folly of Jack's involvement with public time will be more forcefully impressed. But Jack hardly resembles Faustus, and it remains doubtful whether Defoe intended to render the twenty-four years explicitly emblematic by an allusion that would have to be noticed as such in order to work.

Nor does any traditional significance attend the interval mentioned by Roxana when she confesses "that no Woman ever liv'd a Life like me, of six and twenty Years of Wickedness, without the least Signals of Remorse" (p. 188). In

Moll Flanders Defoe heightens the impression of Moll's depravity by making her remark after accepting the banker's proposal of marriage: "If ever I had a Grain of true Repentance for a vitious and abominable Life for 24 Years past, it was then" (p. 144). Here too, if the twenty-four year interval is allusive, nothing in Defoe's text insists upon connections between that period of her life and the most well-known "abominable" misuse of the same number of years. Yet neither her specification of twenty-four years, nor Jack's, nor Roxana's mention of twenty-six years serves to answer questions about chronology as such. Large intervals of time are specified to underscore the moral quality of days that have been so prodigiously wasted.

In such passages Defoe crosses the borderline at which temporal references become statements about the uses of time. He thus invests chronology with meanings it cannot so well communicate in works like *The King of the Pirates*, where coherent dates only serve to make the narrative seem like a more faithful record of reality. The final variety of chronology used by Defoe to suggest moral and psychological meanings, rather than enhance verisimilitude, is biological time.

4

Defoe alludes to familiar models of biological time that were current well into the eighteenth century. In the *Rambler*, no. 151, for example, Johnson remarks that "the writers of medicine and physiology have traced with great appearance of accuracy, the effects of time upon the human body, by marking the various periods of the constitution, and the several stages by which animal life makes its progress from infancy to decrepitude."[50] Bailey provides the usual medical chronology under *age*, saying first that "the Life of Man ... is divided into four different Ages" and then explaining that "*Infancy* or *Childhood*, extends from the Birth to the fourteenth Year. *Youth*, or the Age of Puberty commences at fourteen, and ends at about twenty-five. *Manhood*, terminates at fifty. *Old Age* commences from fifty, and extends till the Time of Death." Chambers repeats the scheme given by Bailey, only stressing a crucial detail by specifying that manhood, which "terminates at 50," is "the virile *Age*," and then adding that "Old *Age, senectus*, succeeds, which is the last: though some divide this into two; calling it *decrepit Age* after 75."[51] Bailey also provides the conventional legal chronology after first explaining that "Age (in *Law*) is used to signify those special Times which enable Men and Women to do that, which they could not do before." Defoe never employs legal models of individual chronology as Richardson does in making *Clarissa* above all what its subtitle proclaims, *The History of a Young Lady*, whose difficulties are almost as much related to her situation in legal time as to her physical age and inexperience. Indeed her youth has one of its most specific meanings in terms of legal complications that add to her distress and illustrate her character when she must decide whether to litigate against her father to assume the estate which she has inherited.

In *Colonel Jack* Defoe plays off biological progress through the four ages of man against contrasting patterns of delayed psychological and spiritual growth without, however, stressing the bearing of these sequences upon Jack's various legal situations. Jack's mind is frequently out of phase with his body. His transportation to Virginia is described as a way of "just beginning the World again" (p. 120). Jack supplements this allusion to a kind of rebirth by saying that he "consider'd my present State of Life to be my meer Youth, tho' I was now above 30 Year old, because in my Youth, I had learn'd nothing" (p. 157). Defoe insists on the regressive pattern. The paradox of a youth who is more than thirty years old is thus stressed when Jack says that he "was now a Planter, and also a Student" (p. 160). When telling of his later travels, Jack comments that he "was a meer Boy in the Affair of Love" (p. 186). His marital misadventures have an adolescent quality of experimentation. At their outset, Jack admits, he "Knew the least of what belong'd to a Woman, of any Man in *Europe* of my Age; the thoughts of a Wife, much less of a Mistress, had never so much as taken the least hold of my Head, and I had been till now as perfectly unacquainted with the Sex, and as unconcern'd about them, as I was when I was ten Year old, and lay in a Heap of Ashes at the *Glass-House*" (p. 186). This boyish unconcern is all the more striking in someone who did not spend his manhood cast away on a deserted island.

Crusoe never admits to such naiveté as Jack professes, only alluding to the absence of women by grimly joking that he "was like to have but few Heirs" (p. 65). He reports that after returning to England "first of all I marry'd, and that not either to my Disadvantage or Dissatisfaction, and had three Children, two Sons and one Daughter" (p. 305). This fruitful marriage is another sign of Crusoe's spiritual progress. Dates given for his birth (1632), shipwreck (September 30, 1659), rescue (December 19, 1686), and departure from England in quest of farther adventures after his wife's death (1694) emphasize that when Crusoe marries he is well over fifty—and thus by conventional reckoning an old man past the virile age. Defoe thus stresses that Crusoe's old age has not meant immediate decrepitude but instead a continuation of his virile manhood. Time has been extended not stolen from him by the providential shipwreck which, by leading him to conversion, puts him into proper relationship to eternity.

Moll Flanders never attains equal spiritual comfort. Neither does she linger in childhood like Jack. She reports staying with her "good old Nurse" until "I was almost fourteen Years old . . . and look'd a little Womanish." Defoe calls attention to this turning-point when childhood gives way to youth by having Moll specify in the next paragraph that her nurse died "about the Time that I was fourteen Years and a quarter Old" (p. 16). This prompts a move into service with a family where Moll stays until she is "between 17 and 18 Years old," by which time, thanks to the Elder Brother, she is no mere girl in the affair of love. Much later, as Moll approaches old age, one of her liaisons brings her to reside "at the Sign of the Cradle" (p. 129). There she has a child with the help of the "Governess, who I had now learn'd to call Mother" (p. 138). Shortly thereafter, Moll reports, "It began to be time for me to leave bearing Children, for I was now Eight and Forty" (p. 150). Here again Defoe invites attention to an important moment in a chronology that is more central to Moll's progress than the location of her life in a particular century.

Of equal concern to Defoe, however, is the psychological distress of approaching old age in isolation like Moll's. Left alone when "it was past the flourishing time with me . . .

Setting & Chronology 77

and the Ruins only appear'd of what had been," Moll neither regrets the past nor plans for her future: "I saw nothing before me but the utmost Distress, and this represented it self so lively to my Thoughts, that it seem'd as if it was come, before it was really very near ... I fancied every Sixpence that I paid but for a Loaf of Bread, was the last that I had in the World, and that To-morrow I was to fast, and be starv'd to Death" (p. 150). With such thoughts she "sat and cried and tormented my self Night and Day" (p. 150). Thus Moll lives in an imaginary future until she attains old age: "I liv'd Two Years in this dismal Condition" (p. 151). Having read three paragraphs earlier that Moll was forty-eight, no reader can mistake Defoe's careful location of her circumstances just at the moment when she starts the last of her allotted four ages.

Moll is exactly fifty years old when she turns thief. Necessity partially explains and to some extent excuses her criminal career. But Defoe's portrait of Moll's mental state on the brink of her first crime goes beyond merely establishing the fact of necessity: he also provides a picture of her disintegrating temporal perceptions. Moll's preparation for becoming a thief has been two years of imagining only future scenarios of "the utmost Distress" that are confused with present time. And Defoe makes this interval of inner temporal confusion coincide with the end of Moll's womanhood. It is the combination of isolation and poverty along with the passage to old age which wrenches her mind into morally false relationships to a future which is prematurely (and thus disastrously) imported into her present by seeming "as if it was come, before it was really very near."

Shortly after the account of that temporal dislocation, Defoe provides a pattern of imagery that underscores the disparity between Moll's physical and spiritual progress. Moll says of her new career: "I was young in the Business" (p. 154). After another explicit statement that her real age is "after 50," the woman whom Moll again calls "Mother" suggests a way of learning how to become a more expert thief: "*Says she*, I cou'd help you to a School-Mistress, that shall make you as dextrous as herself" (pp. 157, 159). During her stay at the home of the Elder Brother, Moll had enjoyed what she considered "all the Advantages for my Education that could be imagin'd"; and these included (apart from what she learned from him) lessons in French, penmanship, dancing and the harpsichord (p. 18). Moll's second education is centered on a curriculum of "shoplifting, stealing of Shop-Books, and Pocket-Books, and taking off Gold Watches from the Ladies Sides" (p. 159). Unlike Jack's student days in Virginia and his eventual discovery of women, Moll's apprenticeship in crime is hardly the realization of experiences that should have come earlier.

She seems to regress and to pick up an alternate but worse line of development. The metaphors that create this impression are among the cyclical patterns that have been well described in recent criticism. But the fact that Moll has crossed the threshold into old age makes a difference that intensifies the horror of her predicament. A misspent youth like Jack's or even Singleton's at least (and by convention) offers the possibility of a penitent old age. But a misspent old age diminishes if it does not remove the probability of any spiritual change. It is hard, therefore, to agree with William Bowman Piper's argument that "neither Moll's age, which Defoe never sees as modifying her powers of thievery, nor her wealth, which presents us with a graph of tedious ascent, gave him any formal aid at all."[52] So far as concerns her age it is just the opposite: Defoe's careful attention to locating Moll's progress and regress through the four ages of man provides one of the formal patterns that distinguishes *Moll Flanders* from his other novels that are also organized episodically within a chronological framework where narrative sequence runs parallel with plot sequence.

Piper identifies another major issue by remarking that "Moll never plans a crime to fill a special financial need nor to allow for any decrepitude of age; she heaps up her hoard of ill-gotten gain with undiminishing vigor."[53] This is more to Defoe's point. Moll's crimes, like the two years of imaginary futures which serve as their prelude, have no valid relationship to either present or future time. They do not even make provision for the disability that will follow if Moll lives into *decrepit age*. Nor of course do they contribute toward preparation for the more important future in what Moll describes as "the other Side of time"—eternity (p. 225). It is only in Newgate that she thinks about "the Word Eternity ... with all its incomprehensible Additions" (p. 225). The crimes are exactly as Piper describes them: pointless and morally askew manifestations of "undiminishing vigor." This part of Moll's old age is morally the reverse of Crusoe's virile old age.

Defoe uses the same technique of specifying progress through biological chronology in different narrative contexts to achieve goals that are formally opposite. Moll's vigorous old age is put into a context where it serves to cast further doubt on a narrator described in the novel's preface as someone who "pretends" to be "grown Penitent and Humble" (p. 3). *To pretend* is defined by Bailey as "to use a Pretence, to make as if; also to assert, affirm, or maintain."

The neutral sense in which *pretends* means only *affirms* was the secondary denotation of the word. Johnson defines *to pretend* as "to put in a claim truly or falsely," but he adds that "it is seldom used without shade of censure." Although Defoe might easily have avoided uncertainty by writing that Moll afterwards *became* penitent, he chose from the outset to raise doubts by using a word that must at least make readers wonder whether her claim to penitence is true or false. And that uncertainty is sustained by a variety of devices, including attention to the disparity between Moll's physical chronology and moral regress when she commences thievery at the start of her old age.

Jack progresses, however, toward a spiritual state which, despite conspicuous regressions, does finally coincide with that most appropriate for his time of life. Defoe's preface to *Colonel Jack* prepares for this closure by describing the story as one in which "*the Penitent shall be return'd like the Prodigal*, and his latter End be better than his Beginning" (p. 2). The vigor of Crusoe's old age is also part of an ending which explicitly conforms to a reassuring narrative model, in his case the *Book of Job*. Defoe surrounds Crusoe with his wealth and his children after making him first suggest the parallel by remarking: "I might well say, now indeed, That the latter End of *Job* was better than the Beginning" (p. 284). Here, as in *Colonel Jack*, allusions to the linear structure of biological time finally reinforce Defoe's portrayal of moral growth. In *Moll Flanders* similar allusions contribute to serious doubts about the protagonist's final state. Thus Defoe's attention to Moll's age—and Crusoe's and Jack's—gives him great aid formally.[54] But it could only do so because Defoe shared with his readers ideas about biological time that were a central part of the eighteenth century's time-consciousness.

3

Time-Consciousness

Before taking up the questions of memory and tempo, I want to remark some additional connections between Defoe's views of time and the temporal structures that characterize his fiction. No invariable relationship exists between beliefs about time and the forms within which those beliefs are expressed. Although it is now possible to describe with some precision the varieties of fictional time, neither critics nor psychologists have yet established much firm knowledge of causal relationships between culturally shared time-concepts and literary forms. Except in the most general terms we cannot yet say how attitudes toward time determine the range of formal possibilities open to an author. Yet there do seem to be significant affinities. Shared views of time within a culture may create expectations about the most desirable ways of dealing with fictional time. Such views may also create expectations about the proper way to read a book. Opinions about the right use of time, for example, will influence the extent to which books of various kinds are read in the first place and, for those which are read, the pace of reading, the extent to which they are thought about after reading, and the amount of pressure for rereading. Time-concepts may determine the interpretive weight placed on beginnings, individual episodes, or endings.[1] All these matters deserve more attention, and I cannot claim to resolve them here, but I do wish to invite further investigation of them by suggesting how Defoe's narratives may have been shaped by the nature and extent of his explicit views about time. I suspect that the very fact of time-consciousness may be as important as the direction it takes in prompting a writer to experiment with various temporal structures. Certainly Defoe was unusually concerned with time. The extent of that concern can be more fully shown by considering Defoe's comment on reading-speed, his statement of relationships between time and eternity, and his dramatization in *Colonel Jack* of how memory evolves to create moral relationships between past and present.

1

Singleton, the Cavalier, Moll, and Roxana are introduced as though they might have existed in real time. Only the *Memoirs of a Cavalier*, however, was taken as a genuine historical document by many eighteenth-century readers. Defoe's major fictions are not equally disguised as true narratives. Nor do their formal properties derive from a uniform attempt to imitate authentic autobiographies.[2] The preface to *Robinson Crusoe* raises this issue only to suggest that whether the story is "history" or "fiction" does not matter: "The Editor believes the thing to be a just History of Fact; neither is there any Appearance of Fiction in it: And however thinks, because all such things are dispatch'd, that the improvement of it, as well to the Diversion, as to the Instruction of the Reader, will be the same; and as such, he thinks, without farther Compliment to the World, he does them a great Service in the Publication" (p. 1). He does an equally great service, that is, whether the narrative is "History of Fact" or merely invented, even though it does not happen to look like fiction. The uses ("the improvement of it") will be exactly the same in either case. This is neither an invitation to regard the story as true nor a plea for suspension of disbelief. It is assurance that the whole question may be put aside. Defoe suggests that *Robinson Crusoe*'s readers need not worry about whether they have crossed the borderline between truth and fiction.

Angus Ross notes that eighteenth-century editions of *Robinson Crusoe* after the first two alter *dispatch'd* to *disputed*: "It seems to mean that since all stories like this are to be read quickly, improvement is equally likely whether the story is true or a romance."[3] This begs the question of what "stories like this" are in Defoe's view—and why he thought they would be read quickly. Ross and other recent editors are right to print *dispatch'd: disputed* makes little editorial or other sense, and it is apparently not Defoe's word. *To Dispatch*, according to Bailey, is "to hasten, to spend or rid off; also to send away in haste; also to kill with speed or quickly." Defoe makes reading-time a primary consideration in discarding the question of whether a narration is history or fiction: works cursorily dealt with are to be measured only by their moral effect.

It is not a bad standard for the modern world of disposable books whose dangers were outlined as early as *A Tale of A Tub*. In putting moral effects above verisimilitude as the right measure of worth, Defoe is within the main stream of eighteenth-century critical concepts. His phrasing is unusual only because it presents the issue as a matter of time, not genres: works that occupy readers for long periods are opposed to works that are "dispatch'd."

Evidence that I consider in chapter 5 shows that although Defoe expected his narratives to be read quickly, it does not follow that he expected them to be read at a uniformly rapid pace. He viewed them as among works to be "dispatch'd" only by comparison with books whose difficult content and absence of illustrative story make for slower going. He also implies a comparison with works such as the Bible or theological discussions that are not finished at one reading. *Robinson Crusoe*, and by implication the other fiction by Defoe which followed it, cannot demand more than one reading either to appreciate artistry (for which no claim is made) or to absorb its lessons. Where any variety of instruction, with or without diversion, is intended, however, there must be intended also an attempt to arouse memories.

Johnson was echoing a view stressed in Christian thought since the chapter on memory in Augustine's *Confessions* when he remarked in the *Rambler* that "it is, indeed, the faculty of remembrance, which may be said to place us in the class of moral agents."[4] Johnson applied this insight to criticism by insisting that the newer modes of fiction developed by 1750 were unlike previous literature precisely because in them "the power of example is so great, as to take possession of the memory by a kind of violence, and produce effects almost without the intervention of the will."[5] Almost without intervention by the reader's will, that is, owing to the fact that he cannot help remembering what he has read. Johnson is mainly considering the novels of the 1740s, and he does not explain their power to stay in the mind or to take violent hold of the memory beyond noting that such effects depend on the choice of protagonists whose situations resemble that of ordinary readers sufficiently for them to identify themselves closely with the stories.

But Johnson's analysis is prophetic in many ways, not least in foreshadowing critical attention to the issue of how memory is related to the reader's ability to control the effects of what he has read. Johnson's observation at mid-century underscores the significance of Defoe's assumption that fiction is a briefly encountered genre whose success will depend on devices that make books memorable.

2

Critics have recently hinted at a few affinities between Defoe's religious outlook and his inclination to write works that focus on memory as a theme or to place thematic demands upon the reader's ability to recall the events of a narrated lifetime. George Starr argues that Defoe's avoidance of tightly constructed plots can be taken as "the expression of a casuistical conception of life without implying that it is peculiar to casuistry.... Whatever larger thematic coherence his books may have, individual episodes tend to be connected chronologically, not causally, and far from helping to organize them into a sustained narrative, casuistry appears to be one of the factors responsible for their disjointedness."[6] One consequence of such fragmented narratives is that unrelated episodes do not easily stay in mind as connected sequences: such events are more quickly forgotten. This attribute of Defoe's temporal structures, however, is at cross purposes with other didactic intentions of his narratives. Starr also demonstrates that Defoe's fiction is often modeled on spiritual autobiographies that depict a search for patterns of religious progress while remembering a life and that encourage readers to adopt a similar retrospective stance.[7] Prior episodes must be recollected to appreciate how they fit into larger moral patterns even when there is little causal connection apparent at first reading or in retrospect.

J. Paul Hunter argues that the model of spiritual autobiography cannot entirely explain Defoe's frequent doubling of temporal viewpoint to conflate accounts of action with retrospective comment on it in *Robinson Crusoe*, where "the deceptively simple chronological record is infused throughout with later interpretation." Hunter also notes that in *Robinson Crusoe* Defoe often depends on the reader's memory to establish implied patterns linking episodes: "Defoe shows the young Crusoe to be dimly conscious only of the most obvious signs of divine concern; less obvious but equally significant signs escape him entirely. Once he has established Crusoe's pattern of perception, Defoe counts on the reader's memory of the before-and-after contrast and usually allows Crusoe to describe events in his uncomprehending state. But Defoe chooses these events with great care so that they bear an intrinsic significance which the reader may perceive even when Crusoe does not."[8] Whatever the exact influence of spiritual autobiography, there is general agreement among critics that Defoe's concern with questions of repentance and providential patterns led him to favor narratives told in the first person from a retrospective viewpoint. The case for accepting this affinity as significant, and very much related to other matters of narrative technique as well, is strengthened by considering Defoe's explanation of man's relationship to time itself.

Defoe reserved this issue for his most famous character. In the *Serious Reflections During the Life and Surprising*

Adventures of Robinson Crusoe there is a poem on eternity as well as a discussion of how time is related to it. These topics are taken up by Crusoe (who in this book more directly than any other character elsewhere is speaking for Defoe) during consideration of how to decide whether a man has lived well. For readers wondering what to make of characters like Moll, Roxana, Jack, or Singleton, the moral basis for deciding whether anyone has lived well becomes the foundation of interpretive strategies in two ways: it provides values by which actions are measured; and, what is equally important, it suggests the most appropriate points during a reading for evaluating characters. To some extent such evaluation is always a continuous process subject to revision at the end. But there will be crucial differences in the extent to which readers are encouraged by signals within a novel to make up their minds about characters early in the book or else to suspend judgment until a retrospective view of all the action is possible.

Jane Austen, for example, builds the ironic structure of *Pride and Prejudice* upon strategies for trapping readers into judging Darcy prematurely, as Elizabeth does. At the end there must be recollection of earlier episodes and reinterpretation of them within the reader's memory as within Elizabeth's. In *Tom Jones*, on the other hand, as John Preston has shown, Fielding creates a plot whose temporal structure involves recall together with rereading for similar purposes of reevaluation to appreciate dramatic irony but which equally depends for its realization upon readers who have at the outset made essentially correct judgments of Tom, Blifil, and the other major characters.[9] Their actions are impossible to foresee in detail—another important part of Fielding's temporal structure, as Preston has also shown

—but do follow from their characters in ways that readers are challenged to predict.

Early in *Tom Jones* Fielding provides incidents compelling readers to see correctly how Tom and Blifil differ. There is also an invitation to anticipate future episodes—as a useful moral exercise—on the basis of this early judgment: "In the Conjectures here proposed, some of the most excellent Faculties of the Mind may be employed to much Advantage, since it is a more useful Capacity to be able to foretel the Actions of Men, in any Circumstance, from their Characters, than to judge of their Characters from their Actions."[10] This emphasis on narrative structures encouraging prediction while in the process of reading (and of living) marks a significant turn away from the Puritan tradition of retrospectively oriented narratives. Although Defoe does sometimes lead readers to guess (or notice that they cannot guess) the next turn of adventures that are often advertized as strange and, above all, surprising, in his narratives he most often resorts to devices that encourage readers to look backward and juxtapose what has been read with what is being read: narrative past with narrative present. In this way Defoe creates exercises in what for him is the more important capacity of retrodiction.[11]

To introduce the poem on eternity, Crusoe states that "the right way of judging men, and the way which alone can be just, is to judge of them by their general conduct; and so a man may in his own mind justly denominate himself: as every good action does not denominate me to be a good man, so neither does every failing, every folly, no, nor every scandalous action, denominate me a hypocrite, or a wicked man; otherwise some of the most eminent saints in Scripture, and of every age since the Scripture was written, are gone to the devil; and 'twill be hard to say there was ever a good man in the world" (*SRRC*, pp. 169–70). Fielding says much the same thing in *Tom Jones* (bk. 7, ch. 1), but without reference to eternity and within a narrative context where the moral nature of each character is clearly signalled at first appearance, where the narrator explains his doctrine of conservation of character and where the effect of insisting that a single bad act does not constitute a villain is therefore primarily to caution readers against altering their favorable initial impression of the protagonist.

Crusoe's remark, with its emphasis on the relationship of time and eternity, provides a rationale for one to consider episodes of a life or a narrative from the perspective of the end without forming any decisive judgment of character until arriving at the last moment. And the moral quality of individual actions could on this view even be entirely evident *without* one's having to answer the question of how to regard the whole series. Crusoe does not provide any clear measure of how many virtuous or vicious actions would tip the scales: only a warning that no one episode is crucial. Defoe's is a more diachronic than synchronic view of both character and morality. It leads readers to suspend judgment until the last page—and then to remember. This view allows as morally (and therefore artistically) valid those narratives like Defoe's that do not easily permit readers to form unequivocal judgments about protagonists. What has often looked to twentieth-century critics like ethical incoherence in Defoe's novels may have seemed necessary for didactic purposes in narratives partly intended to show the hazards of making a judgment too quickly.

Crusoe makes what for Defoe's theology is the necessary

qualification that, because of the disproportion between eternity and even the maximum number of good actions possible during a lifetime which is less than a moment by comparison with eternity, salvation cannot be earned by any number of works. There remains God's "rich unbounded grace, that rewards according to itself, not according to what we can do." At the last judgment a survey of how all the moments of life have been used gives way to a more synchronic standard: "We are to be judged by the sincerity of our repentance" (*SRRC*, p. 171). But this is God's judgment: how "we are to be judged," not how to judge others. Defoe is here arguing for repentance without repudiating his insistence that for judging people (in real life or by implication in fiction) it is best to wait for the end or at least the last possible moment.

Crusoe also describes the "negative good man" who refrains from vicious conduct or even observes the outward forms of Christianity while nevertheless remaining "perfectly a stranger to the essential part of religion." Underlying this problem as Defoe explains it here and dramatizes it elsewhere in his fiction are mistaken attitudes toward time: "Take this man's conversation apart ... what notions has he of misspent hours, and of the natural reflux of all our minutes, on the great centre and gulf of life, eternity? Does he know how to put a right value upon time? Does he esteem it the life-blood of his soul, as it really is, and act in all the moments of it, as one that must account for them? Alas! .... He ... entertains no notion of judgment to come, eternity, or anything in it." Such inability to look far enough ahead is partly a matter of attention deflected from the future outside time by a sense of present individuality: "What room has a man to expiate, in his thoughts upon so immense and inconceivable a subject as that of eternal duration, whose thoughts are all taken up, and swelled top-ful with his own extraordinary self." The difficulty is also a failure of imagination: "Eternity is not a meditation suitable to the man I am talking of; 'tis a sublime thought, which his bloated imagination has never descended to or engaged in" (*SRRC*, pp. 170–72 passim).

To remedy this imaginative defect as well as to emphasize ideas about time by slowing down the pace of Crusoe's discussion, Defoe switches to poetry. I do not claim anything for "Eternity" as a poem, but the fact that Defoe bothered to write it is unequivocal evidence of the extent to which he had time-concepts very consciously in mind during the period of his best fiction. Defoe's poem moves toward a joyous conclusion. There is comfort in reflecting on the "Duration" of "that glorious Place" where the soul may dwell for a "blest Eternity."[12] Throughout the poem and in the discussion which introduces it, Defoe follows the main stream of Christian tradition by distinguishing time from eternity and by affirming that within eternity there are no distinctions between past, present, and future: "To thee things past exist as things that are; / And things to come, as if they were." The majority of theologians agreed with Augustine, not St. Anselm, that although eternity is endless and has always existed, it must not be supposed merely as an existence of the same kind experienced within time where things change and cannot (except by God) be viewed simultaneously with respect to their past, present, and future.[13]

In this Augustinian tradition God, the unfallen angels, and men who are saved are viewed as inhabiting eternity. Men during this life, and devils during their postlapsarian existence inhabit time. There is a beginning as well as an ending to time. In his *Political History of the Devil*, for example, Defoe mentions "the Beginning of Time," and affirms that "God himself was, and existed before all Being, Time, or Place."[14] Therefore, while Defoe stands out because he was so ready to discuss time, his ideas on its nature in relationship to eternity reflect assumptions certainly shared by the majority of his readers. Only the extent, not the direction, of his conscious preoccupation with time as a philosophical concept is in any way unusual.

The image in Defoe's poem of eternity as a "mighty Circle" is also conventional. It suggests that within eternity beginnings cannot be distinguished from endings: "To end, begin, be born, and dye / . . . Are Nonsense in thy Speech / . . . In thee the ends of Nature form one Line, / And Generation with Corruption join." The poem even more strongly emphasizes eternity as the destination of everything within time, and eventually of time itself. Eternity as the creative "mighty Womb" from which will issue "Worlds to come" receives less attention than images of eternity as the "Abyss," "Grave," and "Great Gulf of Nature" that will swallow up first this world then "Time itself." It is not easy to see how insistence on eternity as the grave of time squares with the assertion that "Time when to Eternity roll'd on, / Shall never, never, never waste away." Defoe apparently means that although earthly deeds and thoughts vanish ("however nobly done"), what is done by the inhabitants of eternity cannot disappear.

The statement is preceded by an affirmation that "What we have been, and what we are, / The present and the Time that's past, / We can resolve to nothing here, / But what we are to be in thee, at last." *Resolve* meant "to melt," "to dissolve," and "to analise" (Johnson). Thus existence in time cannot be analyzed or melted down into—that is, understood or turned into anything valuable—"here" in time except in the light of "what we are to be" during a future in heaven or hell throughout eternity. Conduct during this life cannot be judged with absolute accuracy without knowing about that other judgment of "what we are to be" in the eternal future. But no one can say how anyone will fare in the afterlife, not even a novelist portraying fictitious characters. Narrators cannot be placed in the one location that would allow perfectly accurate evaluation of "time that's past." Defoe reveals his sensitivity to this issue when he remarks in the preface to *Moll Flanders* that "we cannot say indeed, that this History is carried on quite to the full End of it, unless they can write it after they are dead" (p. 7). To this extent even the autobiographical stance does not allow a sufficiently retrospective view. Given Defoe's concept of time, all narratives, even third-person accounts, stop before the end. But the closer they and their readers come to considering it the better.

With the disappearance of time as it "drowns and expires" in eternity, there will also be an end of "all the great Actions of aspiring Men, / By which they build that trifling thing called Fame." Hence also the vanity of those "glorious Monuments of Fame, / Which Fools erect t'immortalise a Name." Defoe avoids any echo here of traditional conceits that art will endure forever. He does not even condone attempts to create art in defiance of time. The possibility is dismissed as a grasping after "fancy'd Immortalitie." From this religious perspective on time and eternity, it also follows that no book should aim at permanence. Nor should any book claim greater value than as something dispatched to leave behind memories that in the ideal case turn attention from the author and his work, and the experience of reading, to the reader's future outside time.

3

The memories that best point toward eternity are those involved in repentance. Colonel Jack explains the first step of such remembering when he tells how he found "leisure to reflect, and to repent, to call to mind things pass'd, and with a just Detestation, learn as *Job* says, *to abhor my self in Dust and Ashes*" (p. 308). Maximillian Novak observes that "Repentance . . . is . . . along with faith, the necessary article in Defoe's concept of Christianity," and he adds that Defoe was among those who insisted that "repentance was a spiritual gift of God which need be made only once."[15] But the dramatization of these views in *Colonel Jack* is problematic. Everett Zimmerman finds that "Jack's repentance is the most perfunctory one in all of Defoe's novels."[16] George Starr finds that in *Colonel Jack* "narrative itself has become paramount, and largely eludes thematic control" because Jack's story "preserves distinct vestiges of the spiritual autobiography, but virtually abandons both its characteristic spirit and shape."[17] In *Colonel Jack* Defoe is searching for a new form. What now hinders acceptance of Jack's spiritual change as convincing (although perhaps eighteenth-century readers had less trouble) is apparently a narrative arranged so that its themes must often be used in retrospect to sort out episodes unrelated to them upon first encounter and so that its events are most easily inclined to reorganization in the reader's memory.

In chapter 4 I discuss the narrative techniques involved in this arrangement, which is signalled four paragraphs from the end by Defoe's suggestion on how "all that design to read" Jack's story may (having just finished it) "prepare to do so" (p. 308). Without disputing the problematic nature of *Colonel Jack*, I want to suggest that it deserves recognition as another experiment with temporal structures like those more sucessfully realized throughout *Robinson Crusoe*'s account of conversion and in Defoe's organization of *A Journal of the Plague Year* to follow the sequence of H.F.'s memories instead of the chronological progression of the plague. Before taking up that argument as it relates to narrative techniques, however, I want to use *Colonel Jack* as a final illustration of how Defoe's concern with time led him to concentrate on memory as a theme and also on the problem of how writing can portray remembering.

More than Singleton, Moll, Roxana, or even Crusoe, although not so often as H.F., Jack refers to memory in ways that emphasize his distance as narrator from the events he describes. At the beginning of his account he often sounds like someone describing memories as well as the remembered events. And for the history of his family, Jack has to depend on memories that are not even his own: "All I know of it, is by oral Tradition thus; my Nurse told me my Mother was a Gentlewoman." His only heritage is: "*Remember, that I was a Gentleman*" (p. 3). Moreover Jack is endowed with a better memory than any of Defoe's other characters: "I lov'd to talk with Seamen and Soldiers . . . and as I never forgot any thing they told me, I could soon . . . give almost as good an Account of the *Dutch* War, and of the Fights at Sea . . . and the like, as any of those that had been there, and this made those old Soldiers and Tars love to talk with me too, and tell me . . . also of the Wars in

Oliver's time" (p. 10). These stories serve as odd substitutes for the more normal memories of childhood and family history. Jack gropes for the right words to describe his experience, and can only say that "By this means, as young as I was, I was a kind of an Historian" (p. 11). The uses Jack can make of his memory are thus among the first questions raised by Defoe.

At the end of his narrative, when Jack tells about his repentance, he also explains why he started to write his story, and associates its composition with a period of heightened memory that is the psychological prerequisite for his spiritual change: "Here I wrote these Memoirs having to add, to the Pleasure of looking back with due Reflections, the Benefit of a violent Fit of the Gout, which as it is allow'd by most People, clears the Head, restores the Memory, and Qualifies us to make the most, and just and useful Remarks upon our own Actions" (p. 307). William H. McBurney calls this attack of gout a "device, surely unique in English fiction, for authenticating the narrative and the acuteness of its observations."[18] Everett Zimmerman remarks that Jack is helped toward "dubious" repentance by what is not an "entirely spiritual stimulus."[19] Accounts of the gout which I have seen do not say that it restores the memory. There was agreement, however, that its cathartic effect would often purge unwholesome elements from the body, thus leaving victims in better general health between seizures than they would otherwise have been.[20] It appears that Defoe is not relying on a commonplace connecting gout with memory. He is inventing an acceptable one which allows emphasis to be placed on Jack's memory and thus on the moral role of memory itself.

Whatever the accuracy of Defoe's knowledge of gout,

there was no need for what is clearly an extraordinary device (and one displaying nice medical imagination) merely to authenticate a narrative whose preface insists that because the story is so instructive it is not "of the least Moment to enquire whether the Colonel hath told his own story true or not" (p. 2). Verisimilitude is not what Defoe primarily achieves by making Jack suffer from gout. Defoe's concerns are symbolic. To the extent that gout was regarded, even by some medical writers, as a gentleman's malady, Jack's illness is another sign of his social rise. But that is a peripheral meaning. The psychological effects of Jack's gout are intended as reassurance that his repentance is sincere. J. Paul Hunter has thoroughly documented the point that contemporary theologians "were quick to recognize the possibility of conversions wrought by physical extremity." Among other texts he cites Benjamin Calamy's statement that "there are some particular Times wherein we are more especially called upon to review our Actions . . . such are times of Affliction . . . when we ourselves are visited with any Sickness or grievous Calamity."[21] As in the narration of Crusoe's illness and conversion, Defoe is concerned with the psychological mechanisms involved in repentance and triggered as well by illness as by storms or other providential events. The difference is that in *Colonel Jack* Defoe takes more pains to show the evolution of memory toward its proper spiritual role. He also tries to create the impression that its narrative is an extension of the protagonist's memory and that, for him, writing is part of remembering. But these connections only become explicit—and important for readers to notice—at the conclusion where "These Memoirs" are by apposition linked with the "Pleasure of looking back with due Reflections" which is facilitated by the gout.

Jack then admits that his narrative has left "Room for just Reflections of a Kind which I have not made yet; particularly, I think it just to add how in collecting the various Changes, and Turns of my Affairs, I saw clearer than ever I had done before, how an invisible over-ruling Power . . . orders the Events of every Thing relating to us" (pp. 307–8). This discovery is made while "collecting" memories and writing them down in the narrative which readers are completing when they arrive at the passage telling them when Jack realized God's role in his and every life. Writing and the time taken to do it have played a part in Jack's repentance: his narrative is not merely a report after the fact of spiritual change. This explanation could be taken to account for the uncertain moral focus in some earlier portions of the narrative, although it is only at the end that readers are thus urged to consider the act of writing as an event in Jack's life. But Defoe prepares for *Colonel Jack*'s conclusion by tracing the growth toward moral purposes of Jack's memory.

During the early part of his life it serves no higher end than to make him a strange kind of historian and then remind him of his money and the social position that he regards as his birthright: "I remember'd that I had almost a Hundred Pound in Money in *London*. . . . This whetted my Ambition, and I dream't of nothing but being a Gentleman Officer, as well as a Gentleman Soldier" (p. 105). When Jack prospers as a planter in Virginia there is a change: "I had . . . a secret Horror at things pass'd, when I look'd back upon my former Life." His ability to remember moral principles improves to match his previous total recall for ships and battles: "I continually remember'd the Words of the ancient *Glass-maker* . . . that to be a Gentleman, was to be an *Honest Man*, that without Honesty, Human Nature was Sunk and Degenerated" (pp. 155-56). Jack's memory of moral advice becomes continuous rather than sporadic.

He can then alter his emotional response to past events. After he "continually remember'd" the glassmaker's advice, Jack reports: "It yielded me a greater Pleasure, that I was Ransom'd from being a Vagabond, a Thief, and a Criminal, as I had been from a Child, than that I was deliver'd from Slavery, and the wretched State of a *Virginia* Sold Servant: I had Notion enough in my Mind, of the Hardship of the Servant, or Slave, because I had felt it, and Work'd thro' it; I remember'd it as a State of Labour and Servitude, Hardship and Suffering. But the other shock'd my very Nature, chil'd my Blood, and turn'd the very Soul within me: the thought of it was like Reflections upon Hell, and the Damn'd Spirits; it struck me with Horror, it was Odious and Frightful to look back on, and it gave me a kind of a Fit, a Convulsion or nervous Disorder, that was very uneasy to me" (p. 156). Jack distinguishes between emotions that accompanied events, and subsequent responses. The servitude that caused him greater suffering than crimes did while he was committing them is remembered because of past emotions ("because I had felt it"), yet the recollection is calm: only a memory. But instead of merely remembering his criminal days Jack responds to them with chills and shock. Defoe's redundant use of *fit, convulsion,* and *nervous disorder* slows readers down to underscore a distinction between emotions recollected in tranquillity and memories that elicit morally useful emotions. Defoe's point is that for a moral life the past must sometimes be responded to as though it were a part of the present. The years of servitude are over because they survive only as clear notions, whereas the criminal period of Jack's life must still be reckoned with. It is only ended in the time marked by clocks.

Jack's awakening to the moral uses of the past is not completed at this point, however, despite his progress and despite the example of an ex-highwayman who, after transportation, becomes Jack's servant and tutor. Jack is not immediately disposed to imitation when this "pedagogue" describes his efforts "to look back upon his past Life" and repent (p. 161). But the conversations do reinforce a more nearly continuous activity of Jack's memory in one way: a poetic prayer shown to him by the tutor stays in Jack's mind sufficiently so that he reports remembering its lines "distinctly ever since" and repeating them to himself "a Thousand times" (p. 163). Defoe quotes the poem so that readers may also remember it while understanding that its persistence in Jack's memory plays a significant role in his preparation for repentance. But the poem is not repeated in Defoe's text to keep it alive in the reader's memory or to dramatize further its role in Jack's progress. The immediate prelude to his repentance is a series of confrontations with figures from his past.

In this respect *Colonel Jack* resembles the episodes in *Roxana* after Roxana has given Amy a "general Commission" as an ambassador to the past charged with discovering what has become of the merchant whom Roxana might have married, the prince whom she almost married, the Jew who caused so much trouble, and her first husband, whose reappearance in Paris had been a foreshadowing of later encounters with the past. Roxana's encounters are more disastrous than Jack's, and her final search for lost time only confirms the permanent distortion of her relationships to past and future. Her quest is improperly motivated. She thinks about earlier years mainly because her mind has not matured in phase with her body: "I was as gay, and as young in my Disposition, as I was at five and twenty; and as I had always been courted, flatter'd, and us'd to love it, so I miss'd it in my Conversation; and this put me many times, upon looking-back upon things past" (p. 214). No gout or other disease suitable to her age "restores the Memory" here in a way that might impel Roxana to look back "with due Reflections" as Jack does.

When Jack's "miserable divorc'd Wife" reappears, moreover, their reconciliation and remarriage are a sign of increasing maturity as well as an ethical advance for both (p. 255). She is praised by the plantation manager (who complicates the story by falling in love with her) for talents that include a parallel to what has become one of Jack's most important attributes: "what a Memory . . ." (p. 260). As Jack is about to settle down, two shiploads of transported rebels arrive near his plantation, arousing Jack's fear that, because they were captured at Preston, where he had also fought against the king, they will compromise him. Visions of a future in which he is "discover'd, betray'd, carried to *England*, hang'd, quarter'd, and all that was terrible" inspire further travels leading Jack to the exile where he starts to review his past and write his memoirs (p. 269). This outcome was not foreseen by Jack, who duly notes that "Man, a short sighted Creature, sees so little before him, that he can neither anticipate his Joys, nor prevent his Disasters" (p. 292). Jack also discovers that his last travels were not necessary to avoid impeachment.

His guilt had caused a mnemonic fallacy. After the general pardon that removes Jack's fear of prosecution, he returns to the vicinity of the ex-rebels, and remarks "that tho' before I fancied every one of them would ... remember me, and consequently betray and accuse me; now, tho' I was frequently among them ... nay, tho' I remember'd several of their Faces, and even some of their Names, yet there was not a Man of them, that ever took the least notice of me" (p. 292). Jack draws a conventional moral about "how necessary and inseparable a Companion, Fear is to Guilt" (p. 291). His inclination to imagine that other ex-rebels will have memories as active as his calls attention to his discovery that they do not. Nor does anything suggest they are on the way to repentance. Defoe by this contrast again underscores the role of memory in achieving a moral life.

Nothing in his account of that role is unconventional except perhaps Defoe's invention of heightened memory as a symptom of gout to stress the importance of looking backward during conversion. Nor are Defoe's views on eternity, the right uses of time, and the didactic possibilities of quickly read books any more out of the main stream of early eighteenth-century thought than his typological view of history and his agreement that each life is divided into four ages. The fact that he shared such attitudes with a majority of his readers allowed and surely to some degree encouraged Defoe to experiment as he did with temporal structures well suited to convey those and other related ideas about time most effectively. But it did not compel him to do so. Not all those writers who shared his assumptions were prompted to similar experiments, which is another reminder that we can at best point to significant affinities not invariable relationships between time-concepts and literary forms. I do not claim more for Defoe.

What is nevertheless sufficiently striking to warrant the

claim of significant affinities between Defoe's assumptions and his experiments with temporal structures in literature is the extent of his preoccupation with time. Those who did share his beliefs did not usually take or create so many occasions to express them. It would be hard to name another writer of the period whose works include true histories, fictions dramatizing the role of memory in repentance, meditations on the right use of time, *and* a poem on eternity. Nor is it easy to find another writer who *also* turned at the age of fifty-nine so insistently to autobiographical modes of portraying the whole arc of relationships from birth through old age: a choice that betrays concern with time as other forms do not.

Thus Burton Pike observes that autobiographically oriented authors have in common "an obsessive preoccupation with the chronological aspect of time." He rightly takes preference for autobiographical form as a sign of that obsession even when writers try to escape the linearity of clock-time by devices which desynchronize narrative and plot. Pike also suggests that even true autobiography is "not simply an attempt to retell one's past life on a linear scale, but rather in effect a novel written in the present, with one's past life as its subject. . . . On this deeper level, all autobiography is fiction." In its *effect* creation of a fictional time, that is, because in autobiography the real past exists (as always) only as a construct of memories re-created within a later context: "What we find in autobiographers, therefore, is a fascination with the present which, to vary St. Augustine, screens itself as a fascination with things past."[22] In this way also Defoe's preference for retrospective narrations shaped like autobiographies is another measure of his concern with the structure of experiential time.

The extent to which that concern is explicit throughout his fiction, as well as implicit in Defoe's formal choices, is an argument for including him among modern writers. The accepted standard is that which W. J. Harvey voices by remarking that "an unusual emphasis on the thematic importance of time is one of the distinguishing features of modern literature."[23] Despite obvious historical differences Defoe's fiction deals with time sufficiently to meet our own expectations. Some of the ways in which it does, as well as historical differences that have not been so obvious, can be explored by turning next to memory and tempo.

4
The Reader's Memory

Memorable is one of the words available for praising something while evading the issues of why it is remembered and whether it is always good to make a lasting impression. Some of the memorable scenes in *Roxana* stand out in retrospect because they are what even she calls "dirty History" (p. 75). Moll's marriage to her brother is shocking enough to stay in mind after other episodes fade. John J. Richetti remarks that "Moll spends five years and only about one-quarter of her book as a criminal ... and yet that part of the book is the one that most readers claim to remember, or the part which seems to colour their descriptions of Moll."[1] Crusoe's island adventure has detached itself from Defoe's text to become one of those memories which are the common possession of an entire civilization.

Almost everybody who picks up *Robinson Crusoe* can outline some of its episodes before he starts reading. People come to the text with memories of its story—not of the narrative itself or the entire story that Defoe tells, of course, but of parts that have continued to appeal for reasons partly beyond his control. Those who examine students in classes on the novel can testify that cultural memories which have acquired the force of myth are often unyielding, even when they are discovered to be at variance with their source. Expectations or preferences may determine what is remembered even when perceptions of what is read are not distorted while a book is in hand. It is now hard to make anyone except scholars remember the religious parts of *Robinson Crusoe*. Such variation in what is taken from any book is only partly a matter of individual psychology and culturally determined attitudes. A work's form is sufficiently involved in its afterlife to warrant arguments like those urged by Hans Robert Jauss in favor of an aesthetics as well as a sociology of reception and impact.[2] Attempts to trace the ways in which books are remembered over the years may become a much more significant branch of literary history. Prior to such studies, however, are questions about how books are remembered while they are being read and shortly afterward. Memories called into play during a reading are part of a work's temporal structure.

In *Tristram Shandy*, for example, Sterne not only portrays the quirks of associative memory by showing what happens when Toby and Walter fall victim to it. Readers are also caught up in similar predicaments. From chapter 2 onward, any mention of clocks incites readers to imitate Walter's way of thinking (whether they want to or not) by remembering Mrs. Shandy's question in chapter 1. References to clocks encountered outside Sterne's pages after *Tristram Shandy* has been read may also provoke Shandian associations that are hard to avoid and very much related to Sterne's intentions. Moreover as one reads *Tristram Shandy* it is hard to remember the sequence of narration previous to any given page. Those who try are soon tangled in a series of mnemonic misadventures analogous to Tristram's problems in writing the novel. As they struggle to sort out episodes into a proper chronology in calendar-time or an equally proper chronology in narrative sequence, which has meant reading time (spread over seven years for Sterne's first audience and taking a considerable amount of clock-time for subsequent ones), there is a diminishment of comic distance between Tristram and his readers. Those who supposed themselves leading a more orderly mental life may again (the novel is filled with such traps) find themselves thinking (remembering) along lines uncomfortably close to the confusion which seems so laughable in Tristram's case as he keeps failing to untangle his past.

Even in such extreme situations, however, it is hard to describe the formal structure of all those memories that are part of a proper reading. The reasons are not hard to find. People vary in what they actually remember. Memories often form at the periphery of awareness and are difficult to notice or even unavailable to introspection after they have done their work. There are different kinds of memory. Experimental psychology has not yet arrived at more than useful hints about the question of how memory operates while we are reading complicated works of literature.[3] Until recently that issue has been foreclosed to the discipline of literary study by preference for criticism which begs questions about what is actually remembered by assuming that everything in a text is *or should be.*

Northrop Frye asserts that "the process of academic criticism" begins only after a work has been read to the end so that it can be seen as a unity comprising "a simultaneous pattern radiating out from a center, not a narrative moving in time."[4] This is to impose an equally spatial form upon all texts by describing them as though each of their episodes could be viewed in retrospect and remembered simultaneously with equal vividness. A significant critical departure of the 1970s has been articulated by Stanley Fish, who argues persuasively that readers do and critics should respond to the "temporal flow of the reading experience . . . and not to the whole utterance." He advocates, in opposition to "the atomism of much stylistic criticism," a method that "involves an analysis of the developing response of the reader in relation to the words as they succeed one another in time." In his view the trouble with criticism that treats novels, poems or plays as *objects* of analysis is that "it transforms a temporal experience into a spatial one; it steps back and in a single glance takes in a whole (sentence, page, work) which the reader knows (if at all) only bit by bit, moment by moment."[5] This approach, however, may equally foreclose studies of how books are actually remembered by its assumption that the reader's developing response is falsified or evaded when a critic stands back to describe the patterns that emerge in his mind after completing a text.

There will indeed be problems if the developing response to a text is confused with its emergent patterns as they linger in memory after a book is finished: the real memory of each reader or the artificial memory places of the note card and critical essay. Neither responses while reading nor patterns that emerge in retrospect can be taken as a complete formal description. A temporal method of criticism of the kind advocated by Fish does, however, encourage attention to memories that play some role while a book is in hand. Also implied as a corollary to such attention is the possibility that forgetting may be an appropriate (and certainly very often an actual) response to some parts of a text. Everything may not be remembered all the way through, and previous passages may be recalled to varying degrees as part of the reader's experience. The temporal method of criticism allows for selective remembering, and the critics who practice it are not necessarily dismayed at the prospect of forgetful readers.

Far from denying the importance of a distinction between what happens while reading and what happens afterward, I want to insist upon it. But I also want to suggest that we start considering relationships between the two parts of any reading instead of choosing one or the other as the only proper grounds for criticism. The distinction may allow some debates to be resolved—or at least put in terms that allow the issues on which they depend to become explicit rather than implicit. The question of how far *Moll Flanders* achieves thematic unity and emotional force is one case in point. Another is the nature of Defoe's emblematic method in *Robinson Crusoe*. A third is the question of how Defoe controls tempo.

1

The extent and sincerity of Moll's repentance have been regarded as keys to the question of whether *Moll Flanders* achieves any significant degree of unity. Insofar as the episodes of her life may be viewed as showing a conventional progress toward repentance, Defoe's novel may be accepted as a coherent narrative in which Moll's actions are related to the outcome of her story. After surveying discussions of this issue through 1967, Ian Watt agreed that "Moll Flanders and Defoe both thought themselves sincere about the religious and moral issues raised."[6] But Watt singles out as especially problematic conclusions like those implied by George Starr's argument that "a conventional pattern of spiritual decay supplies . . . thematic coherence despite any amount of incoherence in the outward narrative."[7] For Watt the "real doubt" concerning such arguments in favor of coherence is "just how much of the book" such an interpretation "really accounts for."[8]

It depends upon whether such interpretations are advanced to explain everything as it is encountered while reading, whether they are advanced to account for everything which is "really" in the text and which might be listed in a catalogue of its contents, or whether the interpretations are supposed to account only for what readers actually remember as they read the book and afterward. The last category is the most variable one, but for now it is sufficiently defined as what is recollected by competent readers without photographic memories who have not taken notes as they went through the text. The extent to which any interpretation really accounts for a book will also depend upon whether initial or subsequent readings are in question.

A similar difficulty with *Moll Flanders* was suggested by Watt in an essay which set the terms for much subsequent discussion while also encouraging critics to look more closely at Defoe's accomplishment. Watt points out that Defoe rather equally divides *Moll Flanders* between "over a hundred realized scenes whose average length is less than two pages, and an equally large number of passages containing rapid and often perfunctory connective synopses." This has never been disputed. The effect, according to Watt, is a "fall in tension as we switch from episode to summary—for a minute Moll Flanders will appear brilliantly illumined, only to fall back into the semi-darkness of confused recollection."[9] *Her* recollections in the form of perfunctory synopses, that is. The fall in tension presumably occurs while reading connective material, and that fall has not been denied. Nor would there be much disagreement that throughout Defoe's fiction there are many passages which seem digressive from central themes or otherwise of lesser interest than the episodes for which he is usually praised (and remembered). What results is paradoxical for Watt and probably for any academic criticism of the kind advocated by Frye: "It is certain that it is the fully presented episodes which include all that is vivid and memorable in *Moll Flanders*, and which are rightly quoted by enthusiasts as evidence of Defoe's narrative genius; but they surely forget how large a proportion of the book is occupied by uninspired summary, plaster over an inordinate number of cracks."[10] This is exactly the point which needs more consideration: Defoe's readers do surely forget some matters. But they do not forget everything.

Consequently passages which "elude thematic control," as Starr puts it when describing *Colonel Jack* and *Roxana*, may nevertheless fail to create the obstacles that Watt implies ought to result in less admiration than Defoe continues to receive.[11] Although recent criticism has enhanced our awareness of his narrative genius, the essential paradox was correctly perceived by Watt: works that should—one might have supposed—be regarded as less satisfactory with every advance in the art of coherent storytelling since Richardson and Fielding have nevertheless attracted readers willing to overlook (forget about) the passages in between those which are praised. To some extent in Defoe's case as in that of other writers, this accumulation of praise happens for cultural reasons irrelevant to formal questions. But there remains the paradox of a major novelist who managed to plaster over more "uninspired" passages than others of equal stature in the eighteenth century are given credit for concealing.

To imply that everything "vivid and memorable" occurs

in scene rather than in summary avoids several questions. There is the issue of what part such vivid scenes play when recollected by readers—and by narrators, as they frequently are—during subsequent passages. There is the question of the role played by such scenes after completion of the book. There is the problem of why (and when) Defoe's satisfied readers manage to push so much material out of mind. Watt is right: they do. Among other things the phenomenon may be taken as a sign of Defoe's success in controlling memories of his narratives.

Watt's discussion also takes one step toward exploring the problem of forgetfulness which he raises without identifying it as such. After noting "how large a proportion" of *Moll Flanders* must be pushed out of mind to praise it, Watt asserts that "Defoe, certainly, makes no effort to reduce the amount of patchwork required by consolidating the episodes into as large units as possible." As instances of this omission Watt points to Moll's narrations of her seduction by the Elder Brother and her marriage to her half-brother. The first episode is split into "a very large number of separate encounters between the characters concerned, each of whose effectiveness is largely dissipated as the narrative relapses into bare summary." The narration of Moll's reaction to her incestuous marriage "is split up into so many separate scenes that the emotional force of the episode as a whole is much weakened."[12] Expanded scenes with fewer pages of connective material between them may indeed result in a work whose power is enhanced because the reader's attention is occupied by each incident for longer periods of reading-time. If other aspects of the narrative are handled effectively, there will be more chance for it to sink in and consequently a corresponding gain. Although consolidation

The Reader's Memory 113

into the largest possible units is by no means always a virtue, there are certainly enough advantages to repay consideration of how smaller units can be combined.

In the first place, related scenes will always be consolidated in the reader's memory toward the end of a book and afterward. That is how memory works. Details are combined for assimilation and storage. Connective material drops away so that scenes dealing with the same theme or a particular affair coalesce in retrospect. Transitional passages fade out of the mind, and this brings those of greater interest together to operate more powerfully when remembered in combination. Nothing then separates them to dissipate their impact. It is not just Defoe's admirers who remember selectively. Everybody does unless he takes special care not to. It has often been remarked that artistic renditions may have greater impact than the real objects or situations rendered because the artist filters out irrelevancies. Memories, except for that photographic recall which is not often involved in recollecting books, do something similar. There is a retrospective imposition of patterns:

Where accurate memories are concerned—and I am not now discussing the mental rewriting or distortion that is always possible[13]—such patterns are imposed only in the sense in which all perception involves the imposition of a pattern that will somehow conform to whatever is "out there" to be perceived. It would be most precise to say that accurate memories often involve completion of patterns inherent in a series of passages but only realizable—or at least most powerfully realizable—in retrospect. To this extent remembering is very much part of the entire process of perceiving. Examples in literature range from the juxtaposition of scenes more widely separated in reading-time than in remembering-time to the consolidation of many related scenes or episodes into a single unified grouping under heads like "affair with the Elder Brother" or "years as a thief."

The text may imply categories of consolidation, or it may explicitly provide them, as when Colonel Jack refers to his military adventures and marriages as a twenty-four-year interval "of levity, and profligate Wickedness" or when Moll at one point sums up her previous career as "a vitious and abominable Life for 24 Years past" (*CJ*, p. 308; *MF*, p. 144). Such phrases are one way of encouraging the mental grouping of episodes that were necessarily spread out—and perhaps not so clearly related—as they were read. The question of whether material is under thematic control is thus also very much a question of when it is or is not brought under control during the reader's encounter with a narrative. In the most coherent novels everything will be under some form of apparent control from the outset, but even so the nature of thematic control may shift during and after a reading.

Defoe's avoidance of chapter divisions is another encouragement for readers to combine passages more closely together in retrospect. In works that do provide chapter divisions, they may supply categories that facilitate retrospective consolidation of episodes. Where such help is not available, readers will nevertheless make connections on the basis of other clues, and perhaps be all the more impelled to attend to them because the text is not typographically compartmentalized. Philip Stevick suggests that "Defoe's technique, with its absence of physical division . . . is a remarkably persuasive mimetic structure, fashioned as it is because that is the way experience is felt."[14] The gain, however, is largely in conveying how experiences are felt while they are happening. Whatever else chapter divisions accomplish, they convey a sense of pastness because they mimic the consolidation within memory of previous experiences in ways that allow for more convenient storage.[15] While events are taking place, it is most often unclear how they are finally to be classified and in that sense what "chapter" they are part of.

Defoe's reluctance to provide chapter headings even in retrospective narratives is all the more striking because, as Stevick also remarks, there were precedents for including —and expecting—chapter divisions in stories of all kinds "at least since Homer."[16] Their omission is one more strategy which contributes to the impression that, as Maximillian Novak puts it with reference to other devices, "in a very real sense Defoe's narrative is always occurring in the present."[17] Despite the retrospective viewpoint of Defoe's protagonists, the burden of consolidating narrated events is by the absence of chapters shifted toward readers in a way that, for the entire narratives, imitates encounters with unfolding present experience more than it imitates the portrayal of the narrator's memories. Sometimes other strategies counterbalance this effect, especially in *A Journal of the Plague Year*. For the most part, however, Defoe's omission of chapters in favor of continuous narrative facilitates the reader's inclination to consolidate episodes in memory where they may operate together more powerfully than when encountered separately during reading.

Defoe's most striking episodes are not thus consolidated, however, *only* because any author may depend upon the reader's memory to combine related material. Let us consider one problematic sequence mentioned by Watt, for example. Defoe's narration of Moll's seduction by the Elder

Brother is comprised of separate encounters between the characters concerned, but Defoe encourages readers to consolidate the successive scenes by including allusions that call into play the reader's memory of what has just been read. Even while reading, the narrated moments—and the narratives of them—are superimposed upon one another in ways that combine separate episodes in the reader's experience to a greater degree than might be expected from their successive distribution on the printed pages.

When Moll and the Elder Brother are alone for the first time, she reports that "having me in his Arms he Kiss'd me three or four times . . . and then sitting down, says, *dear Betty* I am in Love with you." Defoe's bridge to the next scene is mostly an account of Moll's state of mind, including her observation that "from this time my Head run upon strange Things, and I may truly say, I was not myself; to have such a Gentleman talk to me of being in Love with me" (p. 21). The brother's declaration from the previous scene is echoed and recalled by the repetition of "in Love." At the next meeting, Moll reports, he "comes into the Room to me directly, and began just as he did before with taking me in his Arms, and Kissing me for almost a quarter of an Hour together" (p. 22). Here both the sense of the passage and the verbal echo "in his Arms" are transformed into explicit allusions to the previous encounter by the phrase "just as he did before." Readers can hardly avoid accepting this invitation to remember the previous scene, which is thus called to mind for comparison with the scene being described and becomes a part of it.

After telling about the rest of the second visit and how in parting the Elder Brother "put five Guineas into my Hand," Moll explains that she includes such details so a proper moral can be drawn if her "Story comes to be read by any innocent young Body." Moll introduces her account of the third visit by saying that the Elder Brother "comes up again in half an Hour, or thereabouts, and falls to Work with me again as before, only with a little less Introduction" (p. 23). The phrase "again as before" invites readers to recollect the previous scene (which in turn by recollection leads to its predecessor) and perhaps even the exact words which are only two paragraphs before the phrase inviting recollection of them: "Taking his Advantage, he threw me down upon the Bed, and Kiss'd me there most violently; but to give him his Due, offer'd no manner of Rudeness to me, only Kiss'd me a great while" (p. 22). Repetition of "Kiss'd me" helps impress the phrase (and the fact) on the reader's memory. Among its other effects reiteration is a way of making something more memorable. Moreover the invited recollections of the second visit serve as an initial description of the *next* scene: the explicitly evoked memory, in other words, becomes part of the description of the following scene.

Readers know what the Elder Brother did "before" and therefore know what he is going to do next. Their memory of the previous passage, however, is only a substitute for another description at the outset of Moll's narration of the next scene. As she goes on to describe what happens, memories of the previous episode serve as explicit definition of the reader's expectations, which Moll's narrative then confirms. It would of course be an innocent reader indeed who could not anticipate in any event the outcome of the third meeting between Moll and the Elder Brother. But Defoe ensures that memories of what the Elder Brother did "before" will provide expectations, and then uses those expectations—which is to say, explicitly evoked memories of the previous scene—as a way of maximizing narrative tension throughout the account of the third meeting.

Placement of the phrase "again as before" is crucial to the effect. By telling what is *going* to happen (i.e. what happened "before") Defoe enhances suspense (and quickens the tempo) by creating an interval of reading-time during which readers know the outcome but must wait *for* it to happen. After being prepared for "a little less Introduction"—and remembering that there was not much introduction to the main business of the previous meeting—the reader encounters a paragraph containing more introductory conversation than he has been led to expect: "And, First, when he enter'd the Room, he turn'd about, and shut the Door. Mrs. *Betty*, said he . . ." (p. 23). During the ensuing conversation, which occupies the rest of the paragraph, readers are likely to keep their memory of how Moll and the Elder Brother most conspicuously fell "to Work . . . before" in mind as an expectation of what will happen when the talking stops.

Anticipation in the form of that memory would not be so likely if the sentence introducing the paragraph starting "And, First" had omitted, as it could easily have done, the phrase "and falls to Work with me again as before, only with a little less Introduction." If Defoe had only wanted to patch the two scenes together with bare summary of events between them, it would have been easier (and quicker for Defoe, whose presumed haste in writing is so often invoked to account for his technique, especially if it looks like a mistake) just to write: "He comes up again in half an Hour, or thereabouts. And, First. . . ." The omission of Moll's allusion to the previous scene would not have altered the reader's expectations by much. It might even seem a better way of enhancing suspense by withholding a clear statement of what is to follow. But in a characteristic small reversal of temporal order, Defoe reveals the outcome first ("falls to Work with me again as before") and *then* tells what led up to that outcome. He thus creates the kind of suspense that comes from one's waiting for something which he knows to be inevitable.

Defoe's narratives most often follow the sequence of plot time: what happened first is narrated first, and the order of narration follows the order of narrated events. But the departures from this chronological order which synchronizes narrative and plot sequence are a significant feature of Defoe's style. They do not call attention to themselves as in the case of works that plunge in medias res and then proceed without much synchronization of narrative and plot sequence. Defoe seldom resorts to entire scenes that are flashbacks or anticipations of the final outcome. Within scenes, however, he may present information allowing the outcome of that scene to be known before the narrative arrives at the scene's conclusion. Thus Defoe achieves by local strategy many of the effects that depend upon that reversal of narrative sequence and plot sequence which allows the reader to be informed about what is going to happen before being told how it comes about.

Novak has pointed out another place in *Moll Flanders* where Defoe narrates "in a manner that skilfully reverses the event" and Moll's forebodings: "It was in vain to speak comfortably to him, the Wound had sunk too deep, it was a Stab that touch'd the Vitals, he grew Melancholy and Disconsolate, and from thence Lethargick, and died; I foresaw the Blow, and was extremely oppress'd in my Mind, for I saw evidently that if he died I was undone" (p. 150).[18] Such reversals deserve more notice than they have received given the general framework of chronological narration in which they are embedded. They allow some advantages of rereading—with knowledge of the outcome—even during a first reading. They replace narrative probabilities with narrative certainty.

C. S. Lewis explained the importance of this when he distinguished between works that cater to mere "narrative lust" —curiosity about what is going to happen—and those which are designed to achieve effects that are not "used up" when the end is known: "You cannot, except at the first reading, be really curious about what happened. . . . The re-reader is looking not for actual surprises (which can come only once) but for a certain surprisingness. . . . In the only sense that matters, the surprise works just as well the twentieth time as the first. . . . It is better when you know it is coming: free from the shock of actual surprise you can attend better to the intrinsic surprisingness of the peripeteia."[19] It is better, that is, when you have memories of what is *going* to happen later in the narrative: when you read the first act of *Hamlet* remembering what happens in the last. Some works like *Pride and Prejudice* depend upon such effects to such an extent that a second reading (or what may amount to the same thing, a remembering of major episodes in the light of their aftermath) becomes a necessary part of their temporal structure.

Although Defoe was the master of strange surprising adventures, he was not simply interested in springing the unexpected upon readers. He avoided that by a variety of devices ranging from title pages summing up the story to anticipatory hints ("as you shall hear in its place") to prophetic dreams and small departures from chronological order of narration. All such devices are ways of creating prior memories of the outcome—of a paragraph or of twenty-eight years on an island. Readers then bring such memories to the narrative sequence when the narrator resumes the telling of events in chronological order. Defoe's reluctance to rely exclusively on effects deriving mainly from curiosity about how things will turn out is also reflected in his preference for first-person narratives. Readers must infer at the outset that Moll has not been hanged, nor Singleton, and that Crusoe has been rescued. There are, to be sure, many places where Defoe does not anticipate what is going to happen, and where suspense builds up on that account to quicken the pace and to create other effects that depend on avoiding what seems the most probable outcome. But there has been insufficient appreciation of his departures from chronological sequence in order to create memories of the narrative future.

After Moll's paragraph describing conversation at the outset of her third meeting with the Elder Brother, she reports that "we had not sat long, but he got up, and stopping my very Breath with Kisses, threw me upon the Bed again." Even without the word *again*, readers could hardly avoid remembering the previous bedroom scenes and noticing their similarity to this one, which also ends short of "that, which they call the last Favour" when the Elder Brother departs after putting "almost a Handful of Gold in my Hand" (p. 23). The similarity of events is enhanced by the verbal echo of "threw me upon the Bed" with "threw me down upon the Bed," and of "Gold in my Hand" with "five Guineas into my Hand." By adding the word *again*, however, as well as by alluding at the outset of Moll's description of the third meeting to what the Elder Brother did "before," Defoe makes the invitations to remember previous episodes an explicit as well as an implicit part of the narrative structure.

Consolidation of these separate scenes in the reader's memory is therefore not left to the likelihood that any scene which resembles previous ones will stir up memories of its predecessors. So far as the text is concerned, allusions to the previous scenes are an intrinsic part of Moll's description of the third meeting. So far as readers are concerned, this means that memories of Moll's narration of previous scenes are an inherent part of the comprehension of the third meeting. There is no way in which her entire account of that scene can be read correctly without remembering the previous scenes. If they are forgotten, the meaning of *again as before* will be lost.

That loss would not interfere with understanding the events of the third meeting, however. What is said and done during that meeting is described fully enough so that anyone given the passage describing it without having read the previous pages, and with the allusions to them omitted, would know what happened during the meeting and would only miss the fact that it does resemble two previous ones. Thus Defoe intends the memories elicited by *again as before* to be part of reading about the third meeting without making those memories necessary to an understanding of the story merely as story. The structure of memories (of previous passages describing previous scenes) created by that allusion to what happened before becomes a stylistic feature in that it marks a characteristic way of narrating events that might have been equally well conveyed as a series of facts without including the phrase that *must*—in order to be understood—trigger memories. Those memories convey meanings that might have been lost had the seduction been portrayed in one expanded scene because they underscore the fact that Moll is falling into a pattern of misconduct. It is to emphasize such patterns—and thus contribute to characterization—that Defoe often includes retrospective allusions which consolidate memories of previous scenes with narration of subsequent episodes.

Critics have remarked the rhythms of similar events that mark Defoe's manner of proceeding in *Roxana, Captain Singleton,* and *Colonel Jack* as well as in *Robinson Crusoe* and *Moll Flanders.* Not all similar episodes explicitly allude to and create memories of each other as in the narration of Moll's second and third meetings alone with the Elder Brother. But individual episodes making up any extended rhythm of similar events by the very fact of similarity will tend to consolidate in retrospect and therefore to create a more powerful impression of what kind of behavior each episode exemplifies. The ethical quality of conduct can be emphasized forcefully by narrating several morally equivalent episodes that repeat one another with only minor variations that tend to drop out of mind as the incidents are remembered. Moll's being kissed by the Elder Brother —or her marriages, her crimes, Singleton's piracies, Jack's military adventures and Roxana's affairs—together with the moral implications will stay in mind vividly even when —and partially because—individual scenes are so alike that it is hard to keep them sorted out and distinct in memory. Such episodes fuse together in retrospect to achieve cumulative effects that are in sum more powerful than any of the individual scenes or even all of them taken merely *as a series.* Instead of remaining a sequence spread out over reading-time (and the book's pages), related scenes combine *at once* in the reader's memory to have an impact which may approach or transcend what might have been achieved by the opposite strategy of presenting one longer scene as a typical example of conduct which illustrates character.

For this reason, the account of Moll's affair with the Elder Brother, split as it is into several scenes that reinforce one another, is a paradigm of much that is best in Defoe's narrative technique. After the Elder Brother leaves the room at the end of his third meeting with Moll, she says that she "thought of nothing, but the fine Words, and the Gold" (p. 24). This invites the reader to think back over what he said. To understand her remark he must either remember what the brother said ("telling me how passionately he lov'd me, and that tho' he could not mention such a thing, till he came to his Estate, yet he was resolv'd to make me happy then, and himself too; *that is to say, to Marry me*, and abundance of such fine things" [p. 23]); or at least remember that there *were* fine words, and thus in more or less detail recapitulate the scene—and perhaps the Elder Brother's fine words from the previous meeting as well ("*he said*, he was charm'd with me, and that he could not rest Night, or Day till he had told me how he was in Love with me" [p. 22]). Here as in many other such allusions, understanding a sentence in Defoe's text cannot be distinguished from recollecting a previous episode. Reading becomes remembering.

In this context Defoe invites readers to exercise in another way their memories of Moll's affair with the Elder Brother: "Thus I gave up myself to a readiness of being ruined without the least concern, and am a fair *Memento* to all young Women, whose Vanity prevails over their Vertue" (p. 24).

Early in the novel Moll is transformed into an emblem of the misconduct that results when vanity prevails over virtue. She becomes a warning and a reminder. To profit from Moll as memento, readers must keep in mind what she has done: all the scenes in which she "gave up" herself "to a readiness of being ruined." To forget how Moll is seduced—or her later misconduct—is to risk the same dangers. All the places in which Defoe's narration pauses while a moral is drawn are also invitations to remember the previous events from which the moral is derived and to which it applies. Whether or not the explicitly didactic statements are taken to heart by readers, each of the lessons which are stated becomes an invitation to recollect and thus consolidate the episodes which lead to an explanation of their meaning.

Throughout the remaining episodes dealing with Moll's seduction by the Elder Brother and her marriage to Robin, textual invitations to remember previous passages are less frequent and less explicit, but nevertheless they are sufficient to consolidate the entire sequence in the reader's memory as a coherent whole with its own cumulative impact, rather than simply a collection of individually striking scenes glued together with perfunctory transitions or merely by connection with the same affair and by their chronological order. After describing her seduction at the Elder Brother's secret rendezvous "where was all the Convenience in the World to be as Wicked as we pleas'd," Moll sums up meetings extending over "near half a Year" by saying: "We had after this, frequent Opportunities to repeat our Crime" (pp. 26–27). Readers must remember the seduction scene to grasp the next development, which Defoe presents as six months in which Moll's present time is occupied mainly with improper "Opportunities to repeat" her immediate past. Robin's courtship of Moll is then introduced in the next paragraph with the explanation that "before this half Year was expir'd, his younger Brother, of whom I have made some mention in the beginning of the Story, falls to work with me" (p. 27). The verbal echo here of the episode in which the Elder Brother "falls to Work with me again as before" will trigger memories that immediately link this development with the previous sequence.

Readers will have no trouble remembering that there is a younger brother, and they would experience no difficulty in following the narrative even if that fact were here introduced for the first time. By adding the phrase "of whom I have made some mention in the beginning of the Story," however, Defoe invites explicit memories of the beginning, and he is also indirectly reminding readers of *what* story Moll is relating and that they are in the midst of at this point in *Moll Flanders*. It is not the beginning of the novel, which is the beginning of the story of Moll's entire life, which she here recalls, but the next beginning: that place where she tells of going into service. In the sentence after she mentions for the first time that "the Lady in the House where I was, had two Sons," Moll starts the story of her affair with the Elder Brother by saying: "The eldest . . . began . . . taking Notice upon all Occasions how pretty I was" (p. 19). It is this passage and the beginning it describes that Defoe recalls.

After eliciting that memory, Defoe invites comparison of the two affairs by underscoring their similarity: "He finding me alone in the Garden one Evening, begins a Story of the same Kind to me, made good honest Professions of being in Love with me; and in short, proposes fairly and Honourably to Marry me" (p. 27). Two ironies are created here. The first is that resulting from the duplication of situations as Robin "begins a Story of the same Kind" which (in a different sense of *story*) readers have just perused and which they are invited to remember for purposes of comparison. The play on *story*—his professions of love, Moll's previous narrative of her affair with the Elder Brother—is one of Defoe's characteristic uses of puns to heighten awareness of the text as something being read ("a Story"), and thus sharpen the reader's memories of it.

All ironies resulting from the induced feeling of "here we go again" depend upon memories of the previous episode which allow its similarity to the succeeding one to be grasped. So do the second kind of ironies resulting from the fact that, as it turns out, these "good honest Professions" really are good honest professions. Robin does want to marry Moll, to her embarrassment and our amusement.

The ensuing tragicomedy depends for most of its irony upon readers understanding—that is to say, remembering—what Moll knows but Robin does not know about her affair with his brother. Thus by a strategy which is frequent in *Moll Flanders* and Defoe's other fiction, ironic effects are sustained by the reader's memory of events unknown to one or more of the characters. Because of such memories, readers appreciate scenes from two or more viewpoints at once (even though there is only one narrative point of view), as when Robin's proposals and Moll's reluctance to marry him are understood with reference both to her love for the Elder Brother and Robin's ignorance of that affair. Whatever calls attention to situational ironies of the kind built into Moll's affair with Robin also evokes memories of the preceding events which create that irony. Such memories also work as devices of consolidation pulling disparate episodes together in the reader's memory whenever situational ironies are perceived.

Throughout the narration of Moll's courtship by Robin, memories of her affair with the Elder Brother are thus in play, although without such frequent reminders of particular phrases and scenes as Defoe included in the account of her seduction. But there are several passages that evoke memories of previous scenes. At the outset of her involvement with Robin, Moll thinks back over her meetings with the Elder Brother and "presently remember'd what I had often thought of, that he had never spoken a Word of having me for a Wife, after he had Conquer'd me for a Mistress" (p. 28). Because their meetings after Moll became his mistress are not described in detail, readers can only accept her recollection of them as correct. But her statement does encourage memories of what the Elder Brother said in the meetings up to—and including—the one in which Moll is "Conquer'd." In those scenes, as readers are encouraged to remember, there was talk of marriage.

When Moll discusses Robin's proposal with the Elder Brother, "he was very kind to me, and kiss'd me a thousand Times. . . . Yet he offer'd no more all the while we were together . . . which I much wonder'd at . . . considering how it us'd to be" (p. 31). The last clause also invites readers to remember "how it us'd to be" in scenes which they have read. After additional discussions in which the Elder Brother urges Moll to marry Robin, there is another meeting which Moll starts to describe by saying: "We fell into the same Arguments all over again, or at least so near the same, as it would be to no purpose to repeat them" (p. 35). To portray this scene Defoe draws upon the reader's memories of the previous scenes in which arguments between Moll and the Elder Brother were given at length. He invites readers to imagine the first part of this encounter by remembering what has already been narrated, and then has Moll continue: "At last, I *ask'd him* warmly..." (p. 35). Nothing encourages readers to spend very long remembering previous arguments, for there is no need to recollect them verbatim in order to envision the start of this scene. But the intrusion of memories will nevertheless slow its tempo and will also result in consolidation of previous scenes with it because memories of earlier arguments are incorporated by Defoe into Moll's description of what happened at the outset.

Throughout the rest of Moll's account of events leading to her first marriage, several scenes are explicitly consolidated by similar allusions to previous ones: "Away goes the old Lady to her Daughters, and tells them, the whole Story, just as I had told it her.... Then he told me the whole Story between *Robin* ... and his Mother, and Sisters, and himself; as it is above.... Brother *Robin* ... having got his Mother's Consent *as above*. ... *as above*, my Husband was so Fuddled when he came to Bed" (pp. 44, 46, 49). Within a general framework where readers must keep remembering the affair with the Elder Brother in order to grasp Moll's state of mind and Defoe's ironies, scenes are even more fully consolidated in the reader's awareness by these smaller invitations to remember.

In the account of Moll's marriage to her brother, the other problematic sequence mentioned by Watt, Defoe reserves for the concluding scenes such explicit invitations to remember statements from previous ones. However the entire episode is consolidated by a similar framework within which ironies arising from disparities between Moll's viewpoint and her husband's before he is told the truth are constant reminders of the situation disclosed in the scene (and hence *of* the scene) where Moll discovers her mother's identity. In the episode of the incestuous marriage as a whole, Defoe resorts to separate scenes to increase the emotional force of the narrated events. Perhaps Watt is right to suggest that even more emotional force might have been achieved by some other strategy. But instead of concentrating the episode into the largest possible units by minimizing the number of scenes, Defoe uses several scenes to convey a sense of the protracted and mounting horror of Moll's predicament. After discovering that she is married to her brother she resolves to conceal the fact, and "thus I liv'd with the greatest Pressure imaginable for three Year more" (p. 74).

While Defoe never attempts to expand reading-time toward an approximation of read-about time as Richardson did, the proliferation of scenes here nevertheless does help to convey a greater sense of the duration of Moll's agony than could easily have been achieved by compressing her discovery and its aftermath into the fewest possible scenes. Readers must exercise some temporal imagination as they register the fact that Moll lived with her secret for over three years. What that meant for her is dramatized by the number of subsequent scenes which portray the resulting situation as she gradually prepares her husband for the truth. After describing her frame of mind, Moll reports that when her husband forbade her return to England "this plung'd me again" (p. 76). *Again* invites readers to remember Moll's previous description of her depression. Its duration is therefore emphasized. These scenes in turn create suspense about when and how she will disclose the truth. Tension—and also emotional force—builds up in ways that would be hard to duplicate with fewer scenes.

The Reader's Memory

As readers wait for the denouement, they undergo something like the agonized waiting that Moll describes. If these pages seem lacking in emotional force, the problem will be readers who cannot take the incestuous relationship as seriously as Moll's other difficulties. If you believe that Defoe was wrong to include incest among Moll's predicaments, then whatever prolongs attention to that episode—including proliferation of scenes describing it—will seem to weaken the novel. This is an objection to lurid incidents however, not structural weakness.

When Moll tells her mother the truth, she responds with a lengthy outburst, saying in part: "*Why we are all undone!* Married to thy own Brother! Three Children, and two alive, all of the same Flesh and Blood! My Son and my Daughter lying together as Husband and Wife! All Confusion and Destraction for ever! *miserable Family!*" In the next scene Moll reports "a second Conference upon the same Subject" during which her mother "fell into her Rhapsodies again" (p. 79). This invites readers to remember the previous outburst and make that memory part of their understanding of the second conference. From this point to the end of the whole episode, when Moll returns to England, several allusions create memories that link scenes more tightly while also increasing their emotional impact.

These allusions reiterate some of Moll's worst fears. Thus she tells her mother how her husband "had threaten'd already to put me into a Mad-house, and what concern I had been in about it, and how that was the thing that drove me to the necessity of discovering it to her as I had done" (p. 80). In a later scene reported by Moll, her mother reproves the husband for "his terrifying and affrighting me with his Threats of sending me to a Mad-house." He responds that "he had no such design as that of sending me to a Mad-house, whatever he might say in his Passion" (p. 82). These exchanges are followed by another backward glance as Moll finally tells her husband the truth "and particularly how my Mother came to discover it to me, as above" (p. 85). Here, too, memories of what was narrated "above" are called upon to complete another scene by serving instead of recapitulation in Defoe's text. Thus, especially toward the end of the episode of Moll's incestuous marriage, Defoe includes allusions creating memories that consolidate related scenes by enhancing their tendency to stay in mind as a unit. By these and similar invitations to remember Defoe often makes linear narrative sequences achieve many of the effects associated with spatial form.

2

The accepted definition of spatial form is that embodied in statements like W. J. Harvey's suggestion that such novels as *Ulysses* and *Dr. Faustus* "derive part of their distinctive quality from the fact that they are very long works designed to be read as though they were very short and could be grasped as unities by a single act of attention."[20] And thus also by a single act of memory. But they cannot be grasped that way. There is no *single* act of attention or memory that would contain *Ulysses* at any conscious level of the mind. Such works depend upon the interplay between devices which invite readers to remember everything at once, and narratives whose length and complexity preclude that from happening but do not discourage the attempt. Joseph Frank conceded as much in the revision of his seminal essay on spatial form when he finally defined it as that of any novel or poem in which writers "*ideally* intend the reader to apprehend their work spatially, in a moment of time, rather than as a sequence."[21] For short poems or narratives this ideal may be realized. As works get longer, it becomes harder to keep everything in mind simultaneously. However the extent to which any narrative induces such efforts to remember separate episodes or its entire text for simultaneous rather than sequential apprehension may be taken as a measure of the degree to which it approaches spatial form.

Defoe's fictions are by no means all equally close to the achievement of spatial form; nor does it serve the same purpose insofar as it is achieved in his works. In *A New Voyage Round the World*, for example, Defoe almost entirely avoids allusions which encourage readers to keep previous episodes in mind as they go through the book. Attention is always pointed forward. At the end, or at any point along the way, readers may recollect what they have read, especially because memories are facilitated by a linear narrative sequence in which events are related in the order of their occurrence in plot-time. But nothing at the conclusion or in the text of *A New Voyage* strongly encourages recollection of the entire narrative or of particular passages for any specific purpose. Here, more than in his major fiction, Defoe reverts to the picaresque structure in which each successive "now" of reading time is a self-contained moment with minimal connections backward or forward. When readers finish the last page, they have completed their business with *A New Voyage Round the World*. Their subsequent memories of it are no part of its formal structure.

At the conclusion of *Colonel Jack* readers are invited to *start* their consideration of what they have just finished.

Not until the fourth paragraph from the end does Defoe extend an invitation that might seem equally (or more) appropriate for a preface. Jack says of his repentance: "It is with this Temper that I have written my Story, I would have all that design to read it, prepare to do so with the Temper of Penitents; and remember with how much Advantage they may make their penitent reflections at Home, under the merciful Dispositions of Providence in Peace, Plenty and Ease, rather than Abroad under the Discipline of a Transported Criminal as my Wife and my Tutor" (pp. 308–9). Jack's advice on the best way of *preparing* to read his story comes after some three hundred pages of narration whose most important reading—that is, its interpretation and application—is thus to occur in the retrospect of memory.

Those who—as they arrive at the conclusion—"design to read" *Colonel Jack* are advised to do so with "the Temper of Penitents": that is, in the frame of mind of those looking over their own lives and past errors while also remembering Jack's life. Implicit in this advice is a suggestion that readers should also adopt a proper attitude toward the future. Bailey defines *repentance* as "such a Conversion of a Sinner to God, by which he is not only heartily sorry for the Evil he has done, and resolved to forsake it, but actually begins to renounce it, and to do his Duty according to the utmost of his Ability, with a stedfast Purpose to continue a faithful Servant of God to the End of his Life." Ideally readers ought to adopt a "stedfast Purpose" of serving God in the future while recollecting their own lives for comparison with Jack's in order to profit from its lessons. Jack recommends "to all that read this Story, that when they find their Lives come up in any degree to any Similitude of Cases, they will enquire by me, and ask themselves, Is not this the time to Repent?" (p. 309). Jack's story is to be read (remembered) by those who recollect their own lives together with his narration to look for similarities ("Similitude of Cases"). Defoe provides an ending to *Colonel Jack* which invites readers to exercise their memories for a morally sound purpose.

At this point during the last few paragraphs the preceding narrative is brought under complete thematic control, although only in retrospect and only to the extent that readers do accept the invitation to remember its episodes in connection with Jack's repentance (and, ideally, their own lives). His spiritual change allows prior episodes to be reclassified as in some measure leading to or away from the right path—even though many of them have played no major causal role in his change and had no particular spiritual significance either to Jack as he lived through the events narrated or to his readers during their progress through the narrative.

At the beginning of *Colonel Jack* Defoe in the preface informs readers that *"the Ends and Designs of the whole Book"* include encouraging the wicked to change by making it *"appear that the best and only good End of a wicked mispent Life is Repentance . . . and that the Penitent shall be return'd like the Prodigal, and his latter End be better than his Beginning"* (p. 2). This creates an expectation that the events of Jack's life will eventually be applied like those in the parable of the prodigal son. *Colonel Jack*'s ending is therefore also an implicit reminder of the preface which establishes those expectations as well as a realization of the narrative model which is proposed at the outset. In the main body of Jack's narrative, however, there are few reminders of the preface, which may therefore drop out of mind. Even so episodes that are not explicitly subordinated to the lessons suggested by the preface and conclusion do not undermine the didactic structure proposed at the outset and confirmed by the ending. Such "neutral" episodes may eventually (in retrospect) reinforce it. Hence Defoe's assurances in the preface that *Colonel Jack* is safe for all readers (unlike *Moll Flanders*, which is introduced as a book that may be dangerous).

The final paragraph of *Moll Flanders* does not encourage recollection of the preceding text. Its last sentence invites readers to guess whether Moll and her husband did carry out their "resolve to spend the Remainder of our Years in sincere Penitence, for the wicked Lives we have lived" (p. 267). Roxana's last paragraph also points attention forward by encouraging readers to imagine for themselves the "dreadful Course of Calamities" that she mentions without describing. When Singleton signs off as "*Your Old Friend*, CAPTAIN BOB," after "having so plainly told you, that I am come to *England*," it is hard to resist speculation about the rest of his life (*CS*, p. 277). The last lines of *A Journal of the Plague Year* encourage memories of what has been read without specifying the purpose of such recollection. They also refer to H.F.'s survival in a way that divides the reader's attention between thinking about the plague and thinking about the chief use to which H.F. (so far as they know) put his remaining years: writing the narrative which has just been completed.

> *A dreadful Plague in* London *was*
> *In the Year Sixty Five*
> *Which swept an Hundred Thousand Souls*
> *Away; yet I alive!*

The last six paragraphs of *Robinson Crusoe* arouse expectations of a sequel to provide the "farther Account" which is hinted at in the last sentence. The ending of *Colonel Jack* is therefore Defoe's most explicit attempt to establish memories of an entire narrative.

Elsewhere Defoe moves toward spatial form by local strategies. These strategies are even more successful, however, in allowing readers to understand several episodes in the light of one another and thus to apprehend large portions of the narrative at once—"in a moment of time rather than as a sequence." When Roxana tells about her affair with the nobleman in Paris, for example, she mentions getting a necklace after delighting him by proving that her beauty was natural, not the result of cosmetics: "It was an undeniable Demonstration, and he kiss'd my Cheeks and Breasts a thousand times, with Expressions of the greatest Surprize imaginable" (*R*, p. 73). As Roxana narrates the incident years later with greater awareness of its depravity, she remarks that she "could not but sometimes look back with Astonishment, at the Folly of Men of Quality, who immense in their Bounty, as in their Wealth, give to a Profusion, and without Bounds, to the most scandalous of our Sex, for granting them the Liberty of abusing themselves, and ruining both" (p. 74). This is the episode's moral.

Roxana enforces it by juxtaposing, as only she and her readers can, a past and future that were unknown to the nobleman as as he gave her the necklace and became more deeply ensnared: "I, that knew what this Carcass of mine had been but a few Years before; how overwhelm'd with Grief, drown'd in Tears, frighted with the Prospect of Beggary, and surrounded with Rags and Fatherless Children" (p. 74). She continues with a paragraph recapitulating what has been narrated up to this point in *Roxana*. Defoe thus makes sure that readers remember Roxana's past (which she conceals from the nobleman) as a morally significant dimension of his relationship with her.

Roxana's body, which she has just described in the height of its unpainted *"Beauty, that ... is the meer Work of Nature"* (p. 72), is called "this Carcass" by the older Roxana as she narrates the episode. Thus Defoe makes readers think of her future death as well as the nobleman's by including a word that turns her body into (for readers) an emblem of mortality—"this Carcass." Roxana repeats the moral in different words: "I say, I cou'd not but reflect upon the Brutality and blindness of Mankind; that because Nature had given me a good Skin" (p. 74). Then she explains why she has included in her narrative so many details of previous affairs: "It is for this Reason, that I have so largely set down the Particulars of the Caresses I was treated with by the Jeweller, and also by this Prince; not to make the Story an Incentive to the Vice, which I am now such a sorrowful Penitent for being guilty of, *God forbid any shou'd make so vile a Use of so good a Design*, but to draw the just Picture of a Man enslav'd to the Rage of his vicious Appetite; how he defaces the Image of God in his Soul; dethrones his Reason; causes Conscience to abdicate the Possession, and exalts Sence into the vacant Throne; how he deposes the Man, and exalts the Brute" (p. 75). Defoe's metaphor here involves a conventional comparison with the sister art that is spatial, not temporal, and in which time must be frozen: to "draw the just Picture" of the nobleman's moral state, Roxana's past must become part of what is portrayed by the narration of her affair with him in Paris.

So must her future and his. To reinforce the forward

allusions of *carcass*, Defoe makes Roxana add another paragraph more explicitly linking past and future with the moment when she receives the necklace:

> O! could we hear now, the Reproaches this Great Man afterwards loaded himself with, when he grew weary of this admir'd Creature, and became sick of his Vice! how profitable would be the Report of them to the Reader of this Story; but had he himself also known the dirty History of my Actings upon the Stage of Life, that little time I had been in the World, how much more severe would those Reproaches have been upon himself; but I shall come to this again. (p. 75)

By wishing it were possible to hear the nobleman's subsequent regrets "now" when the gift is described and the narrative read, Roxana provides the information that he did later reproach himself for his involvement with her. She thus succeeds (as only a retrospective narrator can) in collapsing for readers the temporal distinctions between past, present and future of plot-time: they fuse in a kind of verbal triptych that can be taken in at a glance and that serves to enforce a moral. Within the same sentence, and thus within the same "moment" of reading-time, Defoe combines an allusion to Roxana's (memorable) "dirty History" prior to meeting the nobleman with a reference to what he thought "afterwards."

In the episode two varieties of spatial form are achieved. The first is that which stems from narrating simultaneously events which are separated in plot-time (the nobleman's affair with Roxana and the "Reproaches" which he "afterwards loaded himself with"). The second is that which stems from alluding to previously mentioned events (what Roxana "had been a few Years before": her "dirty History") in a way that incorporates memories of the prior narrative with the experience of subsequent pages and thus combines in the reader's awareness events that were separated in reading-time as well as plot-time. It is the second kind of spatial form which is most characteristic of Defoe's fiction.

The explicit retrospective allusions which create the textual memories necessary for such spatial form range from statements such as those which combine scenes in *Moll Flanders* to more casual reminders such as these from *Roxana* in which Defoe ensures that repetition of information is noticed as repetition by readers: "I can say no more now, but that *as above*, being arriv'd in *Holland*, with my Spouse and his Son, *formerly mention'd*, I appear'd there with all the Splendor and Equipage suitable to our new Prospect, *as I have already observ'd* (p. 329). By themselves such brief reminders of what has already been told would mainly be noticed as a slight personality trait. Roxana is more inclined to such phrases than Crusoe, Singleton, Jack, or Moll; and her allusions to what has been previously narrated are to that slight extent part of her distinctive "voice." But *Roxana* provides a context in which all reminders, however brief, of what has been narrated serve to reinforce the effect of spatial form which is most powerfully created by rhythms of similar incidents and reappearing persons or objects.

David Higdon has shown how the reappearance of the Brewer, the jewels, Roxana's children, and her Turkish costume as well as "the symmetrical repetition of motifs" work to unify *Roxana*.[22] The frequent intrusions of people or things from her past encourage readers to incorporate memories of previous episodes into their understanding of what happens in the latter parts of *Roxana*. Her name also becomes a reminder—and is initially a foreshadowing—of the scene during which she acquires it. To recollect that incident after completing *Roxana* is to think also of its causes and consequences and thus to move toward apprehending the entire work "in a moment of time rather than as a sequence."

Defoe exploits this strategy even more effectively in *Moll Flanders*, where there is no one instant of plot-time or reading-time associated with the way Moll gets her name. When her narration arrives at the period of her criminal career, Moll explains that she had been a thief "upwards of five Year" when her associates "gave me the Name of *Moll Flanders:* For it was no more of Affinity with my real Name, or with any of the Names I had ever gone by, than black is of Kin to white, except that once, as before, I call'd my self *Mrs. Flanders,* when I sheltered myself in the *Mint:* but that those Rogues never knew, nor could I ever learn how they came to give me the Name, or what the Occasion of it was" (pp. 168–69). Here Defoe explicitly dissociates Moll's name from any single episode while nevertheless making it emblematic of what she has been doing for more than five years whose activities are the most characteristic of her life. Readers thus have the strongest encouragement to remember only Moll's criminal years when thinking about her (or the novel), as Richetti has noticed does in fact happen so far as most readers are concerned.

Moll's name is also a reminder of the occasion when she took shelter in the Mint "as before." The previous passage alluded to is brief: "Upon these Apprehensions the first thing I did, was to go quite out of my Knowledge, and go by another Name: This I did effectually, for I went into the Mint too, took Lodgings in a very private Place, drest me up in the Habit of a Widow, and call'd myself Mrs. *Flanders*" (p. 54). This assumption of a false identity, even apart from the coincidence of the name she gave herself and that given her by fellow-thieves years afterward, is so much of a piece with Moll's later dodges that when it is recalled by the phrase "as before" readers easily think of the Mint episode apart from its chronological place in Moll's life and alongside the criminal adventures which it resembles. Readers are not led to regard the ordering of events in calendar time as their most significant attribute or even the most convenient handle for recollection.

A few pages after telling how her associates named her, Moll reiterates "that tho' I often robb'd with these People, yet I never let them know who I was. . . . They all knew me by the Name of *Moll Flanders*" (p. 174). Instead of making readers think of one episode like the dance at which Roxana is nicknamed, or the moment during his childhood when Jack is first called "Colonel," or the page telling when Singleton was first promoted to "Captain Bob," Moll's explanation of the name by which she was known to the other thieves is not only an allusion to an indeterminate period during her years as a thief but also a reminder—because it is a repetition—of the beginning of her narrative. In its first two paragraphs she starts the story of her life by explaining that because her real name "is so well known in the Records, or Registers at *Newgate,* and in the *Old-Bailey* . . . it is enough to tell you, that . . . some of my worst Comrades . . . know me by the Name of *Moll Flanders*" (p. 9).[23] This creates expectations at the start of the novel that her narrative will convey how Moll became so well known at Newgate. Defoe thus invites readers to regard all the episodes before Moll becomes a thief at the age of fifty as leading to that turn to crime and its aftermath even when previous episodes are not causally related to her criminal career or to each other as they might have been in a more coherently organized plot.

The sentences reiterating how Moll got her name are among Defoe's narrative confirmations of the initially aroused expectations. But every attempt by readers to locate *exactly* in either plot-time or reading-time the moment when Moll got her name results only in remembering events spread out both in Moll's narrative and the action which it describes. Readers making that attempt wind up considering the outset of her story, the account of her years as a thief during which (but at no specified moment) she became known as Moll Flanders, and earlier years involving the mint episode. To think of Moll's name and how she got it is to think of several parts of the narrative together.

Similar effects of spatial form are enhanced by all the parallel episodes which become reminders of one another and which are thus invitations to remember together what is initially encountered by readers separately as part of a sequence whose parts are separated in both plot-time and reading-time. Among the parallels which have attracted attention from critics concerned with Defoe's method of unifying narratives that do not have fully coherent plots are Moll's birth and imprisonment in Newgate, her return to Colchester, her return to Virginia, the similar storms encountered by Crusoe, his shipwrecks, his voyages, his Moorish captivity and later "imprisonment" on the island, his relationships with Xury and Friday, and the prophetic dream which foreshadows Crusoe's encounter with Friday. When that meeting is described, Defoe ensures that readers compare event and dream by having Crusoe allude to the dream twice in a way that encourages recollection of it during the narration of Friday's rescue: "Now I expected that part of my Dream was coming to pass, and that he would certainly take shelter in my Grove. . . . So I did not let my Dream come to pass in that Part, *viz.* That he came into my

Grove for shelter" (pp. 202–5). These comparisons evoke memories that emphasize the prophetic nature of the dream and thus underscore for readers the importance (and accuracy) of Crusoe's realization that he "was call'd plainly by Providence to save this poor Creature's Life" (p. 202).

Throughout *Robinson Crusoe* memories of the previous narrative are evoked so that its lessons can be more firmly grasped. Frequent allusions by Crusoe to his father's unheeded advice, for example, keep the opening scenes present in the reader's memory to reinforce the moral which Crusoe draws from the consequences of his disobedience. Other scenes are also recollected. When Crusoe observes the three men whom mutineers intend to maroon, he remarks: "This put me in Mind of the first Time when I came on Shore, and began to look about me; How I gave my self over for lost: How wildly I look'd round me: What dreadful Apprehensions I had: And how I lodg'd in the Tree all Night for fear of being devour'd by wild Beasts." Readers are invited to recollect an earlier part of the narrative so one of its lessons can be reiterated: "As I knew nothing that Night of the Supply I was to receive by the providential Driving of the Ship nearer the Land . . . so these three poor desolate Men knew nothing how certain of Deliverance and Supply they were, how near it was to them . . . at the same Time that they thought themselves lost, and their Case desperate." Memories of Crusoe's arrival on the island are juxtaposed with his description of the three men in order to enforce the moral which he states in the next sentence: "So little do we see before us in the World, and so much reason have we to depend chearfully upon the great Maker of the World, that he does not leave his Creatures so absolutely destitute, but that in the worst Circumstances they have always something to be thankful for, and sometimes are nearer their Deliverance than they imagine; nay, are even brought to their Deliverance by the Means by which they seem to be brought to their Destruction" (p. 252). Here, as so often when the narrative becomes explicitly didactic, Defoe evokes memories of prior episodes to bring together in the reader's mind all the events which point a moral as that moral is stated. This strategy is the narrative equivalent of those emblem books which print a picture and then explain its meaning on the same page so the picture remains in sight while its significance is unfolded. Spatial form is part of Defoe's emblematic method.

3

To a greater extent in *Robinson Crusoe* than elsewhere in his fiction, Defoe evokes memories of the previous narrative in order to invite consideration of possible alternative pasts and futures. Crusoe's speculations on what his fate might have been had he failed to escape from Sallee or been unable to salvage anything from the wreck, for example, invite memories of the prior narrative in order to extend or change its meaning by forcing readers to consider simultaneously what did happen and what might have happened. Such passages are implicit rather than explicit invitations to remember. But it is impossible not to keep in mind what has been previously narrated while reading a passage like the one in which Crusoe says that he "spent whole Hours, I may say whole Days, in representing to my self in the most lively Colours, how I must have acted, if I had got nothing out of the Ship. How I could not have so much as got any Food, except Fish and Turtles; and that as it was long before I found any of them, I must have perish'd first. That I should have liv'd, if I had not perish'd, like a meer Savage" (p. 130). Defoe here compels readers to remember that Crusoe did get a great many things out of the ship, that he was able to obtain food, and that he did not live like a savage. Readers are unlikely to forget these things in any case. But Defoe brings what might be called latent and continuing memories to the forefront of the reader's awareness to exploit them in a way much different from merely counting on general recollections of Crusoe's story. By its arousal of specific memories to conscious attention, this passage conveys simultaneously two different time-levels: Crusoe's real and alternate pasts are put together in the reader's mind for comparison to illustrate the advantages of his situation.

A similar strategy is employed when Crusoe wonders what he has done to deserve his fate and then imagines the voice of his conscience responding: "Ask, Why is it *that thou wert not long ago destroy'd?* Why *wert thou not drown'd in* Yarmouth Roads? *Kill'd in the Fight when the Ship was taken by* the Sallee Man of War? *Devour'd by the wild Beasts on the* Coast of Africa? Or, *Drown'd* HERE, *when all the Crew perish'd but thy self?*" (pp. 92-93). This passage recapitulates a past which cannot be separated any more than Roxana's from the meaning of later parts of the protagonist's life. Crusoe's present moments must always be seen in relationship to the temporal dimension of his own past in order to grasp their significance.

Only in that way can he become an effective emblem reminding readers of what *all* his adventures mean: "I have been in all my Circumstances a *Memento* to those who are touch'd with the general Plague of Mankind, whence, for ought I know, one half of their Miseries flow; I mean, that of not being satisfy'd with the Station wherein God and Nature has plac'd them." This statement with its invitation to recollect "all" Crusoe's "Circumstances" is followed by a clause which recalls particular episodes even while saying that later incidents would enforce the moral equally well: "For not to look back upon my primitive Condition, and the excellent Advice of my Father, the Opposition to which, was, *as I may call it,* my ORIGINAL SIN; my subsequent Mistakes of the same Kind had been the Means of my coming into this Miserable Condition" (p. 194). Crusoe goes on to explain that he has especially in mind his failure to stay on the Brazilian plantation where by farming he "might have been worth an hundred thousand *Moydors*" (p. 195). In the sentence allegorizing Crusoe's disobedience as his original sin, Defoe encourages readers to think of the initial episode in England together with "subsequent Mistakes of the same Kind." Their meaning does not so much depend on causal relationships or other aspects of distribution through time as on their moral identity, which can best be perceived by thinking of them together and comparing them "in a moment of time."

Crusoe describes a sleepless night "in the rainy Season in *March,* the four and twentieth Year" of his stay on the island, and remarks that "it is as impossible, as needless, to set down the innumerable Crowd of Thoughts that whirl'd through that great thorow-fare of the Brain, the Memory, in this Night's Time: I run over the whole History of My Life in Miniature, or by Abridgment, *as I may call it,* to my coming to this Island, and also of the Part of my Life, since I came to this Island." Here again readers are invited to recollect Crusoe's "whole History," although for them, as for him, that exercise of memory has become so familiar by this point in the narration that it is "needless" to outline *each* part of the previous history ("the innumerable Crowd of Thoughts that whirl'd through . . . Memory"). All of Crusoe's past is alluded to at once here in order to draw a moral from the fact that throughout Crusoe's time on the island he was in equal danger from cannibals although without realizing it until after encountering the footprint. To enforce the lesson which may be drawn from that fact —"How infinitely Good that Providence is, which has provided in its Government of Mankind, such narrow bounds to his Sight and Knowledge of Things . . . by having the Events of Things hid from his Eyes"—Crusoe invites readers to follow him in "comparing the happy Posture of my Affairs, in the first Years of my Habitation here, compar'd to the Life of Anxiety, Fear and Care, which I had liv'd ever since I had seen the Print of a Foot in the Sand" (p. 196). The two intervals (before and after) are to be apprehended together by first reducing them to the miniatures painted by memory and then by comparing the resulting pictures.

The effects of spatial form are achieved to the extent that readers follow the narrator's comparison of memory miniatures drawn from different parts of the text. Defoe's strategy might almost have been intended to overcome so far as possible those limitations which John Locke explained in his discussion of memory by remarking on "the narrowness that human minds are confined to here—of having great variety of ideas only by succession, not all at once. Whereas the several degrees of angels may probably have larger views; and some of them be endowed with capacities able to retain together, and constantly set before them, as in one picture, all their past knowledge at once." Locke adds that it "would be no small advantage to the knowledge of a thinking man,—if all his past thoughts and reasonings could be *always* present to him."[24] Defoe certainly understood clearly enough the advantage of striving for an analogous presentation of the past in didactic fiction. There are large parts of *Robinson Crusoe* where Crusoe's past is always present to readers.

A miniature, according to Bailey, is "a painting of pictures in water colours; also very small; a delicate kind of painting, consisting of little points or dots, instead of lines, commonly done on vellum, with very thin, simple water colors." Chambers explains that "*Miniature* is distinguished from other kinds of painting by the smalness and delicacy of its figures, the weakness of their colours, and faintness of the colouring; and in that it requires to be viewed very near."[25] These definitions show how aptly Defoe chose Crusoe's word for describing the operations of memory to stress its role in presenting abridged and faint but nevertheless recognizable images of prior experience. When *Robinson Crusoe* was published, and for some time thereafter, Defoe's metaphor of memory as miniature was very much alive. Even after midcentury Johnson censured usage of the word that did not retain the allusion to painting: "*Gay* has improperly made it an adjective."[26]

In addition to enforcing explicit lessons, Defoe's memory miniatures help to control tempo: as they show what is important by recalling significant episodes, they also slow the reader's progress by forcing attention backward to earlier parts of the narrative. Whether or not the intrusion of such memories compels readers to proceed more slowly as measured by an external clock (there is no evidence on this one way or the other), their subjective sense of duration will be altered. Other things being equal, narratives organized like *Robinson Crusoe* to provide frequent allusions to the past will seem to go more slowly, the time they describe will seem longer, and the events recollected will figure more largely in the reader's awareness than could be accounted for merely by the number of words devoted to the events that are recalled.

In Defoe's fiction memories of the previous text become part of subsequent episodes differently from the connections established by Fielding in those reminders scattered through *Tom Jones* to enable readers to pick up the thread of its narrative: "The reader will be pleased to remember that we left Mr. Jones, in the beginning of this book, on his road to Bristol. . . . The reader may be pleased to remember that, in the ninth chapter of the seventh book of our history, we left Sophia, after a long debate between love and duty, deciding the cause, as it usually I believe, happens, in favour of the former."[27] Such allusions focus attention toward what is going to happen next by making it unnecessary for readers to pause while ransacking their own memories for information on just where and in what circumstances they had last encountered the protagonists. Fielding's references to prior episodes in *Tom Jones* do not significantly create the effects of spatial form.

They enhance appreciation of a coherent plot whose power would be diminished if causal relationships were obscured or the reader's forward motion impeded by frequent recollection of previous scenes to explain their significance. Even the apologue of the Man of the Hill's narrative, although entirely defensible in terms of the formal intentions of *Tom Jones*, has most often been regarded at first encounter as a problematic intrusion.[28] Apologues are most effective if they achieve spatial form by compelling readers to keep (or try to keep) all their episodes in mind at once for application to the explicit lessons which they enforce, whereas action not primarily organized to illustrate points explicitly stated in the text will not, as action, benefit from a presentation which creates the effects of spatial form.

Thus it is not so much the prior meaning as the subsequent role of Sophia's muff toward which Fielding directs attention when he incorporates into his narrative a reminder of earlier episodes involving it: "The reader will be pleased to remember a little muff, which hath had the honour of being more than once remembered already in this history. This muff, ever since the departure of Mr. Jones, had been the constant companion of Sophia by day and her bedfellow by night; and this muff she had at this very instant upon her arm; whence she took it off with great indignation, and, having writ her name with her pencil upon a piece of paper which she pinned to it, she bribed the maid to convey it into the empty bed of Mr. Jones."[29] The muff's previous history must be remembered to understand why Sophia acts as she does and to understand the consequences of her gesture. Readers are not encouraged to stop or slow down for comparison of this and earlier scenes involving the muff, although such comparisons are quickly made. Earlier scenes are recollected mainly in order to sharpen anticipation of what will happen next when Tom finds the muff in his bed.

Only in the unraveling of secrets connected with Tom's birth does attention travel backward so readers understand earlier events in ways that were impossible at first because crucial information was withheld. But reconsideration of Blifil's villainy, Dowling's carelessness, and related matters serves mainly to accelerate the tempo by increasing expectations that Tom will finally marry Sophia. Acceleration is also increased by the places where Tom's various acts of kindness are recalled. Defoe's strategies for evoking memories in *Robinson Crusoe* have effects that more closely resemble some of those achieved by complication of narrative viewpoint in *Clarissa*, where readers must remember more than one account of many important incidents in order to realize everything that took place. Only by comparing Clarissa's description of the garden elopement with that given by Lovelace, for example, can one arrive at a full understanding of what happened as well as the moral and psychological implications.

Thus Clarissa tells of her "panic next to fainting" on first sight of Lovelace, and reports trembling "so, that I should hardly have kept my feet, had he not supported me." Exactly how he supported her is only discovered when Lovelace says in a subsequent letter that on seeing him "she trembled" and "was even fainting, when I clasped her in my supporting arms"—very closely, it would seem, although readers must finally decide what to make of Lovelace's comment: "How near, how sweetly near, the throbbing partners!"[30] Clarissa's failure to stress this embrace in her letter invites interpretation when the omission is noticed in retrospect. But what is most relevant for my subject is the way in which Richardson relies on the accumulation in the reader's memory of previously narrated facts in order to build an entire episode in the reader's mind, not on the printed pages. Crucial parts of *Clarissa* are not fully described and then repainted in miniature.

They take shape in the reader's memory, imposing mnemonic burdens (and pleasures) on a scale not encountered in Defoe's fiction apart from the narration of Crusoe's arrival on his island. Even there the effects are similar only in kind, not degree. Owing to *Clarissa*'s length, one of Richardson's difficulties was that posed by Aristotle for the hypothetical case of a painting on a canvas one thousand miles wide: the whole is too large to be either grasped at once or easily recollected for the purpose of connecting its episodes with the lessons they enforce. Having expanded the portrayal of time by devoting eight volumes to the events of a single year, Richardson achieved temporal verisimilitude of an order never before attempted. But he shared some of Defoe's didactic intentions, and as a result he had to search for a way of contracting events in retrospect so they could be contained in the reader's memory. The gigantic book and its major episodes had to be made small enough to be seen as a whole. Richardson's epistolary method forestalled most of the narrative solutions available to earlier and later writers.

He therefore resorted to another device which he explains in the preface added to *Clarissa*'s third edition: "In the Second Edition an ample *Table of Contents* to the *whole* Work was prefixed to the first volume: But that having in some measure anticipated the Catastrophe, and been thought to detain the Reader too long from entering upon the History, it has been judged adviseable to *add* (and that rather than *prefix*) to *each* Volume its *particular* Contents; which will serve not only as an Index, but as a brief Recapitulation of the most material passages contained in it; and which will enable the Reader to connect in his mind the perused volume with that which follows; and more clearly shew the characters and views of the particular correspondents."[31] The shift from a table of contents serving as forecast, like

Fielding's, to several tables, each serving as recapitulation of one volume and bridge to the next, reveals that Richardson understood the importance for his didactic purposes of creating memories which would "more clearly show" what had already been perused by each reader.

Although his device is not artistically viable, it does imitate the way memory actually deals with past experience by establishing categories that allow events to be stored through a process that involves omission of insignificant details.[32] Each retrospective table of contents becomes an artificial memory working as real memory would by foreshortening events. What has been experienced at large is contracted so that its essential outlines ("the characters and views") come into sharper focus. Like many of Fielding's reminders Richardson's tables are partly intended to allow readers to move forward more easily by seeing how prior events connect to subsequent episodes. But Richardson is even more concerned to establish the temporal distance necessary for perception of whatever is (was) most important. For this purpose many details are best forced out of mind. Critics have so much praised Richardson's skill in writing to the moment that his efforts to include some of the opposite advantages of retrospective narration have been slighted.

Richardson explains another such attempt in his preface: "An ingenious Gentleman having made a Collection of many of the Moral and Instructive Sentiments in this History, and presented it to the Editor, he thought the design and usefulness of the Work could not be more strikingly exhibited, than by inserting it (greatly enlarged) at the end of the last volume. The Reader will accordingly find it there, digested under proper Heads, with References to the

Pages where each Caution, Aphorism, Reflection, or Observation, is to be found, either wrought into the *practice* of the respective correspondents, or recommended by them as useful *theory* to the Youth of both Sexes."[33] In this collection the "Instructive Sentiments" that were too numerous to be remembered are brought together and rearranged in what amounts to another artificial memory. Its purpose includes exhibiting "the design . . . of the work" in the sense of moral intentions, not artistic shape. The analytical rearrangement "under proper Heads" instead of (like the tables of contents) in a series following narrative sequence also amounts to a reading like that encouraged (but not supplied) at the end of *Colonel Jack*. Moreover sentiments that may not have been apparent in the course of each episode are formulated in retrospect and provided along with page numbers to ensure that readers can remember events in connection with lessons that may *only* be evident in retrospect when *Clarissa*'s moral design can be grasped entire and retroactively used to understand fully "the *practice* of the respective correspondents." Owing to the page numbers, no sentiment need be considered apart from the event which elicits—or should elicit—it. Nor does any episode which may give rise to an important sentiment run the risk of failing to do so. That, at least, is Richardson's theory.

Such explicit encouragement to reread as a substitute for remembering suggests that Richardson expected difficulties not taken into account in Johnson's advice to "read him for the sentiment, and consider the story as only giving occasion to the sentiment."[34] There is no problem in reading simply for the emotional experience and in that way treating *Clarissa* as sentimental fiction. But Johnson's definition of *sentiment* is "thought; notion; opinion." Insofar as "Moral and

Instructive Sentiments" are at issue, Richardson did take steps to deal with a very real problem. The artificial memories grafted onto his text are intended to prevent story from overwhelming explicit moral and instructive sentiments as in fact, however, it always does, given the nature of Richardson's innovations in *Clarissa*.[35]

Critics have therefore been inclined to ignore Richardson's artificial memory places. Abridgments of *Clarissa* for classroom use omit the tables of contents. Even modern reprints of the entire text including tables of contents omit the "Collection of . . . Moral *and* Instructive Sentiments, Contained in the PRECEDING HISTORY."[36] It should at least be more widely recognized that Richardson's additions were intended to be part of the completed work as it would be encountered by readers, and they were not merely added as extrinsic and thus optional study aids. To agree that we find them redundant because we prefer to read for Richardson's psychological mastery of story, and then turn away in embarrassed silence from *Clarissa*'s framework of preface, postscript, tables, and collected sentiments may not do him justice. It certainly does not enhance our understanding of relationships between memory and literary form. Richardson's tables and collected sentiments were an effort to accomplish what Defoe could achieve more adroitly in narratives on a smaller temporal scale where story and sentiment, narration and memories of it, were in more equal balance. By the same token Defoe was unable to go so far as Richardson in making the reader's memories an integral part of the technique for presenting story alone.

In the account of Crusoe's establishment on his island Defoe most effectively resorts to a "cumulative" method of narration. There he goes over an episode from several viewpoints to build a more nearly complete picture of events in the reader's memory than exists in any one version of it on the novel's pages. Crusoe remains the writer of each version, however; and the variations are in temporal viewpoint, not persons telling about the same events. First Crusoe describes the voyage, the storm, the loss of his shipmates, his arrival on shore, salvage of material from the wreck, construction of his cave, and the daily routine of this initial phase of his isolation up to his meditation on how fortunate he was to get so much out of the ship when the odds against doing so were an hundred thousand to one.

After about twenty pages in which these topics are covered (in order "to come . . . by the just Degrees, to the Particulars of this Part of my Story" [p. 38]), Crusoe states that, because his solitary life on the island may be without precedent, he will narrate it from the beginning in chronological order: "And now being to enter into a melancholy Relation of a Scene of silent Life, such perhaps as was never heard of in the World before, I shall take it from its Beginning, and continue it in its Order" (p. 63). Crusoe has already narrated it in chronological order from its moral and psychological beginning: both the remote beginning of his "original sin" of disobedience, and the immediate beginning when ("as I had once done thus in my breaking away from my Parents" [p. 38]) he sailed away from Brazil in search of profit. This initial narration of events from the decision to leave Brazil stresses the ethical equivalence of Crusoe's first departure from home and the slaving voyage that brings him to the island.

Similarities are especially emphasized by mentioning the coincidence of times: "I went on Board in an evil Hour, the [   ] of [   ], [   ], being the same Day eighth Year that I went from my Father and Mother at Hull, in order to act the Rebel to their Authority" (p. 40). In the first edition of *Robinson Crusoe* the date of sailing from Hull is printed in full when that episode is narrated ("the first of *September* 1651" [p. 7]). But in the first three editions, only spaces appear in the sentence mentioning the later coincidence of times. In the fouth and later editions, either Defoe or his printers replaced those blanks with appropriate particulars: "the first of *September,* 1659."[37] I assume that here as elsewhere Defoe's first edition is closest to his textual intentions. Whatever his reasons may have been for leaving out the exact date, that omission has the effect of stressing the coincidence of times, not time itself, thus keeping the reader's attention on moral issues rather than matters of chronological verisimilitude. That is also where the emphasis falls, though somewhat less strongly, when the blanks are filled in.

Calendar-time is marked conspicuously at the outset of Crusoe's second narrative, however, which covers events from his arrival on the island up to the point where he is prepared to keep a journal. The start of that project is not located in time beyond Crusoe's statement that with his cave in order "now it was when I began to keep a Journal of every Day's Employment" (p. 69). But in the sentence after Crusoe says he will go back and write about his silent life "from its Beginning, and continue it in its Order," readers are informed that "it was . . . the 30th. of *Sept.* when, in the Manner as above said, I first set Foot upon this horrid Island, when the Sun being, to us, in its Autumnal Equinox, was almost just over my Head, for I reckon'd my self, by Observation, to be in the Latitude of 9 Degrees 22 Minutes North of the Line" (pp. 63–64). Inclusion of the phrase "in the Manner as above said" shows that neither Defoe nor Crusoe is starting over again owing to some strange forgetfulness that there has already been one narrative of the arrival. The repetition is intentional, and it invites attention to itself as a deliberate strategy.

The previous narrative is explicitly recollected so that the reader's memories of it will become part of the second account, in which the writer thus assumes memories of the first and builds upon them by providing additional details. The next paragraph describes construction of Crusoe's calendar with its inscription: "*I came on Shore here on the 30th of Sept. 1659*" (p. 64). Twice in the following six pages the date is mentioned again: "Sept. the 30th. . . . *September* 30, 1659" (pp. 69, 70). These reiterations make it harder for readers to forget when Crusoe's silent life began. The dates also underscore the fact that it *is* a major beginning. They are used as much to help convey that meaning as to establish verisimilitude. Whatever is given a date or whose time is somehow marked thereby has its importance stressed: witness the naming of Friday. In his case the principle is carried to a brilliant extreme by choice of a recurring day rather than a unique date. Crusoe's explanation seems to reverse the hierarchy by which time signals importance instead of conferring it; but the fact remains that one of Defoe's most original strokes was to render a character unforgettable and stress his significance by identifying him with a time: "I made him know his Name should be *Friday*, which was the Day I sav'd his Life; I call'd him so for the Memory of the Time" (p. 206).

Other details omitted from Crusoe's first narrative of his arrival on the island are also added in the paragraph after his calendar is described: "Among the many things which

I brought out of the Ship in the several Voyages, which, *as above mentioned*, I made to it, I got several things of less Value . . . *which I omitted setting down before;* as in particular, Pens, Ink, and Paper . . . three or four Compasses, some Mathematical Instruments . . . Books of Navigation . . . three very good Bibles . . . a Dog and two Cats" (p. 64; italics mine). The two allusions to Crusoe's first account are reinforced later in the same paragraph by a third reference to what he "observ'd before," thus sustaining memories of the previous account while also in effect affirming that it was not incorrect, but simply incomplete.

This point is crucial to an understanding of the purposes for which Defoe elicits memories which become part of the formal structure of *Robinson Crusoe*. Homer O. Brown is right to suggest that "the differences between . . . accounts of [Crusoe's] first days, mainly concerning whether he wept with joy or with terror, despair or thanksgiving, whether he slept on the ground or in a tree, are less significant than the fact that there *are* differences."[38] But the effect of those differences is not (as Brown suggests) to transform Defoe's narrative into an eighteenth-century anticipation of Sartre's dramatization in *Nausea* of disparities between lived and recorded duration. The discrepancies which stand out in *Robinson Crusoe* lie between Crusoe's first two versions of his arrival on the island and the paragraph in which he gives a sample of the journal that he might have written had he started earlier while still in "too much Discomposure of Mind" to provide anything but a journal "full of many dull things" (p. 69).

Dull, according to Bailey, meant "heavy, sluggish, stupid." Unlike the actual journal which Crusoe kept, which follows next in his narrative, the journal which he did *not* write would have been filled with unintelligent observations: "For example, I must have said thus. *Sept.* the 30th. After I got to Shore and had escap'd drowning, instead of being thankful to God for my Deliverance, having first vomited with the great Quantity of salt Water which was gotten into my Stomach, and recovering my self a little, I ran about the Shore, wringing my Hands and beating my Head and Face, exclaiming at my Misery, and crying out, I was undone, undone, till tyr'd and faint I was forc'd to lye down on the Ground to repose, but durst not sleep for fear of being devour'd" (p. 69). This sample of a hypothetical journal invites memories of what happened according to the previous two accounts of Crusoe's arrival.

In the first there is no mention of vomiting: only a reference to being "half-dead with the Water I took in," which leaves open the possibility that he may have vomited. But Crusoe does report that just after landing safely on shore he "began to look up and thank God that my Life was sav'd" (p. 46). Shortly afterward, however, according to the first account, Crusoe decided that he "had a dreadful Deliverance: For I was wet, had no Clothes to shift me, nor any thing either to eat or drink to comfort me. . . . And this threw me into terrible Agonies of Mind, that for a while I run about like a Mad-man" (p. 47). The running about is consistent with "crying out, I was undone, undone." Differences between running around instead of being thankful to God, and looking up to "thank God that my Life was saved," might be dealt with by one's assuming either that the imaginary journal should be taken to mean that Crusoe was not being *sufficiently* thankful during the entire first day or else by one's assuming that the imaginary journal is wrong or that the first account is mistaken. No way of thinking about the discrepancies makes them go away. Nor is it possible to dispose of the most conspicuous disagreement, over where Crusoe slept: it might be possible to try by assuming that the earlier account fails to mention that Crusoe first tried to rest on the ground *before* deciding to climb a tree and that the imaginary journal breaks off before completion by adding that after being "forc'd to lye down on the Ground to repose" without success, Crusoe *then* thought of sleeping in a tree. But this line of speculation cannot fully reconcile the versions of Crusoe's first day and night.

Instead the effort to do so, which readers can hardly avoid making, merely confirms Crusoe's opinion that the imaginary journal is unsatisfactory. Inaccuracy seems to be one manifestation of its dullness—unless, of course, the other accounts are assumed to be wrong. But Defoe inclines readers to reject the hypothetical journal by calling it dull and by saying that in any case it did not really exist. Nothing encourages anyone to accept its version of events as the most accurate one. By calling attention to the hypothetical journal, Defoe introduces into *Robinson Crusoe* a brief uncertainty which is intended to be noticed as such while readers try to make sense out of the "dull" journal that was never written—until more than twenty-eight years after its time and then only as an example of what should not have been said (and was not).

Brown asks "what are we to make of this confusion, other than to see it as an emphasis on the elusiveness of even the facts of this narrative and an admission of an irreparable tear between the written account and the naked, lived moment?"[39] But the confusion which Defoe introduces about what happened on the first day ashore has the opposite effect of confirming the reader's trust that any journal written in a suitable frame of mind *can* record experience faithfully—and that Crusoe's narrative is an accurate statement of what he experienced on the island. Defoe thereby underscores both the importance and the feasibility of writing about events accurately for later interpretation. By compelling readers to ask themselves what really happened during Crusoe's first hours on the island and thus also forcing readers to consider the significance of those moments several times (as Crusoe does), Defoe encourages his audience to duplicate—and to notice that they are duplicating—the mental operations involved in the Puritan spiritual autobiographer's exercise of looking backward to find the religious meaning of events. Sometimes, Defoe suggests via the unwritten journal's inaccuracies, events might not even be perceived much less understood correctly while they happen or too soon afterward. In the Puritan tradition of diary-keeping that underlies Defoe's impulse to provide a journal and its unwritten counterpart at this point in Crusoe's narrative, any gap between written account and lived moment will only show the superiority of writing as an instrument for revealing the providential pattern of events that cannot ever be understood merely as present experiences.[40]

Confidence in Crusoe's actual journal is established, moreover, immediately prior to the description of his conversion, where it is especially important for him to be regarded as in every sense a reliable narrator: one who gets his facts right and also avoids "dull" interpretation that might deviate from proper moral judgments. The first report of Crusoe's arrival mentions his sleeping in a tree. Also mentioned is the awakening next morning: "When I came down from my Appartment in the Tree" (p. 48). The journal which Crusoe *did* keep is introduced as a "copy"—presumably exact—of that made on the island, and its relationship to the previous narrations of Crusoe's arrival is called to the reader's attention: "In it will be told all these Particulars over again" (p. 69). In the second paragraph of the journal Crusoe says of his first day on the island that "at the Approach of Night, I slept in a Tree for fear of wild Creatures" (p. 70). Much later in the text, after he has finished giving a transcription of the journal, which had to be stopped after his ink ran out, Crusoe mentions among his memories while looking at the men stranded by mutineers "how I lodg'd in the Tree all Night for fear of being devour'd by wild Beasts" (p. 252). These reiterations confirm one another by their agreement, and in doing so cast further doubt on the "dull" journal that was never kept.

The second paragraph of the actual journal is also consistent with the first narration of Crusoe's arrival. Although there is no mention in the journal of the moment immediately after landing when Crusoe "began to look up and thank God that my Life was sav'd," the journal does not contradict this account of Crusoe's initial impulse of thanksgiving: it only records that "all the rest of that Day I spent in afflicting my self at the dismal Circumstances I was brought to, *viz.* I had neither Food, House, Clothes, Weapon, or Place to fly to, and in Despair of any Relief, saw nothing but Death before me, either that I should be devour'd by wild Beasts, murther'd by Savages, or starv'd to Death for Want of Food" (p. 70). By specifying in the first narrative that Crusoe's thanks were given *some minutes* after he escaped death, that is, immediately after landing, Defoe allows readers to accept the journal account as concentrating on what it specifies as "*all the rest of that Day.*"

The journal may thus be taken as omitting any description of the first few minutes after landing, just as the second account of Crusoe's arrival altogether omits description of the entire first day (and night) by giving only the date when he arrived "in the Manner as above said" and then jumping in its second paragraph to describe what happened "after I had been there about Ten or Twelve Days" (p. 64). Defoe makes these narratives reinforce and supplement rather than contradict one another by specifying time-intervals so carefully that the accounts will seem to focus on different moments of the same episode. Another effect of this skillfull manipulation of temporal emphasis is to expand the reader's impression of the subjective duration of Crusoe's initial experiences on the island. Something of how that time flowed for him is indirectly conveyed by showing readers that those days can be described again and again without mere duplication of the first account, with more details emerging each time that part of Crusoe's past is revisited.

The second paragraph of the journal also echoes, and thus recalls, Crusoe's statement in the first narrative that "after" he had taken some comfort in being alive, he nevertheless saw no "Prospect before me, but that of perishing with Hunger, or being devour'd by wild Beasts; and that which was particularly afflicting to me, was, that I had no Weapon . . . and this threw me into terrible Agonies of Mind" (p. 47). In addition to saying essentially the same thing in slightly different words, this sentence from the first narrative and that from the journal both include the word *afflicting* and the phrase *devour'd by wild Beasts*. Thus by verbal duplication at its outset, as well as by reiteration of content, the journal creates a sense of déjà vu. As it continues in many subsequent entries to cover ground previously covered, and mention events already alluded to or described in detail, it creates a similar stirring of memories and consequently creates for Defoe's readers a sense of their having been there earlier.

By the time they start the journal, readers will feel that they share some of Crusoe's memories of his first days on the island. As they again encounter descriptions of those days, readers feel small shocks of recognition which have the cumulative effect of endowing *Robinson Crusoe* with the power of a self-confirming narrative. In it, as in nearly any fiction, there is no way of checking veracity by comparison with another account known somehow to be true. Nor of course is there any need to. But the appearance of truthfulness is, as critics have remarked, often crucial to the effects of Defoe's fiction even for readers who accept it as fiction. In *Robinson Crusoe* one of the devices that most successfully sustains that appearance is Defoe's arranging his narrative so that the mental acts involved in verification inevitably occur each time the book is read. After the first account of Crusoe's arrival subsequent accounts are compared with it and with each other—more or less carefully, but to some extent by each reader at every reading. The agreement—or disagreement in the case of the imaginary journal against which readers are warned—becomes in effect a measure of Crusoe's reliability as a narrator. Thus Defoe mobilizes the reader's memories to create a situation which imitates what happens when any account claiming truth is tested for accuracy.

That test must be made by comparing the account in question with facts otherwise known and taken for true:

that is to say, so far as the psychology of the process is concerned, by comparison with memories accepted as true memories of the events in question or of a faithful account of them, whether those memories were acquired by personal experience or exposure to narratives whose veracity has been established. Whatever the other complications involved, there is eventually entailed in verification the mental operation of comparing one set of memories against another generated by the account in question. If there is no external check (i.e. source of memories taken for true and covering the same events), then internal consistency becomes a paramount test.

The ideal situation in that case would be one in which it is possible to ask for repetition of the narration to see whether essentially the same story emerges each time. If so, and there are no external grounds for doubt, credibility is enhanced. When such conditions are duplicated in *Robinson Crusoe* by telling some of its "Particulars over again," Defoe creates a structure of memories which enhances the verisimilitude of his entire narrative while also slowing its pace by focusing attention on the central event of Crusoe's establishment on the island. Elsewhere in *Robinson Crusoe* and throughout Defoe's fiction whenever parts of the narrative are recalled, there are similar alterations of pace to focus more attention on important events. This is often done for didactic purposes to create the effects of spatial form that are a significant part of Defoe's emblematic method. But the narrative where control of tempo is crucially related to Defoe's formal intentions is *A Journal of the Plague Year*.

5
Tempo

Any narrative divided into 365 parts to match days evenly distributed through clock-time will not encourage much experimentation with tempo. Partly for that reason, perhaps, *A Journal of the Plague Year* is not a journal. There is no series of dated entries recording events of the plague as they occur, or even giving the exact chronological location of the narrator's experiences. If Defoe had wanted to stress the variance between the title and form of this narration, he might have brought Simon Forecastle ashore again to complain, as he did to the editor of Mist's *Weekly Journal:* "I Can but admire at your Impudence, in making use of the Word JOURNAL." What bothers Simon is the absence of details, without which he finds the paper "truly a very empty Week's Work." "You tell us something of Ships coming into such and such Ports, but don't let us know when they anchor'd or moor'd; and of Pyrates, *Danes, Dutch,* and *Salleemen* being taken, but not a Tittle of Giving Chace, whether they were Boarded, driven to close Quarter, fir'd Broadside and Broadside, or struck at the first Gun." Forecastle is annoyed to find only reports of what finally happened, without mention of how long any action took or exactly when it was completed.

As an example of what true journalists might aspire to achieve, Forecastle gives extracts from his own sea-journal: "4 half 2 clapt a Bomb-boat aboard, the Captain bought two

Penny worth of Cabbages, and the Boatswain's Mate two Gallons of Geneva: At 4 the Ships Steward devoured 15 Biscuits, and the Man was relieved in the Long-boat; the Wind coming forward we curst the Cook and got the fore Tack aboard: At 12 the Larboard Watch came upon Deck, and a Midshipman tumbled down the Cock-pit Ladder."[1] This unvaried flow of pointless detail tells clearly enough why Defoe refused to cast any of his fiction entirely in the form of a journal. The parody—which continues through seven entries—also shows that Defoe made his choice after considering the alternative.

His retrospective narratives claiming to record events long after their occurrence not only provide temporal distance that allows for variation of pace by elimination of meaningless trivia, but they also manage to avoid many of the difficulties which prompted Richardson's move toward the development of journalistic forms. In the preface to *Clarissa* he argues with understandable overstatement that "*much more* lively and affecting . . . must be the Style of those who write in the height of a *present* distress; the mind tortured by the pangs of uncertainty (the Events then hidden in the womb of Fate); than the dry, narrative, unanimated Style of a person relating difficulties and dangers surmounted, can be; the relater perfectly at ease; and if himself unmoved by his own Story, not likely greatly to affect the Reader."[2] Certainly there could hardly be a more crucial question than whether a narrator appears "unmoved by his own story." *Dry*, according to Johnson, meant "without tears; jejune; barren; plain; unembellished; without pathos." His definition of *jejune* ("dry; unaffecting") is illustrated with a sentence from Boyle: "You may look upon an inquiry made up of meer narratives, as somewhat *jejune*."

Richardson was not alone in doubting that a "narrative" style could easily achieve the pathetic. Johnson defines *narrative* (adj.) as "Storytelling; apt to relate things past." In these terms Defoe usually chose—and it *was* a choice, not his only available option, as the Forecastle parody and Crusoe's journal demonstrate—a narrative style.

But not one that is uniformly dry or unanimated. *Clarissa*'s brilliance lends force to Richardson's argument that a retrospective narration may not be the best way to "affect the Reader." Too much temporal distance can indeed blunt emotional response. But Freud's observation that time does not exist for the unconscious mind goes far to explain why memories may shatter the tranquillity of recollection and be told or even imitated in fiction with enough power to elicit strong emotions from any audience.[3] The ability of retrospection to abolish many emotional distinctions between past and present has been so well dramatized by writers in the line of Sterne and Proust that no one takes Richardson's statement as a general principle, although it remains the most important eighteenth-century definition of the issues at stake in choosing the temporal locus of narration.

Bailey mentions another meaning of *dry:* "empty, flat." Richardson's metaphor thus hints at a second charge against retrospective narration: that it will not only tend to be unaffecting, but will be uniformly so. Hindsight will level everything in view. There will be no hills or valleys, no high spots or low spots. The pace will be too steady. There will be no variation in tempo. This problem, as the Forecastle parody suggests, is hardly confined to retrospective narratives; and it is certainly not inherent in them. But the difficulty will not be trivial if it arises, and it has seemed one to which Defoe was especially prone.

Louis Landa, for example, remarks in the introduction to his excellent edition of *A Journal of the Plague Year* that "we find in the *Journal* the same homely style of the novels... the refusal to vary pace or manipulate for effects. Defoe's language moves on doggedly at one level. Because he will not heighten the emotion, incidents must carry their emotional weight in and of themselves" (p. xxxv). The choice of incidents with varying emotional weight and their placement will influence pace, and they can be counted among the manipulations responsible for the emotional effects that appear in Defoe's best writing. His manner of describing events is no less important to the tempo they set. Defoe takes many steps to vary or sustain the pace within episodes and throughout larger sections of his narrations. *A Journal of the Plague Year* is not still regarded as his supremely moving achievement primarily because its subject remains inherently affecting in a century like ours. And yet there are far from insignificant reasons why Defoe's stylistic manipulations to vary pace have not been apparent to us. It is worth reopening the question of how, especially in *A Journal of the Plague Year*, Defoe sets the tempo of his fiction to enhance both its emotional and representational power.[4]

1

Captain Singleton endures hardships with courage that is reflected in his refusal to describe them in ways that overtly elicit tears or even much sympathy. His manner of writing might be chosen to represent at its driest the "unanimated Style of a person relating difficulties and dangers surmounted." Here, for example, is the passage where Singleton recollects his first sight of the African desert over which he safely travelled:

> Having with infinite Labour mounted these Hills, and coming to a View of the Country beyond them, it was indeed enough to astonish as stout a Heart as ever was created. It was a vast howling Wilderness, not a Tree, a River, or a Green thing to be seen, for as far as the Eye could look; nothing but a scalding Sand, which, as the Wind blew, drove about in Clouds, enough to overwhelm Man and Beast; nor could we see any End of it, either before us, which was our Way, or to the right Hand or left: So that truly our Men began to be discouraged, and talk of going back again; nor could we indeed think of venturing over such a horrid Place as that before us, in which we saw nothing but present Death.
> I was as much affected with the Sight as any of them, but for all that I could not bear the Thoughts of going back again. I told them we had march'd 700 Miles of our Way, and it would be worse than Death to think of going back again; and that if they thought the Desart was not passable, I thought we should rather change our Course, and travel South till we came to the *Cape of Good Hope*, or North to the Country that lay along the *Nile*, where perhaps we might find some Way or other over to the West Sea; for sure all *Africa* was not a Desart. (p. 79)

When he writes this passage, Singleton knows (as do his readers) that the African dangers have been surmounted. But the landscape is described without any sense that its features have dimmed in Singleton's memory. Nor does he wish that he might convey the scene more vividly. Singleton's account suggests that what he experienced at the edge of the desert remains available to retrospection in ways that neither present safety nor passing time can diminish. Yet those memories play no role in his later life.

In *A Journal of the Plague Year* Defoe resorts to more explicit statements of how the most horrifying moments from the narrator's past continue to haunt him while remaining beyond his (or anyone's) power to communicate fully to those who were not there. Defoe also appeals more openly to the reader's emotions. Thus while Singleton only says that a view of the desert "was indeed enough to astonish as stout a Heart as ever was created," H.F. remarks that "to hear the miserable Lamentations of poor dying Creatures" calling for ministers and warning others not to delay repentance "would make the stoutest Heart bleed." He then adds: "I wish I could repeat the very Sound of those Groans, and of those Exclamations that I heard from some poor dying Creatures, when in the Hight [sic] of their Agonies and Distress; and that I could make him that read [sic] this hear, as I imagine I now hear them, for the Sound seems still to Ring in my Ears" (p. 104). Alliterations (*S*ound . . . *s*ome . . . *S*ound *s*eems *s*till; *h*eard . . . *H*ight . . . *h*im . . . *h*ear . . . *h*ear) are reinforced by repeated words (*I, could, Sound, those, of, hear*) as well as a phrase (*poor dying Creatures*) echoed from the first part of H.F.'s paragraph in a way that duplicates something like what is being described insofar as its repetitive quality can be imitated. Defoe creates a structure of sounds to ring in the reader's ears. H.F.'s point, however, is that the worst lamentations heard during the plague year cannot be duplicated even though he cannot put them out of mind: "I imagine I now hear them."

Appreciation of the paradox may slow readers as they also try to imagine "the very Sound" which they have been told cannot be repeated for them or by anyone after the plague is over. Even to H.F. the sound only "seems" present. It really is not. Insistence upon the irrevocable pastness of the actual events described by his sentence is one way of heightening awareness of their true nature by presenting them as special cases without precluding the possibility that another plague—but only another plague—could replicate them. Here and elsewhere H.F. describes "Agonies and Distress" unique to plague-time. The horrors may recur if the plague returns, but they can only be described inferentially by showing that someone who witnessed them can hardly remain unmoved by his own story of those days. What happened still seems part—and by implication an affecting part—of H.F.'s present, not just remote events whose increasing distance diminishes their emotional impact as the years go by: "The Sound seems still to Ring in my Ears." Insofar as the implications of this fact sink in, readers are given pause. The sentence may not be read any more slowly than others of equal length and complexity. But its import will alter its apparent pace.

The extent to which the tempo of H.F.'s sentence slows will also depend upon the strength of the reader's aural imagination, just as the pace and emotional force of Singleton's description of the desert depend primarily on his appeal to the visual imagination. Those who respond to Defoe's structure of sounds by "hearing" the alliterations and other echoes within H.F.'s sentence will experience some further deceleration even during a silent reading. This effect is not independent of content, which largely determines whether a given pattern of sounds will contribute to acceleration or deceleration. Either way, however, the effects of verbal rhythms upon pace will be less pronounced for those whose imagination is primarily visual, not auditory, or for those who practice twentieth-century modes of "speed" reading.

Singleton's passage only invites attention to a represented sound when he describes as a "howling" wilderness that

African landscape spread out "beyond" the hills from whose summit the scene is regarded at the time of first encounter and in retrospect. Defoe's biblical metaphor is easily—and therefore quickly—translated into an allusion to the very familiar noise of the wind. Nor is there any difficulty in grasping the connotations of a landscape which appears to howl like an animal. What mainly slows the pace of Singleton's description are the difficulties in visualizing precisely what he mentions: *no* tree, *no* river, *no* "Green thing to be seen, for as far as the Eye could look." That distance remains indeterminate. So does the size of the wilderness —"vast." Singleton and his men could not "see any End of it, either before . . . or to the right Hand or left." Neither can readers who try to envision the scene.

Its effects are like those which Burke explained when he remarked that although few things are really infinite, "the eye not being able to perceive the bounds of many things, they seem to be infinite, and they produce the same effects as if they were really so. We are deceived in the like manner, if the parts of some large object are so continued to any indefinite number, that the imagination meets no check which may hinder its extending them at pleasure."[5] The sublime landscape which Singleton describes offers a similar invitation to limitless imagination of what it looked like. Attempts to picture it may be extended at pleasure and theoretically without end in the reader's time.

This possibility is if anything enhanced by what *is* visible: "nothing but a scalding Sand, which, as the Wind blew, drove about in Clouds." The adjective thus tells what the sand can do because of its heat, but it tells nothing more about its appearance. There are no limits for any reader trying to imagine clouds of burning hot sand. During Singleton's description, readers are not compelled—or even typographically permitted—to pause any longer than usual (however long that might be as measured by a clock) at the termination of phrases and sentences. But the open-ended visual imagery makes the passage in every sense arresting.

The need to resist endlessly imagining what is described slows the tempo, as does the possibility of finding emblematic significance in the wilderness imagery and on that account connecting the episode to the various patterns of moral symbolism in *Captain Singleton*. Defoe thus controls subjective pace although, as in the case of H.F.'s sentence, there is no available way to measure the reader's sense of deceleration. It may vary according to how the passage is interpreted. But some slowing down is inescapable, and it becomes apt preparation for a longer than usual end-of-sentence pause when Singleton's first paragraph closes by saying that in the desert whose appearance has just been described he and his men "saw nothing but present Death."

Strong emotions are implied and may easily be guessed. But Defoe does not spell out what the men felt about the prospect of present death. He leaves that for readers to infer during the interval—which may therefore become extended—between the end of Singleton's first paragraph and the start of his second one. That space (time) offers the typographical opportunity for an indeterminate pause. Readers will not be inclined to stop altogether for reflection as they might at the end of a chapter, however. Instead there will be at least two responses that further slow the tempo of Singleton's narrative here. The first occurs when one reads the phrase "saw nothing but present Death." After the previous account of what the men could literally see from their hilltop, readers are prepared for another statement of what was visible, and they must at the end of the phrase accommodate to it as a metaphoric statement. This too is easy enough, but it does require an effort that will contribute to the arresting quality of arriving at "Death."

The second accommodation involving "saw nothing but present Death" occurs when readers finish Singleton's next phrase: "I was as much affected with the Sight as any of them." How much? Whether or not readers have paused (or slowed) to guess at just what Singleton's men felt upon deciding that the desert offered only death, the remark comparing his reaction to their emotions forces awareness that the men *were* "affected" by what they saw. The comparison also compels some estimate, no matter how fleeting, of just how "much affected" Singleton and his men were by seeing the desert. Readers will consider, or reconsider, the implications of what is stated in the previous sentence. Their forward motion is briefly reversed and may be further delayed when they recollect Singleton's report "that truly our Men began to be discouraged." The possibility must be entertained that their discouragement is the emotion in question which Singleton shared. If so he is resorting to understatement. Something stronger than discouragement is the most likely reaction to a vision of "nothing but present Death." But whatever the reader decides, the need to decide something more than what the text states about Singleton's state of mind further slows the tempo of Defoe's passage.

So do the words "with the Sight," which are not strictly necessary: Singleton's meaning would be equally clear if he had only written "I was as much affected as any of them." But here Defoe's characteristic allusion to a previous part of the text compels remembrance (of "the Sight" which has just been described) that also turns attention backward for an instant, thus making the sentence go more slowly than it otherwise would. This effect, like the others which I have analyzed, makes no appreciable difference in the clock-time occupied by a reading of Singleton's passage.

In Singleton's first paragraph there are, however, two phrases whose inclusion does provide an amount of amplification that, in relationship to the total number of words involved, significantly protracts the clock-time necessary for reading the passage by adding words that are not needed merely to communicate an accurate impression of what the desert looked like: "not a Tree, a River, or a Green thing to be seen, for as far as the Eye could look" is synonymous with "nothing but a scalding Sand," and might have been omitted. So might the phrase "either before us, which was our Way, or to the right Hand or left." Singleton's passage, and the essential nature of the landscape he describes, would be equally clear if he had only written: "It was a vast howling Wilderness; nothing but a scalding Sand, which, as the Wind blew, drove about in Clouds, enough to overwhelm Man and Beast; nor could we see any End of it: So that truly our Men began to be discouraged." This shorter version takes less clock-time, and thus moves at a more rapid objective tempo. The difference as measured by a stopwatch timing a reader of Defoe's version and the abbreviated one would not be great. The amount of absolute time involved in many of the passages whose tempo I am considering here is small. But in context, and taken together, the choices which Defoe made to protract or compress his sentences play a significant role in setting their objective pace and that of the narratives in which they occur.

Subjective tempo, however, is by no means always synchronized with, or ever primarily dependent upon, the amount of reading-time necessary. In the longer passage from *Captain Singleton* as Defoe wrote it, tempo is slowed more by the nature of what is said in the amplifying phrases than by the mere fact of their inclusion to occupy readers for additional clock-time and thus to alter the ratio of reading-time to read-about time.

Certainly Defoe often varies that ratio to good effect in his fiction, thereby controlling its pace. Crusoe's repeated accounts of his establishment on the island are only the most conspicuous of Defoe's larger strategies for suggesting the importance of an episode by keeping the reader's attention focussed on it for an extended period. Crusoe's discovery of the footprint is another such protracted moment. The switches from summary narration and indirect accounts of what people said to scenes with much dialogue achieve similar variations of pace. In *A Journal of the Plague Year* H.F.'s discussion with the Waterman is an excellent example of this strategy. So (in different fashion) is the elaborate—and protracted—account of how three men escape from London to survive the plague.

This incident occupies so much reading-time in proportion to the total narrative that some critics have found the variation from H.F.'s main subject (and tempo) excessive. I do not think it is, for reasons that I will suggest later; yet the objection and the grounds for possible disagreement with Defoe's strategy of narrative digression do serve as a reminder of his inclination to match reading-time to what he considered the importance of an incident or topic. It is true that throughout his major fiction such variations play a less significant role in controlling pace than other strategies which alter subjective tempo by complicating or simplifying content: Crusoe's debate with himself over the legality of shooting savages, for example, or the many other places where, as George Starr has shown, casuistical patterns of thinking greatly complicate the reader's apprehension of events and slow his pace accordingly.

In Singleton's passage Defoe's open-ended imagery, the switch to metaphoric statement, the symbolic overtones, and the indirect suggestion of how "much affected" Singleton was all create complications that slow subjective tempo. Readers will not regard these complications as difficulties or even much notice most of them, because in fact they do not pose any *problems* during an ordinary reading of the kind which I am conducting here in slow motion. But the complications nevertheless make Singleton's passage seem to proceed more slowly than would another of comparable length and meaning which avoided open-ended imagery, did not require readers to infer anything beyond what was spelled out for them, and resorted exclusively to literal statements or even entirely to metaphoric statements, thus requiring no accommodation from one mode of discourse to another.

The meaning of such a passage could only be comparable, however, and not exactly the same. Tempo, like other aspects of form, contributes to meaning. Slowing down to focus on an event is one way of suggesting its importance. The devices which make a passage arresting or which accelerate it partly do so because of what they communicate; they also in some measure add nuances of meaning by their effect on tempo. To alter them and the pace which they set is to vary meaning as well. By including "not a Tree, a River, or a Green thing to be seen," Defoe not only slows the pace to emphasize what the desert looked like, how important its appearance at that juncture in the story is, and why Singleton's men thought it "such a horrid Place." Its appearance and horror are sufficiently communicated by mentioning clouds of scalding sand "enough to overwhelm Man and Beast." Singleton's list of what was missing—trees, rivers, green things—tells something of what he longs to see. However, it tells most about what, even as a retrospective narrator, he finds noteworthy when describing the scene years after first viewing it.

Whether he commented *then*, in Africa, on the absence of trees, rivers, and green things is left unclear. Singleton does not say that he made the observation at that moment, while looking out beyond the hills, although readers are free to infer that he did. But he locates other responses unequivocally in the past by reporting on the men's discouragement, on their talk of going back, on how hard it was to "think of venturing over such a horrid Place," on how much affected he *then* was by the sight, and on what he said to urge the men forward. His insistence years later on the absence of trees, rivers, and green things—the fact that he slows his pace as writer and ours as readers while mentioning the point—hints at emotions which continue to surround the episode in Singleton's mind. He is not just—or perhaps not at all in the phrase mentioning trees, rivers, and green things—reporting on what he then thought. He is registering how the scene continues to strike him in retrospect. Unlike H.F., however, Singleton does not say that the sights or sounds of a terrible period from his past continue to stay with him. He merely demonstrates that they do.

Readers are left to infer what that reveals about his emotions. H.F.'s sentence telling how the lamentations continue to ring in his ears offers a more explicit invitation to make inferences about his emotional response to the past, as well as about what that response, in turn, implies about the period he describes. One is encouraged to speculate about the emotional state implied by Singleton's next remark— that he "could not bear the Thoughts of going back again" —and by his report that he therefore told his men that "it would be worse than Death to think of going back again." This speech is arresting, and all the more so because of its concision and the way Singleton reports it without further comment. His narration here and elsewhere in *Captain Singleton* provides additional confirmation of George Starr's argument that for Defoe's protagonists "the act of recounting their lives, no less than the struggles they narrate, represents an effort to achieve control over experience."[6] The signs of that effort create appreciation of the strong emotions involved both during the adventures described and to a significant though lesser extent afterward.

Singleton's laconic argument that going back would be worse than death reveals the strength of his emotions (as well as his courage) more forcefully than any extended explanation could easily do. His refusal as narrator to comment from a safe distance in time on what he then felt amounts to an endorsement of the response: there is *still* nothing more to say, and no reason to suppose, even with the advantages of hindsight, that he put the matter too strongly. But to say all this explicitly would have been to weaken the impact of the implied emotions. Defoe's fiction at its driest is seldom either unanimated or without power "greatly to affect the reader."

The force of his prose often derives as much from the retrospective point of view as from the adventures themselves. The narrators' visible effort to control experience by giving appropriate shape to their written recollections implies that pasts like theirs cannot be altogether put behind. They must still be reckoned with during—and by means of—the act of writing. Even after difficulties and dangers appear surmounted, there is in the moral universe of Defoe's fiction no such thing as a "relater perfectly at ease." Crusoe and Jack are closest, but they are in no position to look back altogether calmly on the spiritual difficulties which they have met. From those dangers neither they nor anyone can ever be entirely free this side of time. Perfect ease can only be expected in Eternity. And about that part of the future, neither Moll, nor Singleton, nor Roxana can put their minds very much at ease.

H.F. has less cause for spiritual uneasiness when looking backward. Yet the plague is the most uncontrollable of all the experiences described in Defoe's fiction, and it therefore seems more than coincidental that H.F.'s narration bears least resemblance to the conventional literary forms by which the past is ordered and thus brought under some measure of control. The narrative sequence in *A Journal of the Plague Year* does not often follow the chronological order of narrated events. Hence the journal does not facilitate a clear understanding of mere chronology, how the plague spread from week to week, although that can (with difficulty) be discovered from what H.F. says. Nor does he provide a topical organization following throughout any logic of necessary progression from topic to topic: there is only an arbitrary pattern dictated by the associative train of his own recollections during which one memory leads him to another and then often leads back to events already discussed.

H.F.'s story of the plague departs equally from the available genres by avoiding the day-by-day pattern of a journal, by avoiding the shapes of spiritual autobiography where events are subordinated to their role in the writer's progress toward a proper religious outlook, and by conspicuously avoiding the appearance of a conventional history. Yet history books were among Defoe's favorite reading, and he was an experienced writer of historical narratives. Tyna T. Orren argues persuasively that *A Journal of the Plague Year* offers valid knowledge of the past as true histories do but that it is not designed to resemble such forms of historical narration as Defoe knew and adapted in *The Storm* and *The History of the Union of Great Britain*.[7] Insofar as *A Journal of the Plague Year* departs from previously available forms without taking a new shape which obviously "contains" experiences in an orderly way, it seems all the more appropriate as the reflection of a time that was unlike other times by virtue of being so highly disordered.

2

Although *A Journal of the Plague Year* apparently is Defoe's most incoherent work because of its departure from the familiar shapes of accepted genres, it nevertheless calls frequent attention to itself as writing: by the mortality tables designed to be read on a page, not spoken aloud; by the lord mayor's orders reprinted as originally published; and by such other verbal "illustrations" as H.F.'s reproduction of superstitious charms against the plague and his copy of the inscription found on a gate outside London. The rest of Defoe's fiction is closer to what Colonel Jack calls "oral tradition." But this is a matter of degree. While Defoe adopted homiletic and dramatic techniques to serve his purposes, all his writing is designed to be read in the pages of a book. Print was his medium, not the stage or pulpit. He explained the differences at the beginning of *The Storm* by asserting that "Preaching of Sermons is Speaking to a few of Mankind: Printing of Books is Talking to the whole world. The Sermon is a Sound of Words spoken to the Ear, and prepar'd only for present Meditation, and extends no farther than the Strength of Memory can convey it." The terms of this distinction are another reminder that Defoe's works have closer affinities to the spoken word than most later fiction. He viewed writing as a more permanent kind of talking. Accordingly the interplay of effects most characteristic of speaking with those peculiar to writing assumes a greater role in Defoe's control of tempo.

His readers are often encouraged to imagine themselves listening while someone talks to them. This situation—insofar as it *is* imagined—will impose some upper limit on the subjective pace of Defoe's prose. More often noticeable, however, are the places where the conceit of a speaking (not writing) narrator intrudes to slow passages for greater emphasis. Of her Turkish costume, for example, Roxana remarks: "There was good Reason why I shou'd not receive any Company in this Dress, *that is to say*, not in *England; I need not repeat it; you will hear more of it*" (p. 248). The impression of a speaking voice contributes to the way that this sentence arrests attention.

It is debatable whether the italics here and in similar passages were intended by Defoe or supplied by his printer. Even adopting the conservative view urged by Starr, however, and discounting accidentals of any kind as evidence of authorial intention in Defoe's work, one sees that the consistent italicizing of phrases like *you will hear more of it* may still be taken as evidence that readers were expected to notice and adopt the convention of a speaking narrator.[8] The italics call attention to such phrases. If supplied by Defoe's printers, who were the first to read his texts and who shared an interest in making them satisfy the expectations of subsequent readers, the italics may be all the more significant as evidence that an eighteenth-century audience was expected to—and did—slow down to notice the places where printed words were most obviously designed to evoke the sense of a speaking voice. On this issue, at least, we can safely rest with James Thorpe's argument that authorship is a joint matter, with editors and printers contributing their share to the finished work.[9] By the phrases themselves, however, if not also by suggesting italics, Defoe certainly took pains to create the impression of Roxana's talking.

Scattered throughout her narrative are remarks that sustain that impression: "As you shall hear.... *As you shall hear.... As I said before.... As you have heard....* How I kept my Husband from discovering my Disorder, *you shall hear presently....* In this Posture that Matter stood when that unhappy Girl, *who I have said so much of*, broke in upon all our Measures, *as you have heard*" (pp. 138, 268, 294, 295, 297). Cumulatively such phrases create an aural context even for those reminders of the narration as written sequence which Roxana provides in phrases like "*as above*" or "*as is mention'd above.*" These are primarily spatial metaphors invoking awareness of the book as physical object. But in context such phrases, together with phrases like "*as I may in time relate more particularly*" (p. 302) refer as much to the time occupied by talking. All Defoe's invitations to imagine a voice are also invitations to make the subjective flow of reading-time conform to the rhythms and pace of conversation.

Roxana's narrative is presented more as an event occupying her speaking-time and the reader's "listening-time" synchronously at whatever pace she sets than as a record abstracted from her passing moments for contemplation on the printed page as rapidly or slowly as readers care to go. They do, of course, have that choice of reading speed in their own control. But Defoe encourages them to set or—what is equally important—to perceive the slower tempo of conversation. Although Roxana does refer occasionally to "the Reader of this Story" (p. 75), she and her readers are brought metaphorically into the relationship of speaker and auditors. *Roxana*'s implied audience is comprised of listeners.

Consequently even references to what "you shall hear in its Place" (p. 102) become not so much allusions to places farther along in the printed book, places in an ordering of pages (although that meaning remains) as references to something more like memory places.[10] Roxana even refers once to an adjustment of the ratio between narrating-time and narrated time, thus revealing Defoe's awareness of how objective tempo may be controlled by decreasing the ratio of reading-time to read-about time: "Tho it took up *Amy* almost a Month . . . to put off all the Appearances of House-keeping, as above; it need take me up no Time to relate it" (p. 211).[11]

Acceleration is not always so clearly signalled, even in *Roxana*, which imitates the spoken word more closely than *Captain Singleton, Colonel Jack*, or *Moll Flanders*. Robinson Crusoe often reminds his readers that they have a book in their hands. Thus he introduces his section headed "*The* JOURNAL" by saying that "I shall here give you the Copy": something to look at, not hear. Even on the island, with no prospect of readers, it afforded comfort when "I drew up the State of my Affairs in Writing, not so much to leave them to any that were to come after me, for I was like to have but few Heirs, as to deliver my Thoughts from daily poring upon them, and afflicting my Mind" (p. 65). What he then wrote (before starting the journal later) is reproduced for readers by Crusoe in two columns ("like Debtor and Creditor") headed "Evil" and "Good." The columns not only show exactly what Crusoe wrote on the island. By slowing the tempo of his narrative they stress the importance of the incident and its moral: "That there was scarce any Condition in the World so miserable, but there was something *Negative* or something *Positive* to be thankful for in it" (pp. 66–67). The presence of good and evil in the same situation is represented by the simultaneous presence of both columns on the same page: readers can see them as well as read them. Before and after reading them, one sees the columns at once and takes them in at a glance, thus registering the fact of their coexistence.

They form a kind of picture (made up of words) whose meaning is explained immediately afterward in the manner of those emblem books whose relationship to Defoe's spatial form I have already suggested. Upon first encountering the columns, however, readers must slow down or pause while deciding how to proceed. Everything under "Evil" may be read down the page and then everything under "Good." Or readers may proceed down the page alternating between what is under "Good" and "Evil" in each "entry" as if they were printed like this: "*I am cast upon a horrible desolate Island, void of all hope of Recovery. But I am alive, and not drown'd as all my Ship's Company was. I am singl'd out and separated, as it were, from all the World to be miserable. But I am singl'd out too from all the Ship's Crew to be spar'd from Death; and he that miraculously sav'd me from Death, can deliver me from this Condition*" (p. 66). If printed this way, which is the likeliest order of an actual reading of what is contained in the columns, the entries would contain the same words and thus convey the same meaning insofar as their meaning as individual words is concerned. But the tempo of the passage as Defoe intended it to be printed (in columns) would be lost, together with the meanings conveyed by that tempo. There would be less slowing, and possibly even some acceleration because readers would have no choice of how to proceed and therefore no need to slow for a decision. Also lost would be the spatial effect of being able to glance back over the columns after reading them, and pausing or slowing then while "seeing" their coexistence as emblematic of the moral which Crusoe provides.

EVIL.	GOOD.
I am cast upon a horrible desolate Island, void of all hope of Recovery.	But I am alive, and not drown'd as all my Ship's Company was.
I am singl'd out and separated, as it were, from all the World to be miserable.	But I am singl'd out too from all the Ship's Crew to be spar'd from Death; and he that miraculously sav'd me from Death, can deliver me from this Condition.
I am divided from Mankind, a Solitaire, one banish'd from humane Society.	But I am not starv'd and perishing on a barren Place, affording no Sustenance.
I have not Clothes to cover me.	But I am in a hot Climate, where if I had Clothes I could hardly wear them.

I am without any Defence or Means to resist any Violence of Man or Beast.	But I am cast on an Island, where I see no wild Beasts to hurt me, as I saw on the Coast of *Africa*: And what if I had been Shipwreck'd there?
I have no Soul to speak to, or relieve me.	But God wonderfully sent the Ship in near enough to the Shore, that I have gotten out so many necessary things as will either supply my Wants, or enable me to supply my self even as long as I live.

By this verbal "illustration," as well as in other ways, Defoe implies for *Robinson Crusoe* an audience of readers, not listeners.

Crusoe often has them in mind, as when he remarks of his efforts of potmaking: "It would make the Reader pity me, or rather laugh at me, to tell how many awkward ways I took" (p. 120). In the context of such references to readers, "tell" does not mean "speak aloud." Nor does it evoke a voice to slow readers into conformity with its imagined rhythms. It is not the sounds of Crusoe *speaking* as narrator that set or modulate the basic tempo of his narration, which Defoe intends readers to accept as a written account of a "silent Life" (p. 63). Defoe breaks that silence, however, with the sounds of several voices whose intrusion varies the pace of Robinson Crusoe to emphasize its lessons long before that dramatic occasion when Friday "spoke some Words to me, and though I could not understand them, yet I thought they were pleasant to hear, for they were the first sound of a Man's Voice, that I had heard, *my own excepted*, for above Twenty Five Years" (p. 204). Crusoe's own voice must be imagined at those moments of narrated (not narrating) time when he did speak aloud during the years when he "was alone, circumscribed by the boundless Ocean, cut off from Mankind, and condemn'd to what I call'd silent Life" (p. 156).

On seeing a shipwreck, for example, Crusoe responds with "earnest Wishings, That but one Man had been sav'd! *O that it had been but One!* I believe I repeated the Words, *O that it had been but One!* A thousand Times" (p. 188). The italics and repetition stress the intensity of Crusoe's longing for companionship. So does Crusoe's famous account of how "the Desires were so mov'd by it, that when I spoke the Words, my Hands would clinch together, and my Fingers press the Palms of my Hands, that if I had had any soft Thing in my Hand, it wou'd have crusht it involuntarily; and my Teeth in my Head wou'd strike together, and set against one another so strong, that for some time I cou'd not part them again" (p. 188). Defoe encourages readers to switch from imagining what Crusoe silently thinks (his "earnest Wishings") to what he says aloud ("when I spoke the Words") without varying by much the content of thought and speech. The objective tempo is slowed by triple repetition of one phrase. This will also make the passage seem to go more slowly because for a time it does not progress to a new statement. The subjective tempo is further decelerated for those readers with sufficient aural imagination to "hear" (and read at the pace of someone who is speaking) what Crusoe "spoke." Defoe's exploitation of the slower rhythms of speech to contrast with the more rapid pace of reading (and thought) is evident because the words "that but one" are in each phrase. Consequently the main differences are in imagining them thought and in imagining them spoken aloud.

Elsewhere Defoe emphasizes some of Crusoe's most important moments by reporting that he does speak or that he seems to hear voices. "Now, said I aloud, My dear Father's Words are come to pass: God's Justice has overtaken me. . . . Then I cry'd out, *Lord be my Help, for I am in great Distress.* This was the first Prayer, if I may call it so, that I had made for many Years" (p. 91). After reporting his "Thoughts" by the sea shore which lead him to question God's justice, Crusoe reports that his conscience began to rebuke him "and methought it spoke to me like a Voice; WRETCH! *dost thou ask what thou hast done!*" (p. 92). Imagination of the entire rebuke as coming from a spoken voice rather than merely as (what Crusoe also calls them) "these Reflections" adds weight to the passage by encouraging readers to take it at the slower pace of speech (p. 93).

There is greater alteration of tempo when Crusoe gives the exact words that are to be imagined as spoken than in passages where readers are only invited to imagine that Crusoe says something but are not given a transcript of what was said: "This touched my Heart very much, and immediately I kneeled down and gave God Thanks aloud for my Recovery from my Sickness" (p. 96). What Crusoe says in his prayer of thanksgiving is omitted. But the fact of praying "aloud" suggests the importance of both his prayer and the entire episode. Defoe uses speech, whether quoted verbatim or indirectly reported, to emphasize significance. When something is said aloud, readers are invited to pay close attention and they must accordingly slow their pace.

The degree of deceleration thus induced will not be the same in every context, however. There may also be other devices which quicken the reader's attention sufficiently to create an over-all acceleration despite any slowing down to accommodate dialogue. But imagination of something spoken aloud usually contributes appreciably to setting the tempo of passages where speech is reported or quoted. Thus at one point during Crusoe's isolation he thinks of giving "Thanks to God for bringing me to this Place" but is "shock'd ... at that Thought, and ... durst not speak the Words: How canst thou be such a Hypocrite, (said I, even audibly) to pretend to be thankful for a Condition, which however thou may'st endeavour to be contented with, thou would'st rather pray heartily to be deliver'd from" (pp. 113–14). The effect of this and similar passages in which Crusoe reports what he *said* ("even audibly") in response to what he *thought* is to vary the tempo of *Robinson Crusoe* by providing the equivalent of dialogue in a situation of "silent" and solitary life when in fact only monologues were possible. Readers must imagine many sounds—and alternations of silence and speech. The silence of Crusoe's island life is not literal but symbolic.

So, very often, are the sounds. The importance of Crusoe's first "terrible Dream," for example, is underscored not only by the sights described in his account of dreaming that he "saw a Man descend from a great black Cloud, in a bright Flame of Fire," but also by the fact, which readers are invited to imagine along with further visual details, that the apparition "spoke to me, or I heard a Voice so terrible, that it is impossible to express the Terror of it; all that I can say, I understood, was this, *Seeing all these Things have not brought thee to Repentance, now thou shalt die:* At which Words, I thought he lifted up the Spear that was in his Hand, to kill me" (p. 87). By first mentioning "a Voice so terrible" that its impact cannot be fully described, Defoe prepares readers to exercise their own imaginations to invoke such a voice. There would have been less encouragement to do so if the voice had been characterized after, instead of before, the statement of what it seemed to say. Here, on a small scale but nevertheless effectively, Defoe builds suspense and slows pace by delaying a quotation while focusing attention on it to create expectation. He prepares readers to "hear"—and thus take more slowly—what the apparation says by stressing that its message is delivered aloud. Or at least—Crusoe himself is uncertain of this point, which calls further attention to it—the apparition causes Crusoe to *hear* a voice, even if in the dream there were no real sounds: "He spoke ... or I heard." Whether there were actual sounds matters less than whether Crusoe understands the message; and his understanding is signaled by the fact that Crusoe "heard."

Behind the equation of understanding with hearing, and thus also behind Defoe's invitations to "hear" as a way of slowing down to register the significance of an episode, lies the long religious tradition of the importance of the Word. Walter J. Ong argues for the continuing relevance of that tradition to literature during the postrenaissance transformation from oral to visual media. He also argues that emphasis on seeing printed words eventually encouraged a shift away from typical or emblematic characters and away from focus on various kinds of simultaneity including, presumably, such uses of spatial form as I have identified in Defoe's fiction. But Ong insists that the switch toward atypical (and thus more nearly time-bound) characters with little symbolic import, and toward linear narratives with plots that place overwhelming emphasis on the importance of sequence and natural causality in man's relationship to time, was not accompanied by disinclination to accept the primacy of the Word in Christianity. Nor was there any immediate displacement of the accompanying assumption that such primacy was related "in some mysterious way to sound itself," which thus maintained a significance now lost. Ong warns particularly against supposing that "because the eighteenth century was a significant watershed dividing residually oral culture from typographical culture, it thereby eliminated all oral residue from Western Society."[12] This caution is especially worth remembering while considering Defoe. His fiction, more successfully than any later in the century except *Tristram Shandy*, adapts oral forms to typographical media by combining strategies from traditions of speaking and traditions of writing to work together, instead of concentrating mainly on one or another mode of appeal within the framework of printed pages.

In *Robinson Crusoe* Defoe's most explicit reminder of the religious background of attention to the primacy of the Word (and corollary emphasis on the significance of sound) comes during Crusoe's illness. He tells how unresponsive he initially was to the passage which he noticed on opening a Bible at random: "*Call on me in the Day of Trouble, and I will deliver, and thou shalt glorify me*" (p. 94). The biblical source of these words, their italics, and their obvious relevance to the situation in which they are noticed by Crusoe all invite particular attention from Defoe's readers: they can hardly avoid slowing their pace upon arrival at this quotation even though Crusoe does not speak it aloud. But the very silence of his reading seems to hint at a spiritual problem when he adds that "the Words were very apt to my Case, and made some Impression upon my Thoughts at the Time of reading them, tho' not so much as they did afterwards; for as for being deliver'd, the Word had no Sound, *as I may say*, to me" (p. 94). Crusoe's inability to apply the passage is symbolized by his metaphor of the word's silence to him. He does not "hear" words whose application he cannot grasp. They remain silent. Sound is meaning.

By stressing Defoe's use of this metaphor and recalling its general background, I do not mean to suggest that sounds are equally portentous everywhere in his fiction. But for many reasons, and with results that have been insufficiently appreciated, Defoe was highly alert to the imaginative uses of represented sound as well as to the rhythms of printed sentences in controlling tempo.

Take, as a final example from *Robinson Crusoe*, a comic incident also involving what Crusoe and his readers hear—or think they hear. He describes what happens after arriving at his bower exhausted one day and falling asleep:"Judge you, if you can, that read my Story, what a Surprize I must be in, when I was wak'd out of my Sleep by a Voice calling me by my Name several times, *Robin, Robin, Robin Crusoe,* poor *Robin Crusoe,* where are you *Robin Crusoe?* Where are you? Where have you been?" Readers must first try to imagine the voice which is reported, and for want of any information to the contrary at this point in the passage they will probably suppose it human, as they may when Crusoe reports that "the Voice continu'd to repeat *Robin Crusoe, Robin Crusoe*" (p. 142). Readers might, however, recall the apparition from Crusoe's dream and wonder if another such "terrible Vision" (p. 88) is starting. If so a corresponding "Voice so terrible" must be imagined. But Defoe's text does not explicitly invite that comparison. And the sympathetic attitude of the voice quoted here implies something different.

Speculation is cut short when Crusoe next reports that he "saw my *Poll* sitting on the Top of the Hedge; and immediately knew that it was he that spoke to me; for just in such bemoaning Language I had used to talk to him, and teach him; and he had learn'd it so perfectly, that he would sit upon my Finger, and lay his Bill close to my Face, and cry, *Poor* Robin Crusoe, *Where are you? Where have you been? How come you here?* And such things as I had taught him" (pp. 142–43). This flashback to the education of Crusoe's parrot compels readers to a complicated adjustment of the way in which they imagine what is said. The reported voice becomes a conflation of the parrot's—however that is imagined—and Crusoe's own voice. His thoughts are thus again made audible.

Also dramatized are the unspecified but clearly numerous occasions during the previous island years when those thoughts were uttered for the sake of Poll's education and whatever relief that afforded Crusoe. His mood during many days undescribed elsewhere in the narrative is implied by the way Poll's voice conflates Crusoe's awakening in the bower with earlier times when Crusoe said what he awakes to hear the parrot saying. Here too Defoe creates a sense of implied duration that contributes to the temporal verisimilitude of *Robinson Crusoe* by making readers aware of time (given to Poll's lessons) that is not narrated but whose existence is made to seem real because of its result (Poll's remarks). Vivid dramatization of an effect evokes some realization of the time given to causing it. Readers are slowed down in this passage not only by repetitions which protract it in clock-time and which thus decelerate objective tempo by increasing the ratio of narrating to narrated time with respect to Crusoe's awakening in the bower. The passage will also seem to go more slowly by virtue of the complicated aural imaginings elicited and because it evokes open-ended imagination of the time that Crusoe occupied by teaching the parrot.

There is deft characterization here as well. Crusoe's explanation of how the parrot had "so perfectly" learned "such bemoaning Language" portrays his own self-pity with fine comic detachment that is altogether endearing. There may even be another shade of self-deprecating comedy in the bird's emblematic associations: "A Parrot (Hieroglyphically) was pictured to represent an eloquent man; because no other bird can better express itself" (Bailey). The parrot's discourse shows the turn of Crusoe's eloquence during his "silent" life.

Another reiteration that the parrot only speaks what Crusoe had thought and said earlier further slows the pace of this episode to underscore what it reveals about his character and frame of mind: "As I was well satisfied it could be no Body but honest *Poll* . . . holding out my Hand, and calling him by his Name *Poll*, the sociable Creature came to me, and sat upon my Thumb, as he used to do, and continu'd talking to me, *Poor* Robin Crusoe, and *how did I come here?* and *where had I been?* just as if he had been overjoy'd to see me again; and so I carry'd him Home along with me" (p. 143). The shift to indirect reporting of what the parrot says slows the subjective pace even more as readers notice that "How come you here" is changed to "How did I come Here" and "Where have you been" is changed to "Where had I been."

Defoe's shift from *you* to *I* completes the conflation of voices and times: Crusoe's thoughts metamorphosed into the parrot's speech are finally transformed back into a phrase most easily taken as Crusoe talking to himself: "How did I come here?" But in a kind of double-take which further slows their pace, readers must remember that it is still the parrot who is being quoted. This final superimposing of times and voices again encourages the reader's temporal imagination: how *often* did Crusoe wonder about his predicament? Defoe then evokes the entire incident more concisely later when Crusoe (as retrospective narrator safely off the island) invites open-ended speculation about Poll's future: "He liv'd with me no less than six and twenty Years: How long he might live afterwards, I know not; though I know they have a Notion in the *Brasils*, that they live a hundred Years; perhaps poor Poll may be alive there still, calling after *Poor Robin Crusoe* to this Day" (p. 180). Here Defoe suggests an implied future duration amusingly haunted by sounds which echo past moments of Crusoe's silent life. This suggestion, like the brief mention of Crusoe's farther adventures at the end of *Robinson Crusoe*, contributes to its temporal verisimilitude by implying a fictive future to succeed the narrated past and narrating present.

As readers are imagining Poll's voice again, projected here beyond that present ("this Day") into an indefinite future, Crusoe adds: "I wish no *English* Man the ill Luck to come there and hear him; but if he did, he would certainly believe it was the Devil" (p. 180). To appreciate Crusoe's last touch of comedy on the topic of his parrot, Poll's voice must be imagined once more, but this time as it might be heard (and misunderstood) from the viewpoint of yet another stranded Englishman, in a hypothetical future.

Defoe's narrative proceeds without any break to catalogue the fate of Crusoe's other animals: "My Dog was a very pleasant and loving Companion to me, for no less than sixteen Years of my Time, and then dy'd, of meer old Age; as for my Cats . . ." (p. 180). Such continuities of narrative flow from topic to topic have puzzled modern readers accustomed to finding typographical clues that help them respond properly to variations in tempo. Consequently the extent to which Defoe does control tempo, especially within episodes, has been less often remarked than places where he does not arrange material to provide what are now customary visual signals placed to alter the reader's pace or arrest his attention. George Sherburn observed that because Defoe avoided chapter divisions, his writing "lacks an easy mechanical aid in emphasizing dramatic moments as well as preparation for and punctuation of minor climaxes."[13] But as Sherburn implies, Defoe chiefly falls short in supplying easy mechanical aids: paragraphing is another. The burden of responding to narrative tempo is shifted to readers more strongly than in most later fiction. It is also true that the over-all tempo of Defoe's narratives does not vary so much as many critics would now prefer. There is no disputing that preference, insofar as it is a preference. But I want to dispel the usual accompanying assumption that Defoe never significantly varies the tempo of his fiction. As Sherburn also assumes, and others after him without much pursuing the consequences for tempo, there *are* highly dramatic passages, long and short, that do call attention to themselves and thus vary the pace of Defoe's narratives to good effect even in the absence of those visual aids that could help readers respond properly.

And in other less mechanical aspects of narration, especially within episodes, Defoe far from neglected strategies more varied than creation of "dramatic moments" to arrest attention. Laughter, to cite the example closest to hand, certainly follows any imagination of Crusoe's hypothetical stranded Englishman coming on Poll and mistaking him for the Devil "calling after *Poor Robinson Crusoe.*" It at least evokes a smile. The conceit is both sufficiently open-ended and sufficiently amusing to cause some deceleration of subjective tempo. The lack of interruption on the printed page between Crusoe's speculation and the next sentence telling about his dog and cats does not mean that readers must push on steadily without some pause for appreciation of the comedy or that, if they do push on, both sentences will seem to go at the same pace. Shifts to and from a comic mode (of which there are many examples throughout Defoe's fiction) alter tempo as effectively as the verbal repetitions and as those appeals to visual and aural imagination that are most characteristic of Defoe's methods for avoiding dull uniformity of pace.

3

Although Maximillian Novak is correct in arguing that Defoe's "main achievement was to slow up the reader's time by various forms of repetition," Defoe's contribution to "slowing the pace of fiction, making it into that sluggish form known as the novel," was not only a matter of resorting more fully than others had before him to devices of repetition. Nor does it completely account for Defoe's representational power to show, as Novak also persuasively does, that in many scenes like Colonel Jack's famous account of losing his money in the tree, "Defoe achieved what Conrad said the novelist should do. He made his readers see and feel as they had never done before."[14] Conrad also insisted that it was the artist's subordinate task "by the power of the written word, to make you hear."[15]

Defoe's fiction deserves equal credit for its achievement in varying tempo by appealing to the pleasures of the aural imagination. He does make us hear—but only if we can "listen" while silently reading—or if we are willing to read him aloud. Part of our difficulty in recognizing this aspect of Defoe's accomplishment may be traced to the well-known psychological differences between those who think visually (apparently a majority of literary critics) and those who think verbally and are inclined to augment their response to sentence rhythms by imagining sounds when they are described. Also involved is the cultural phenomenon that Walter J. Ong describes as "a widespread reorganization of the sensorium favoring the visual in communication procedures—that is, favoring the visual in association with the use of words."[16] Defoe's writing so much reflects that shift toward emphasis on the visual that Novak is right to claim priority for its power to make readers see (or think they see, because events are described fully through the protagonist's responses: Crusoe makes the footprint seem vivid by explaining his reactions to it).[17] But sounds were also evoked skillfully by Defoe. This may have been more apparent to his own contemporaries in an era when the shift toward visual effects was underway (and articulated by Addison among others) but less important than it afterward became.

Reading some of Defoe's passages aloud compels recognition of how much they do vary in pace, how important it is to alter the tempo of speaking accordingly, and how little justice is done to his prose if it is all spoken (or silently read) at one level. I recommend this experiment, especially for the *Journal*. Many novelists would benefit equally from being read aloud, of course; and I only want to insist that Defoe is among that number for reasons that go beyond the advantages conferred on most prose by such reading. There are some visually oriented novels intended for silent reading, and for which an oral "performance" would be ruinous, just as there are many works that vary their tempo by devices for which reading aloud would bring small gain. Defoe, however, writes as though he assumes readers inclined to "hear" as well as "see," and perhaps even willing to engage in the now suspect custom of reading aloud to themselves, their families, or their friends.

After H.F. wishes that he could repeat and make his readers hear sounds of the plague still ringing in his ears, he adds in the next sentence (which is set off visually as a separate paragraph for emphasis): "If I could but tell this Part, in such moving Accents, as should alarm the very Soul of the Reader, I should rejoice that I recorded those Things, however short and imperfect" (p. 104). Bailey defines *accent* as "(with *Rhetoricians*) a Tone or Modulation of the Voice, used sometimes to denote the Intentions of the Orator or Speaker, to give a good or ill Signification to his Words." Johnson defines *accent* as "1. The manner of speaking or pronouncing, with regard either to force or elegance. ... 3. Poetically, language or words; 4. A modification of the voice, expressive of the passions or sentiments." H.F. is not using the word metaphorically in Johnson's third sense to mean he wishes that he could find the right words. He is using *accent* more technically to suggest that he would be happy with a written account (in which he "recorded those Things") if that account could be spoken aloud in the tones most likely to be moving. But H.F. cannot do it that way. Much as he would prefer to "tell" about the plague's most alarming events in accents designed to make his audience respond emotionally, he must write instead. His wish to speak aloud, however, is Defoe's invitation for readers to supply the modulations that no writer can put in his pages.

Other passages create similar invitations. Thus after telling of his first visit to the burial pit, H.F. remarks (in another sentence set off as a separate paragraph for emphasis): "This may serve a little to describe the dreadful Condition of that Day, tho' it is impossible to say any Thing that is able to give a true Idea of it to those who did not see it, other than this; that it was indeed *very, very, very* dreadful, and such as no Tongue can express" (p. 60). Here Defoe suggests that reiteration may sometimes come even closer than any single description can to conveying "a true Idea" of what is most dreadful. Although he does not say why this can happen, H.F.'s statement implies the explanation by illustrating how repetitions allow a single idea more time for emotional impact by slowing readers down to concentrate on a word (and thought) for longer periods while also inviting them to supply mentally (or aloud if they decide to speak the passage) those variations of accent that may communicate emotions most powerfully.

The trouble with such reiteration was remarked by Aristotle when he pointed out that speeches by professional orators are "good to hear spoken, but look amateurish enough when they pass into the hands of a reader. This is just because they ... contain many dramatic touches, which, being robbed of all dramatic rendering, fail to do their own proper work, and consequently look silly. Thus ... constant repetitions of words and phrases, are very properly condemned in written speeches: but not in spoken speeches—speakers use them freely, for they have a dramatic effect. In this repetition there must be variety of tone, paving the way, as it were, to dramatic effect."[18] Defoe writes without any sign of concern that his repetitions will be "seen" as faulty instead of "heard" as moving. Nor does he seem to worry that his audience will not slow appropriately as well as imagine proper accents when encountering phrases like H.F.'s *very, very, very*. Well into the eighteenth century there is evidence of a consensus that even where passages do not so conspicuously call for reading aloud by imitating or alluding to speech, the appropriate tempo for such a reading will be apparent to anyone of good taste, whether or not he has been instructed in rhetorical delivery.

Lord Kames, for example, considers the question of reading aloud under the heading "Beauty of Language," and he starts by conceding that "the only general rule that can be given for directing the pronunciation, is, to sound the words in such a manner as to imitate the things they signify." This conventional mimetic theory of pronunciation is rendered usable when Kames suggests possible variations in tone (we would say pitch), emphasis (stress in modern vocabulary), and speed (an issue which twentieth-century linguists avoid): "In pronouncing words signifying what is elevated, the voice ought to be raised above its ordinary tone; and words signifying dejection of mind, ought to be pronounced in a low note.... In Dryden's ode of *Alexander's Feast*, the line, *Faln, faln, faln, faln*, represents a gradual sinking of the mind; and therefore is pronounced with a falling voice by every one of taste, without instruction." Kames recommends strongest emphasis for "words that make the greatest figure," adding that resemblance between sound and sense is also governed by "slow or quick pronunciation: for though the length or shortness of the syllables with relation to each other, be in prose ascertained in some measure, and in verse accurately; yet taking a whole line or period together, it may be pronounced slow or fast. A period accordingly ought to be pronounced slow, when it expresses what is solemn or deliberate; and ought to be pronounced quick, when it expresses what is brisk, lively or impetuous."[19] In this view what mainly sets the proper speed for any sentence is not syntax or punctuation but content, which also determines the distribution of emphasis and variations of tone.

Kames does not extend his analysis beyond these basic considerations or to units larger than the "line or period." But individual sentences achieve much greater prominence as pacesetters when read aloud than when seen as part of a passage scanned visually on a page. Kames also takes for granted that subjective pace (whether "deliberate" or "brisk") will be obvious and should determine the objective speed of reading aloud. Neither he nor, so far as I know, any eighteenth-century critic doubted that the art of pronunciation is mainly a matter of matching the pace (and tone) of what is spoken to that first perceived while silently reading. But whatever advantages Defoe may have gained from audiences closer than we are to oral traditions of storytelling and reading, his variations of tempo are nevertheless designed to work during silent reading even if they are most apparent (especially to us) when taking his pages at the pace of actual speech, which not only goes more slowly but more conspicuously depends upon the speaker's own sense of timing to convey intended meanings by matching his pace to that of the text.

Even if we grant an audience responsive in this way to variations of tempo, however, there still remain serious questions about how Defoe first brings readers to "hear" when they are not reading his prose aloud or encountering passages that unmistakably imitate speech and thereby enforce a slower tempo than surrounding narrative. J. H. Plumb's assertion that in *A Journal of the Plague Year* "we hear again the shrieks of the dying and the lamentations of the living" is considered by George Starr, who agrees with Plumb's description of the effect, but asks "in what sense do we 'hear' them?"[20] Noting how often Defoe's narrator mentions shrieks, cries, and other noises, Starr observes that "for the most part these are not auditory descriptions at all: they specify nothing about the sounds themselves, but refer instead either to the impact they made on the narrator, or to the circumstances under which he infers they were uttered." Starr includes this point in his analysis of how Defoe's prose most "often presents not things but people perceiving things, so that both the existence and the nature of the things are established by indirection, by showing us people in the act of perceiving them."[21] Among its other advantages such indirection, which is the strategy by which Defoe usually makes readers imagine either sights or sounds, allows for greater control of subjective tempo than could be achieved by descriptions that leave nothing to the reader's imagination.

Such objective accounts, more fully cataloguing the attributes of whatever is seen or heard, would not so much encourage readers to pause or slow down while making an effort to envision what has been suggested by indirection. Pace would accordingly be altered mostly by manipulation of typographical clues such as paragraph and chapter divisions, or by piling up clauses, sentences, and paragraphs or cutting them down to occupy more or less of the reader's clock-time, and thus mainly alter objective tempo. Consider, for example, the passage in which H.F. writes that "People might be heard even into the Streets as we pass'd along, calling upon God for Mercy, thro' Jesus Christ, *and saying*, I have been a Thief, I have been an Adulterer, I have been a Murderer, and the like; and none durst stop to make the least Inquiry into such Things, or to administer Comfort to the poor Creatures, that in the Anguish both of Soul and Body thus cry'd out" (p. 34). This is an auditory description only in the minimal sense of specifying that it is what people were "*saying*" that could be "heard even into the Streets." Pace is slowed for emphasis mainly by the three clauses which stand out from their surroundings because of their parallelism. They will take up more clock-time than two or one, and they will seem to go more slowly than other parts of the sentence because the second and third echo their predecessors as much as they progress to new information: "I have been . . . I have been . . . I have been." The sounds themselves are only characterized as expressions of "Anguish both of Soul and Body." There is no attempt to make readers understand what the voices were like as voices, apart from what they say, because nothing is indicated about loudness or other attributes.

The final three words throw attention backward by inviting recollection, as Defoe so often does. "Thus cry'd out" will trigger at least a fleeting memory of "I have been a Thief, I have been an Adulterer, I have been a Murderer," thus further decelerating the reader's progress while that memory flashes across his mind. Addition of the entire final clause was unnecessary to finish describing what was said or to stress the point that no one dared "administer Comfort to the poor Creatures." Readers do not need more information than is provided up to these words in order to grasp the situation of these "poor Creatures" and find it moving. Defoe's addition of a final clause directing attention backward by further characterization of what has already been sufficiently described to elicit sympathy is a skillful manipulation for effect, designed to heighten emotion while slowing pace. So is the inclusion of three parallel quotations. But the slowing here is mainly a slowing of objective tempo (although significant within the small time-frame of the sentence), because the passage occupies more clock-time than it would have without the repetitions and the invitation to think back over what was "thus cry'd out."

Both objective and subjective tempo are slowed when H.F. writes: "Passing thro' *Token-House-Yard* in *Lothbury*, of a sudden a Casement violently opened just over my Head, and a Woman gave three frightful Skreetches, and then cry'd *Oh! Death, Death, Death!* in a most inimitable Tone, and which struck me with Horror and a Chilness, in my very Blood" (p. 81). This is an auditory description first in the minimal sense of telling that there *were* sounds: three screams (not two or four) followed by the quoted words (not others). Defoe slows objective pace by repeating one word three times, and also by the additional clock-time required for the redundant phrase "and a Chilness, in my very Blood." Subjective slowing of tempo in this sentence is equally significant, however; and it derives from the nature of what is reported and the way it is described.

"*Death, Death, Death!*" arrests attention more than most other possible words could have. So does the fact that H.F.'s sentence is also an auditory description in the less minimal sense of characterizing sounds themselves in two ways: positively—by describing with clinical precision their impact on H.F.; and negatively—by stating explicitly that what he heard was "a most inimitable Tone." *Horror* meant "such an Excess of Fear as makes a Person tremble;" *horrour* "in medicine" meant "a shivering or trembling of the Skin over the Whole Body, with a Chilness after it" (Bailey). H.F. mentions his "Chilness" to emphasize that he responded physiologically as well as psychologically to the sounds. And while this is certainly (and very effectively) a description of the sound in terms of its perception by H.F., the sentence is perhaps also as much an objective description relying on simple but clear medical terminology to specify the observable clinical effects ("Chilness") of "a most inimitable Tone." Defoe's insistence that the sound itself cannot be described invites imagination of what it might be like, and it causes some corresponding pause or deceleration of subjective pace while the reader is trying to grasp the impossibility of hearing anything like it outside of plague-time.

Defoe heightens the effect of that sentence by starting the next paragraph with an allusion back to it and then by providing dialogue that must be imagined as spoken aloud and that further arrests the reader's attention on what could be heard during the plague: "Just in *Bell-Alley*, on the right Hand of the Passage, there was a more terrible Cry than that, tho' it was not so directed out at the Window, but the whole Family was in a terrible Fright, and I could hear Women and Children run skreaming about the Rooms like distracted, when a Garret Window opened, and some body from a Window on the other Side the Alley, call'd and ask'd, *What is the Matter?* upon which, from the first Window it was answered, *Oh Lord, my Old Master has hang'd himself!* The other ask'd again, *Is he quite dead?* and the first answer'd, *Ay, ay, quite dead; quite dead and cold!*" (p. 81). The sounds of this dialogue arching back and forth between windows above Bell-Alley are precisely located in space. It is easier to envision the spatial gap which they bridge, and register the information conveyed, than to imagine exactly the "more terrible Cry" which precedes the dialogue. But Defoe's comparison of that sound with the previous "inimitable Tone" invites an attempt to do so whose inevitable frustration creates the slower subjective pace of descriptions that do not satisfy the reader's longing to understand fully what he is reading about.

Elsewhere in *A Journal of the Plague Year* Defoe slows the pace by including similar invitations to think about what cannot be completely imagined: "It is impossible to describe the most horrible Cries and Noise the poor People would make at their bringing the dead Bodies of their Children and Friends out to the Cart" (p. 178). Such explicit disclaimers challenge readers to make some attempt of a kind that is more obliquely invited in places like H.F.'s description of a man who "by the insufferable Torment he bore, daunced and sung naked in the Streets" (p. 177). Sung what?

Omission of any attempt to describe the song or its sounds creates the kind of open-ended image that, whether aural or visual, involves all but the most passive readers in some effort to imagine additional details, and it therefore slows subjective pace in a way that more complete descriptions would not. The effect is similar to that achieved for different purposes by Wordsworth in "The Solitary Reaper" when he encourages readers to speculate about the content of a song whose words are not provided. The device is of course more conspicuous (and more conspicuously signaled) in that short poem than in Defoe's equivalent strategies in *A Journal of the Plague Year*.

Its over-all pace, however, is to a significant degree set by the proliferation of descriptions that are in some way incomplete. When H.F. first mentions "the famous *Soloman Eagle*," for example, he is described as going "about denouncing of Judgment upon the City in a frightful manner; sometimes quite naked, and with a Pan of burning Charcoal on his Head: What he said or pretended, indeed I could not learn" (p. 103). The last clause of this description contributes no additional information about the content of Eagle's denunciations of London. Quite the reverse: that clause calls attention to the incompleteness of the very general phrase which tells what Eagle said, and it accordingly slows the pace of H.F.'s account by inviting speculation as well as by protracting the clock-time during which the reader's thoughts are focused on one topic.

"The poor outrageous Creature which danced and sung in his Agony" is mentioned more than once by H.F. along with similar examples of extremes to which people were driven, including the case of a man who "being tyed in his Bed, and finding no other Way to deliver himself, set the Bed on fire with his Candle, which unhappily stood within his reach, and Burnt himself in his Bed" (p. 177). This mercifully incomplete description is only the most striking of those passages which heighten emotion and arrest attention by their power of suggestion.

It is not merely the incidents themselves, however striking, but also the manner in which Defoe describes them which creates the distinctive tempo of such passages. He controls subjective pace as much by withholding details (and thus stimulating some effort at imaginative completion) as by repetitions that turn attention backward while also slowing objective pace by keeping the reader's mind occupied with the same incidents for additional clock-time.

The question of frequency is also involved. No critic has yet ventured a theory of the relationships between frequency and tempo. Consider, however, the deceleration of subjective pace invited by H.F.'s account of times when "the Funerals became so many, that People could not Toll the Bell, Mourn, or Weep" (p. 170). Defoe's insistence upon these silences is another kind of auditory description: specific because the absence of sound (no bells, no weeping) is an objective fact. What is crucial to the effect of this and similar passages, however, is the invitation to imagine many times of silence, not just one particular occasion. But no limits are set for the interval described. Because Defoe withholds a precise answer to the question "how many times?" the passage becomes temporally open-ended.

Gérard Genette has explained the four possible variations of narrative frequency: (1) something which happens only once may be told once; (2) something that happens more often may be narrated as often as it happens; (3) something that happens once may be narrated more often; and (4) events that happen more than once may be narrated only once.[22] As Genette nicely suggests by his comparison of Balzac, Flaubert, and Proust, this classification allows significant discrimination among works that differently represent time by resorting to one or another combination of the available narrative frequencies. The scheme deserves wider application, and it can certainly be extended to account for some of the major differences in tempo among Defoe's works. His Forecastle parody, for example, shows in extreme form what results when the first and second modes of frequency are combined so that every incident no matter how trivial is duly narrated once ("the Captain bought two Penny worth of Cabbages"), while recurring events ("at 12 the Larboard Watch came upon Deck") are told as often as they happen.

By comparison with *Robinson Crusoe* and *A Journal of the Plague Year* certainly *Captain Singleton*, *Colonel Jack*, *Moll Flanders*, and *Roxana* maintain a more rapid objective tempo because for these Defoe chose mostly the first mode of narrative frequency and he provided mainly a one-to-one ratio of event to narration. Significant events are narrated once in correspondence with their occurrence, while trivial happenings that may be presumed to have occurred often are omitted from the narration. Defoe provides effective variation within this framework, however, by repetitions that have the effect of telling some events more than once. He also includes single reports that stand for whole classes of events. But among the autobiographical fictions it is in *Robinson Crusoe* that Defoe most significantly varies tempo by combining the first, third, and fourth modes of frequency in ways that amount to a departure from the basic framework of one-to-one ratio between event and narration. Crusoe's shipwreck and establishment on the island are told more often with the consequences for tempo as well as verisimilitude that I have discussed; and there are many passages in which Crusoe describes a daily or seasonal routine while also making clear that the account is to serve as a description of what he did during many years when that routine was his custom. Readers are invited to take the described day—or season—as typical, and they imagine it to be multiplied by the duration of his stay alone on the island.

It is in *A Journal of the Plague Year*, however, that Defoe shifts most sharply from a predominantly one-to-one ratio between events and their narration. He provides frequent repetitions while also including a large number of typical descriptions which readers must take as standing for whole classes of recurring events. Far from being trivial, such events are what by their frequency as much as their nature most characterize the plague year: death above all. Each death that is described must be imagined as representative, not merely as particular; and that necessary effort of imagination slows the pace while adding to the horror of each description by compelling realization that the kind of agonies described were in fact never confined to the moment which H. F. has singled out for narration.

The extent to which repetition alone slows both objective and subjective tempo has been often remarked by critics dealing with time in literature. Apart from Genette's consideration of Proust, there has been little exploration of the effects achieved by various choices among possible frequencies, especially in a rare situation like that created in *A Journal of the Plague Year* by Defoe's combination of repetition with numerous passages whose narrated events must be understood as recurring. Despite the repetitions which characterize *A Journal of the Plague Year* such events are not described as often as they are said to have taken place, and they are sometimes only described once. The general effect is to make Defoe's narrative move more slowly than it would if there were fewer typical episodes included and identified as such either explicitly or by means of syntax, as in the description of Soloman Eagle as someone who "went about denouncing of Judgment upon the City [how often?]

"... sometimes quite naked, and with a Pan of burning Charcoal on his Head" [when?]. This sentence is among the many that do not narrate one occasion, but that invite imagination of an indeterminate number of similar events.

Defoe also creates an oppressive density of bizarre and terrible events that readers are made to sense as having existed alongside those that are narrated. The effect is entirely appropriate because it enhances the representational as well as emotional power of *A Journal of the Plague Year*. In order to understand that time, readers must feel an almost constant pressure of other events whose nature is made clear by H.F.'s frequent assurances after describing particular episodes that "I cou'd give a great many such Stories as these . . . which in the long Course of that dismal Year, I met with" (p. 52). Defoe makes the narrative move slowly not only by repetition but by insisting on the reality and the implied presence of these untold tales, which for a reader of any imagination will add their own weight of horror to the emotions elicited by what *is* described.

Many of those descriptions also imply durations beyond what is narrated, with effects beyond what might be expected in proportion to the amount of narrating time (and reading-time) which they occupy. After describing the time when no bells sounded at funerals, for example, H.F. goes on in the same paragraph to tell how, during the plague's height, "People sat still looking at one another, and seem'd quite abandon'd to Despair; whole Streets seem'd to be desolated, and not to be shut up only, but to be emptied of their Inhabitants; Doors were left open, Windows stood shattering with the Wind in empty Houses, for want of People to shut them" (p. 171). Here, too, the auditory description is specific only insofar as it implies the silences of people looking at one another in despair—and the other silences of desolate streets. The sounds of this period are not described beyond the author's obliquely inviting readers to slow down while imagining for themselves the adroitly implied contrast between empty houses devoid of human sounds, and the noise of windows "shattering with the Wind." Tempo is effectively slowed, however, by the fact that readers must imagine that sound as continuing over a large but unspecified time-span.

Perhaps Defoe's most effective local strategy of openended auditory description combined with narration in that mode of frequency which provides one account of events that took place more often is in the stunning narration of H.F.'s second visit to the burial pit. Everything described in his relation of that night must also be taken to represent what happened during a larger interval. In this case Defoe specifies the time involved by having H.F. report that from the 4th of September to the 20th "they had thrown into it 1114 Bodies" (p. 59). In addition to striking details of the pit's appearance at night when the dead-carts arrive, Defoe includes in the scene a grief-stricken man whose family is about to be buried, and who "said nothing as he walk'd about, but two or three times groaned very deeply, and loud, and sighed as he would break his Heart" (p. 61). His absence of speech is Defoe's invitation for readers to speculate (as H.F. at first does) about the man's situation.

There would be less motive for one to enter his mind and sympathetically identify oneself with him if Defoe had put into his mouth words like those ascribed elsewhere to victims of the plague. In the context of the burial-pit scene, it would only diminish, not heighten, emotions to have anyone say something like "*Death, Death, Death!*" The man's intensity of grief is suggested by H.F.'s indirect account of an apparently heart-broken sigh—and also by the more objective enumeration of his groans and description of them as deep and loud. These sounds are specified about as fully as existing vocabulary allowed, but in a way that is indeed less concerned with rendering their attributes than with focusing attention on them to invite imagination of what they meant.

H.F. rivets attention on this man by reporting that after his family was "shot into the Pit promiscuously. . . . He cry'd out aloud unable to contain himself; I could not hear what he said, but he went backward two or three Steps, and fell down in a Swoon" (p. 62). Any attempt to guess "what he said" only underscores the inadequacy of language to such moments. By again resisting the temptation to supply words in a situation whose pathos would be diminished by any imaginable phrase, Defoe portrays the entire burial-pit scene more powerfully.

Its impact is then heightened by recollection of the episode when H.F. says that after he returned home "the poor unhappy Gentleman's Grief came into my head again, and indeed I could not but shed Tears in the Reflection upon it, perhaps more than he did himself" (p. 63). Readers must also remember, and slow their forward speed while thinking longer about what happened at the burial pit, just as H.F. does.

Inspired by his memory to seek the man out, H.F. finds him in the Pye Tavern sitting "still, mute and disconsolate" surrounded by scoffers "ridiculing the Man, and his Sorrow for his Wife and Children" (pp. 64–65). His silence contrasts with the oaths and raillery of these scoffers as described by H.F. up to the moment when they too are struck down by the plague "and were every one of them carried into the great Pit" (p. 67). The blasphemies in which they indulge make their fate seem entirely deserved, and the sense that justice is at least occasionally served by the plague gives momentary relief to the reader's sense of unmitigated horror. In this way, too, Defoe varies pace—but only to heighten effect.

Such variation intensifies the emotional effect of reading about so many deaths: that only a few of them seem poetically just acts of divine retribution merely adds to the pathos of what has been told about the "poor unhappy Gentleman's Grief" and the other bereavements among the virtuous which it symbolizes. Defoe creates similar variation in tempo by including several narrations that are different in kind from the most frequent episodes. There is the traditional comedy of a drunken piper found asleep and put into the dead cart by mistake. After telling how he startled its attendants by awakening to ask where he was, the anecdote accelerates to its punch line: "*But I ain't dead tho', am I?* says the Piper; which made them laugh a little" (p. 91). This comic incident provides laughter of a sort that does vary pace—but in a way that contributes to the grim atmosphere of H.F.'s narration.

He says when first mentioning the story of three men who survived by fleeing London that "several Stories were told of such; some comical, some tragical" (p. 57). Anticipation of reading a narration with for once a happy outcome provides some forward thrust of the reader's expectation which is, however, counterbalanced by H.F.'s repeated delays in getting to the story that he keeps promising. Making readers wait so long for this episode adds to their sense of slow motion. When H.F. finally starts telling about the three men, it soon becomes clear that their adventures are going to end happily and that they will therefore be among the few "comical" anecdotes whose outcome (as well as linear narrative-sequence corresponding to the chronological order of events) allows some escape for readers from the slowly moving proliferation of "tragical" incidents that are very much alike. But, again, the relief of experiencing a quicker pace while following a journey outside London only calls attention by contrast to how slowly the account of what happened inside London moves. Therefore, while Defoe speeds up the subjective pace by making readers anticipate seeing the scoffers punished, the piper's awakening, and the escape of three men, the end of these and similar episodes which create a sense of acceleration is always a return to the slow pace that Defoe establishes as the norm in *A Journal of the Plague Year:* its tempo shows how time seemed to flow during "the long Course of that dismal Year."

4

Defoe is as careful to include statements about the tempo of the plague itself and how time was experienced by those who survived as he is to create a narrative which makes the reader's time move at a correspondingly slow pace. In *A Journal of the Plague Year* to a greater extent than elsewhere in his fiction, Defoe achieves what he is often reproached for having neglected: portrayal of duration, the *way* time passes or seems to pass.

The durations that concern him, however, are as much

public and objective as private and subjective. Defoe portrays relationships between both varieties of time. H.F. not only reports what happened during the "long" plague year: he also specifies the rate of events and insists that the import of that rate must be understood in order to grasp the nature of London's ordeal as well as the main reason why it was possible for the city to endure as it did. Thus, very early in his narrative, H.F. mentions various portents of both the plague and the fire to stress the different pace of those disasters: "before the Pestilence" there was a comet "of a faint, dull, languid Colour, and its Motion very heavy, solemn and slow: But . . . the Comet before the Fire, was bright and sparkling . . . and its Motion swift and furious" (p. 20). Defoe amplifies the point by H.F.'s explanation that "one foretold a heavy Judgement, slow but severe, terrible and frightful, as was the Plague; but the other foretold a Stroak, sudden, swift, and fiery as the Conflagration" (p. 20). This distinction between the rate of the fire and that of the plague establishes expectations about the tempo of the events that will be narrated. It also prepares readers to understand why a slow-moving narrative would be appropriate or even necessary for the topic in hand.

Toward the end of *A Journal of the Plague Year* Defoe makes H.F. reiterate another point that has been much insisted upon throughout: "I cannot but mention again, tho' I have spoken several times of it already . . . that . . . the Progression of the Distemper . . . began at one end of the Town, and proceeded gradually and slowly from one Part to another, and like a dark Cloud that passes over our Heads, which as it thickens and overcasts the Air at one End, clears up at the other End" (p. 212). In addition to stressing again how "gradually and slowly" the plague came and went,

Defoe's metaphor of comparing it to a passing cloud provides indirect reassurance that to describe a phenomenon without clear-cut divisions between beginning, middle, and end it is appropriate to write a narrative without sharp edges in the form, say, of chapter divisions like those in *The History of the Union*. Nor is there in *A Journal of the Plague Year* any narrative division of the plague year into conspicuous turning-points until close to the end, when H.F. tells of an unexpected decline in mortality which led to a dramatic "Change that appear'd in the very Countenances of the People, that *Thursday* Morning, when the Weekly Bill came out" (p. 245). Until this passage the boundaries of the plague's different phases are neither quite so apparent even in retrospect, nor so localized in time as "that *Thursday* Morning." Readers are made to understand that the plague reached its peak in August and September. But no single moment stands out as marking the arrival of that phase.

One effect of a narrative so well arranged to mirror events with the amorphous edges of a slowly passing cloud is described by Tyna Orren when she observes that, even more than elsewhere in his fiction, Defoe "holds the reader tightly in a flow of experience that he can only break out of by a kind of rebellion. The reader is thus prevented most of the time from standing back and viewing the *Journal* as a unified whole. He is prevented, that is to say, from doing ... precisely what ... a historian does with evidence concerning the public past when he shapes a sequence of events into a coherent narrative, so that at every point in the *Journal* the reader is tied to the present moment ... just as the recorder of minutes or the writer of an individual journal entry always is."[23] In this way Defoe achieves some of the effects of journalistic concentration on whatever present moment is in question within a narrative that does not take the form of dated entries and whose viewpoint is retrospective.

Defoe's freedom to juxtapose so many similar anecdotes from different stages of the plague and to recur so often to the same topics has another effect that Tyna Orren has identified. She remarks that in plotted narratives like *Tom Jones*, in which causal relationships are clear and narrative sequence mainly corresponds to the chronology of narrated sequences, the past has a double significance for readers: what has already been read corresponds to what is in the character's past during plot-time, while "the reader's future—what he hasn't got to yet—corresponds to the participant's future; the present moment is felt to arise out of the past and to be a bridge to the future so that the reader remembers the past as what initiated the present and looks to the future for what will bring the whole sequence to its logical conclusion and make clear its meaning." But H.F. even reverses cause-effect sequence by reserving for the last part of his book the most extensive discussion of what caused the plague to spread after it first began. Readers therefore have difficulty recalling exactly where in the narrative sequence (their reading-time) a topic has previously occurred, and "the matter's reappearance only reinforces the effect that the *Journal*'s anecdotal construction has . . . of upsetting [the reader's] sense of getting somewhere: he got to a discussion of shutting up houses some time ago, and now he has got to the same place again. His awareness of the past is less a distinct *memory* than a sense of *déjà vu*."[24] Consequently the effects of spatial form created in Defoe's autobiographical fictions are not duplicated in *A Journal of the Plague Year*.

The over-all impression created as readers go through its

pages is of a time when death and suffering of unparalleled intensity were to be found throughout large areas of London. Some events are placed at the beginning or middle of the plague or within its closing days. Anecdotes which cannot be assigned to particular moments in its chronology are so numerous, however, that what remains uppermost in the reader's mind is a sense that most of what is described might have occurred at almost any time. Narrated events therefore coexist in the reader's memory of the narrative (both during and after reading it) instead of distributing themselves along a time-line in retrospect. To that extent *A Journal of the Plague Year* does achieve a significant degree of spatial form.

Except for H.F.'s narrative about the three men who escaped from London, however, there is little encouragement to hold in mind entire *sequences* like Crusoe's running away to sea while contemplating them in miniature to grasp some moral. Instead Defoe compels readers to experience—as Londoners did—a time when events "proceeded gradually and slowly." Despite the mortality tables—and partly because there are too many of them to keep firmly in mind without a photographic memory—the tempo of that motion is made easier to apprehend and remember than any particular sequence in either reading-time or read-about time. Defoe thus shifts emphasis from the chronology of what took place within the narrated time-spans to the quality of experienced duration throughout "the long Course of that dismal Year."

The achievement has been regarded as paradoxical. F. Bastian, for example, praises Defoe's general success in portraying the plague year without, however, allowing him much credit for planning: "He triumphs in the *Journal* despite the almost complete absence of a plan."[25] But the effects which allow that triumph are enhanced by the invisibility of Defoe's plan and by the avoidance of a conventional plan: any obvious linear organization allowing every incident to be placed along a time-line, or any topical organization where there is a logical and therefore predictable progression from topic to topic, creates anticipation of what may come next in the ordering of logic or chronology. And such anticipation itself works against the sense that a narration is proceeding "gradually and slowly." A slow tempo can be created within such conventional arrangements but not so easily: they are more likely to provide an overview which helps narrative acceleration or (if the action is not much extended in time) freezes time altogether. Also more difficult to convey by such predictable plans would be any emotional understanding of a year that was itself unpredictable. Because readers are seldom sure where H.F. will jump next in terms of topics introduced or moments during the plague year singled out for discussion, the experience of reading the *Journal* corresponds more exactly to the sensations of those who lived through what Defoe also characterizes as "this Surprizing Time" (p. 19).

There is an even more important advantage to Defoe's avoidance of any conventional plan like the ones he was perfectly able (and willing) to employ in *The Storm* and *Due Preparations for the Plague*. In them no reader can mistake the organizing plans which are explicitly announced. But these works are not among his triumphs. By choosing, and perhaps *only* by choosing a procedure which Bastian and others have correctly seen as a distinct combination of narrative and apparently disorganized commentary which makes *A Journal of the Plague Year* unique,

Defoe could better portray the actual rhythm of the plague.

The plague was not spread through all London simultaneously. Defoe explains this repeatedly, and he sums it up in clarifying his partially misleading metaphor of the plague as a slowly passing cloud: "So while the Plague went on raging from West to East, as it went forwards East, it abated in the West, by which means those parts of the Town, which were not seiz'd, or who were left, and where it had spent its Fury, were (as it were) spar'd to help and assist the other; whereas had the Distemper spread it self over the whole City and Suburbs at once, raging in all Places alike, as it has done since in some places abroad, the whole Body of the People must have been overwhelmed" (p. 212). Although it is true that *A Journal of the Plague Year* displays greater unity of time, place, and action than Defoe's fictional autobiographies spanning many years in lives of surprising variety, that unity is only apparent in retrospect. London, seen from inside its boundaries throughout the plague year as H.F. reports it, was neither a single place nor even a collection of places undergoing the same experience "at once."

This creates a problem for any eye-witness account that has only a single narrator, even one writing from the comprehensive viewpoint allowed by retrospect and even one so given as H.F. was during the narrated time to walking around collecting information. It was easier for Defoe to convey the more nearly instantaneous devastation outlined in *The Storm*, because that was by comparison more nearly a single moment: one week from start to finish of the high winds, with the great storm itself striking on November 26, 1703, between midnight and 6:30 A.M. There were during the week and during that night many different but simultaneous sequences of individual adventures or larger events like the escape of the British home fleet. And when there is such unity of time as the storm displayed, there is not much need to portray either objective or subjective duration.

Quite the contrary. Because the storm's pace was rapid, like the fire, Defoe's narrative problem was the opposite of that which faced him in writing *A Journal of the Plague Year:* it was necessary to find some way of stopping time. Only by doing so could a multiplicity of events crowded into the same short interval be understood in their synchronic relationships to each other. And those relationships are of the essence, because what defines speed is not only short absolute duration but a high ratio of events to a given interval. Individual sequences like the escape of the fleet could be narrated diachronically, but they had somehow to be shown (and grasped by readers) as occurring at the same time as other separately narrated episodes. Where so many threads must be woven together to show how much happened simultaneously, however, the acceleration of events cannot easily be reflected by means of a narrative that seems to move rapidly. Individual episodes may go along briskly, but the narrator must often recur to the beginning to pick up and carry forward another incident, and therefore he cannot achieve acceleration to match the pace of events taken together. When dealing elsewhere with longer expanses of time and less diversity of action, Defoe accelerates pace in conformity with the rapid tempo of narrated events: most successfully at the end of *Roxana* by creating suspense about Susan's fate. In order to deal with the rapid tempo of the storm, however, Defoe made it easy for readers to do what *A Journal of the Plague Year* discourages: to stand back and take in the major outlines of what happened throughout England, thereby registering how very much did take place "at once."

A more static narrative with an entirely visible plan is perhaps the most obvious way to cope with the problem of conveying simultaneity as the major temporal dimension of depicted events. This in any case was Defoe's choice in *The Storm*. Preliminary chapters entitled "The Natural Causes and original of Winds" and "Of the Opinion of the Ancients, that this Island was more Subject to Storms than other Parts of the World" are followed by a descriptive chapter, "Of the Storm in General." This allows readers to have its major events in mind early in their progress through the text. Then "A Pastoral, occasion'd by the Late Violent Storm" supplies a poetic interlude which is succeeded by a discussion "Of the Extent of this Storm, and from what Parts it was supposed to come; with some circumstances as to the Time of it." The last part of the book is headed "Of the EFFECTS of the Storm," and the narrator promises divisions "into the following Chapters or Sections, that I may put it into as good Order as possible":

1. Of the Damage in the City of *London*, &c.
2.   in the Countries.
3. *on the Water*   in the Royal Navy.
4.   to Shipping in general.
5.   by Earthquake.
6.   by High Tides.
7. Remarkable Providences and Deliverances.
8. Hardned and Blasphemous Contemners both of the Storm and its Effects.
9. Some calculations of Damage sustained.
10. The Conclusion.[26]

Perusal of this plan and the chapters in which it is partially carried out is like viewing in succession dozens of snapshots taken in different places on the same day. There is little sense of movement through time. As the account shifts from place to place, space becomes its most important dimension.

Nor is there much emotional involvement. Readers are disengaged from the narrated events not only because the events are inherently less distressing than those of the plague year but because Defoe arranges *The Storm* in open conformity with the impersonal order of logical analysis by first taking up causes and then proceeding to effects instead of winding along the pathways of the narrator's memory as *A Journal of the Plague Year* so often does. For *The Storm* Defoe also chose the least complicated mode of narrative frequency: events that happened once are narrated once. There are some minor departures from this mode, but topics are not brought up over and over. The resulting gains in clarity are achieved at the expense of emotional force.

The reasons, so far as they concern time, are explained by the conventional and valid doctrine which Kames summed up in warning that passions cannot be raised "by painting to such a height as by words: a picture is confined to a single instant of time, and cannot take in succession of incidents. ... But seldom is a passion raised to any height in an instant, or by a single impression: our passions, those especially of the sympathetic kind, require a succession of impressions; and for that reason, reading and acting have greatly the advantage by reiterating impressions without end."[27] Spatial form in itself of the kind which Defoe partially achieves in *The Storm* cannot create the impact of narratives that also manage, as *A Journal of the Plague Year* does by its higher frequency of repetitions, to provide what seem more like "impressions without end." A corollary of this emotional gain is that narrated time does not seem stopped, as it had to be for the most accurate representation of events that co-existed during the storm's rapid passage. In the *Journal*, represented time seems to move slowly, because reading-time does.

And because that sense of slow motion is so much created by recurring topics, and by narrated events that often seem like those previously narrated, Defoe's portrayal of passing time in *A Journal of the Plague Year* not only heightens emotional impact but allows readers to experience a duration that corresponds about as closely as the aesthetic experience of any reading-time could to the distinctive way in which moments passed and were filled by recurrent rhythms during London's plague. Defoe suggests the distinguishing feature of that particular duration by his explanation of the passing-cloud metaphor, and he also suggests it by such elaborations as H.F.'s catalogue of how the plague "began at St. *Giles*'s, and the *Westminster* End of the Town, and it was in its Height in all that part by about the Middle of *July*, *viz.* in St. *Giles* in the *Fields*, St. *Andrew's Holborn*, St. *Clement-Danes*, St. *Martins* in the *Fields*, and in *West-minster:* The latter End of *July* it decreased in those Parishes, and coming East, it encreased prodigiously in *Cripplegate*, St. *Sepulchers*, St. *Ja. Clarkenwell*, and St. *Brides*, and *Aldersgate;* while it was in all these Parishes, the City and all the Parishes of the *Southwark* Side of the Water, and all *Stepney*, *White-Chapel*, *Aldgate*, *Wapping*, and *Ratcliff* were very little touch'd; so that People went about their Business . . . and conversed freely with one another in all the City, the East and North-East Suburbs, and in *Southwark*, almost as if the Plague had not been among us" (pp. 186–87). This and similar extensive lists convey geographical facts about the plague which reveal its manner of existence in time: as a rhythm of recurring sequences, each rising to a similar crescendo and then diminishing.

That mode of duration, however, while characteristic of London's plague year, is not a feature of all plagues. Defoe understood this very well, as he understood so many other aspects of existence in time; and he stresses the difference by his comparison with "some Places abroad"—he mentions Naples—where the plague struck everywhere "at once, raging in all Places alike" in a more rapid and less rhythmical tempo. Like the storm and the fire those other plague-times were more nearly simultaneous experiences for the populations involved. To show a time marked instead by slow sequences that started over and over in different places, thus making the plague year seem "long" as measured by its impressions left in the memory of a survivor and reflected in his narrative, Defoe provides a work whose structure, verbal rhythms, imagery, manner of describing events, modes of frequency, and resulting pace all combine to create for readers not only emotions appropriate to the subject, and remarkably correspondent to those experienced during plague time, but also a corresponding duration.

6
Implications

The success of Defoe's ambiguous time-schemes in reinforcing the rhetorical intentions of *Roxana, Colonel Jack, Captain Singleton,* and *Moll Flanders* suggests that we may better comprehend how eighteenth-century fiction evolved if we look more closely at its temporal settings and their effects. We may also extend our methodology for dealing with time in literature. More often than critics have remarked, with consequences that remain to be explored in fiction after Defoe, narratives hover just outside present time without resorting to past or future settings. By refusing to supply complete references to years, for example, Richardson takes the action of *Clarissa* outside, but not very far outside, historical time in a way that reinforces other mythic elements of his novel while also maintaining its immediacy. He shifts emphasis from historical time to mythic time. *Clarissa* thereby becomes a step forward in presentational realism through expanding narrative scale while also achieving effects that we can now recognize as depending on modes of representing time which are by almost any definition unrealistic. Thus J. Paul Hunter, in contrasting Fielding's telescopic views of large time-panoramas and Richardson's microscopic approach to the intensive portrayal of small periods expanded, remarks that "it is finally misleading to think of what Richardson . . . does" as realism because his "enlargement and savoring of the moment ... radically distorts in order to reveal."[1] By such distortion, as well as by giving an internally consistent chronology which is detached from any particular year and thus is transformed into an emblematic time-sequence, Richardson brought to new perfection not only the portrayal (by enlargement) of how individuals experience time, but also what Frank Kermode identifies as the traditional gratifications of "sham temporality, sham causality, falsely certain description."[2]

Of course at the level of particular episodes Richardson shows his awareness of the deceptiveness of causality, and he dramatizes the fact that in subjective experience of passing time causation may be impossible to discover precisely where it is crucial. There is no more brilliant illustration of this in English literature than the garden elopement-scene in *Clarissa*. In retrospect Clarissa sees that day, and the minutes with Lovelace before and while running off with him, as one of those "points of time" on which (as she puts it) one's subsequent worldly happiness may depend. Yet there is no indication of clock-time within the scene. Nor is it ever made clear to readers exactly when during that unspecified amount of time the point of no return has passed either psychologically or in objective fact up to the moment when the coach sets out. Viewed in retrospect, the whole day dwindles for readers and characters alike to a time which is crucial. Its large causes and consequences become apparent. Viewed from within by protagonists and readers, the time of the actual turning point, and thus the clear line between causes and their effects, becomes elusive. Temporal boundaries disappear.

Clarissa as a whole, especially when it is considered in retrospect, nevertheless shows a world in which cause does lead to effect, and where both can be specified, given a vantage at sufficient temporal distance from the events in question. To that degree, at least, Richardson is reassuring despite a tragic mode that does not emphasize providential orderings of the kind dramatized in some of Defoe's fiction. His narratives with their more picaresque structures often show a world where mere sequence of before and after may be as much the norm of ordinary human experience as awareness of causal relationships with invariable if not always welcome chains of consequences linking past and present into significant unities of the kind implied by more coherent plots. This is surely one source of Defoe's appeal for the twentieth century. But if the temporal unities created by the linkage of cause and effect are illusory for reasons that Hume and his successors have explored, those illusions are, as Kermode suggests, gratifying versions of temporality to contemplate in fictions. We need these shams for comfort, and we resist writers like Robbe-Grillet who match fictional time to philosophical understanding of what may underlie temporal perception. These aspects of fictional time are now well understood in connection with the temporal orderings created by coherent plots. But I reiterate Kermode's insight to stress the context within which I am stressing the need for additional investigation of those corollary gratifications provided by temporal settings.

As I hope Defoe's example sufficiently demonstrates, temporal settings must only be definite enough to provide resting-places for the mind so that it has the illusion of relating to a specific time even though that time may be detached from particular moments in order to universalize a narrative. This too is understood in principle, but critics have not often enough considered the implications. Nor has there been much attention paid to the devices by which various degrees of disengagement from particular settings can be achieved. *Tom Jones*, for example, is usually described simply as a novel whose main action takes place during forty or so days at the most threatening moment of the Jacobite rebellion, thereby allowing topical satire.

Less often remarked is the extent to which Fielding as well as Richardson makes choices, although different choices, that keep action within the eighteenth century while severing its ties to particular years in order to maintain significant temporal distance between plot events and the flow of calendar time. That time is, in the first place, not marked by dates throughout *Tom Jones* but is implied by allusions to events like the rebellion which do have dates. And no such events are mentioned at the outset. Fielding begins Tom's story by summing up Allworthy's life to "about five Years before the Time in which this History chuses to set out."[3] That time is not pinned down by a date. Neither is Tom's birth. Nor are the calendar years in Tom's life to the day of his setting out on the road after being expelled from Paradise Hall in what readers only discover is 1745 by inferring that date from Tom's encounter with soldiers going to fight against the rebels. Tom's fall is into the world of time.

Before that point in the story it is not calendar—and thus historical—time which is paramount but biological time. Readers learn first about Tom's birth, marriages and deaths which preceded it, and the events of his youth. It is thus most exact to say that Tom falls from private time into involvement with the public time marked by wars and the reigns of monarchs. Each life cycle is so much the repetition of a timeless pattern, however, that to focus on the initial stages of it as such early in a novel, while also avoiding any mention of dates, achieves maximum detemporalization even for those later portions of the plot which *are* affiliated to a particular historical moment.

The sense of Tom's birth as the commencement of a familiar cycle despite unusual circumstances is intensified by Fielding's allusions to death at the outset of *Tom Jones:* seriously to the death of Allworthy's wife, comically to the end of Captain Blifil. His tombstone departs from the convention of including dates although it glances very far forward by insisting on Blifil's expectation of a joyful rising. His ironic epitaph, for all its hilarity, is no less important than mention of Allworthy's wife as a memento mori: it is only less disturbing. And therefore it is more effective in stressing the reassuring continuities displayed by each progress through the ages of man, although of course readers hope that Tom will have better progress and a happier ending.

Those critics who have remarked the importance of Fielding's topical commentary and celebration of his own time in *Tom Jones* are right. But what finally stands out in his use of the '45 as its focal point in calendar time is the way that Fielding prepares a context which transforms the particular historical moment into an emblematic time which serves most importantly to underscore Tom's affirmation of the social order by offering him a chance to show his allegiance to king and country. Fielding avoids taking Tom close enough to the real events of the rebellion to deflect attention from the general fictional time created early in *Tom Jones.* Nor does Fielding bother to reconcile the introduction of that historical moment with the generalized chronology established initially. By alluding to calendar time, Fielding does not enhance verisimilitude. He weakens it in order to achieve what for him are more important goals, among them explicit consideration of man's relationship to time.

Thomas Cleary notes that Fielding's announcement (7:9) of the time of action not only "places Tom's meeting with the soldiers in the last week of November or the first week in December 1745, the period in which the Pretender's army was near Derby, . . . it disrupts violently the novel's much-praised chronological consistency, for the chapter headings to Books VI and VII indicate that exactly three weeks and one day elapse between this meeting and the night of Allworthy's recovery which is described as 'a pleasant evening in June' . . . a discrepancy of four months has bothered scholars who celebrate the novel's chronological consistency." Moreover Fielding's "anti-Jacobite satire is found as consistently and anomalously confined to the central books as the specific historical background."[4] Fielding's allusions to calendar time are therefore not only conspicuously restricted to one part of *Tom Jones:* they create anachronism.

Not parachronism or prochronism but misplacement of events with respect to one another: Fielding puts November or December three weeks after June. As so often for Defoe, however, the pejorative connotations of "anachronism" are misleading. Fielding's discrepancy is only problematic for modern critics. And while it is certainly a feature of *Tom Jones*, that discrepancy is better regarded as a clue to Fielding's thematic intentions (although anachronism was not necessary to realization of them) than as a lapse from efforts at temporal realism. Cleary argues persuasively for the inconsistency as evidence of revision: "Taken together, the oddities of chronology, characterization, and structure in the novel, the digressive qualities of virtually all of the passages in which its anti-Jacobite satire is found ... strongly suggest the imposition of a specific historical background as well as anti-Jacobite (or anti-opposition) satire on its central third in the course of a partial and hasty revision carried out during the first half of 1748."[5] Whatever its order of composition, *Tom Jones* can only be seen as deficient in temporal setting, because anachronistic, if chronological consistency is taken as among Fielding's primary intentions. If not, as might be equally suggested by the fact that a writer so generally scrupulous and attentive to time-relationships of other kinds was content to let the anachronism stand even if he was writing hastily, then the anti-Jacobite and other topical allusions in Tom Jones are less problematically (and I think in the light of Defoe's example most properly) regarded as subordinate to the larger issue of man's relationship to time.

This view of Fielding's intentions is also confirmed by Henry Knight Miller's thorough study of connections between *Tom Jones* and the romance tradition. Of the anachronism which has been troublesome to previous critics, Miller remarks that there is "no real explanation for this impossibility." He nevertheless insists that "it was a happy error" because "not only is each season precisely appropriate for its contextual action—summer for rutting, winter for judgment—but the abrupt collision of winter upon summer most effectively marks the dislocation of Tom's Edenic world, as it also marks a radical leap from the romance world of temporal imprecision into the calendar world of an actual and geographically determinate England in late 1745." Miller regards Tom's sudden departure into winter as "a typical romance use of the temporal as symbolic background," familiar to readers of works like *Sir Gawain and the Green Knight*.⁶ So it is.

With an eye on romances alone, however, Miller does not go beyond a cautious statement that "the temptation is strong to say that Fielding planned the whole thing just this way . . . the 'error' remained uncorrected in subsequent editions." Nor does the romance tradition, if that were Fielding's only precedent, allow very confident acceptance of Miller's argument that "the radical time-leap . . . could be an aspect of the regeneration or redemption of Time itself." This interpretation is worked out through Miller's resort to Mircea Eliade's scheme of departure from and return to *ille tempore*, a Golden Age: in this case Tom's banishment from and "return to the world of Paradise Hall . . . and therefore a redemption—though not for Fielding, an abolition—of Time, by 'sacralizing' the transitory shifting moment of the temporal through an incarnation of the changeless vision of the Ideal." From the perspective of romance backgrounds, Miller is "reluctant" to pursue his reading, which he finds "rather too anthropological and 'modern' in conception."⁷ Defoe's example, however—surely representative of a precedent quite as operative as the romance tradition for Fielding and his readers—should encourage less tentative adoption of Miller's suggestion that *Tom Jones* is intended to show what we would call the redemption—but not the abolition—of time.

The way in which Fielding maintains awareness of time as the context within which—and by means of which—the complications of his plot are resolved, thus affirming time's redemptive role in human affairs, can be seen by looking more closely than is customary at the way the action of *Tom*

Jones is actually affiliated to calendar time: not so abruptly as attention to Fielding's anachronism suggests, although it is true that until Tom's banishment from Paradise Hall readers are not invited to notice significant connections between fictional and historical time. It is the Man of the Hill whose birth is assigned a date: 1657. This is the only date in *Tom Jones*, thus Fielding's most prominent invitation to notice the way its action is attached to calendar time. The date invites attention to history while also very much widening the novel's temporal setting and connecting that setting to biological as well as political time: when encountered by Tom in 1745 the Man of the Hill would be eighty-eight years old. The scope of *Tom Jones* is consequently extended backward in a way that is as significant as the more open-ended forward extension implied at the end by the narrator's report that Tom and Sophia have a boy and a girl. Despite confinement of its central events to 1745, *Tom Jones* covers actions ranging from 1657 through the birth of Tom's children and therefore, by implication, into a future beyond its terminus of narration and publication in 1748.

In providing this scope without calling attention to it at the outset or connecting plot-time throughout to particular days and months of calendar-time, Fielding made choices that were by no means inevitable when narrating one part of a single life. Philip Stevick observes that "the very amplitude of *Tom Jones* testifies to Fielding's pleasure in seeing causal patterns and complex chains of events in terms of their unity and coherence."[8] Equal pleasure, and equally reassuring chains of sham causality, could have been created, however, without reaching back to 1657. In fact one moral of the Man of the Hill episode—that involvement with human society is better than withdrawal from it—could (as Cleary remarks) have been made as effectively without including any allusions to specific dates or real historical events. But it is in the context of such allusions that Fielding can most effectively raise the question of man's relationship to time.

After showing Tom's disapproval on learning that the Man of the Hill has withdrawn so totally as to remain ignorant of even the two Jacobite rebellions, "one of which is now actually raging in the very Heart of the Kingdom," Fielding turns attention backward to Monmouth's rebellion: the Man of the Hill tells of his escape after being wounded at the battle of Sedgemore (p. 363). Cleary shows how puzzling this turn of the narration has remained in the eyes of Fielding's critics: "The closing section of the Man of the Hill's Tale, itself a much-censured digression . . . seems digressive even within the context of the tale . . . the elongation of his tale past his escape from London vice and return as a contrite prodigal to the country robs it of even the relative structural shapeliness of Wilson's tale in *Joseph Andrews*, which it resembles greatly until the Man of the Hill describes meeting his old gaming companion and turning patriotic rebel. Though this 'coda' to the tale provides the final explanation of the misanthrope's complete withdrawal from the world as well as the occasion for political satire, a similar effect might well have been produced by a briefer, less circumstantially described and political example of the depths of human ingratitude."[9] This is correct. But affiliating the Man of the Hill's retreat with a specific historical moment well known to Fielding's eighteenth-century readers yet very far away in calendar time for them establishes a reference-point that gives more than abstract or mythical meaning to Tom's astonishment: he wonders how anyone living alone could "have filled up, or rather killed, so much ... Time" (p. 367).

Although Fielding repudiates such retirement, he also affirms through the Man of the Hill's reply that solitude properly used is valuable because it allows contemplation of God and eternity by disengaging men from "the pleasures, the silly Business of the World," which "roll away our Hours too swiftly from us." The Man of the Hill insists that "the Pace of Time" cannot "seem sluggish to a Mind exercised in Studies so high, so important, and so glorious!" (p. 368). To this statement, but not to the idea that all of life should be spent in contemplative retreat, Tom agrees. His adventures on the road and in London are by this dialogue explicitly subsumed under the general heading of proper and improper employment of time. So are previous episodes in *Tom Jones.* More specifically, and in a way that shows the relationship of temporal setting to Fielding's artistic preoccupation with the question of tempo, Tom's adventures become illustrations of right and wrong ways to keep time from seeming too "sluggish" or, conversely, from passing "too swiftly" because devoted to worthless pursuits.

At the level of theme, no less than in narrative technique, *Tom Jones* is among the eighteenth century's most significant invitations to consider "the Pace of Time." Only *Tristram Shandy* raises the issue as insistently. Certainly Fielding's concern with moral aspects of "the Pace of Time" accounts more fully than critics have been inclined to remark for his experiments in accelerating narrative tempo. By arranging episodes so that more and more events are crowded into ever-contracting periods of plot-time, Fielding dramatizes the ways in which hours "roll away... too swiftly" when misemployed, as they so often are by Tom, especially at Upton and in London. Some of his misguided encounters show, among other things, intervals filled with too much of the "pleasures, the silly Business of the World." Typical is the hurry of Tom's affair with Lady Bellaston. So is the simultaneous appearance in Molly's bedroom of Tom and Square. Of course, as critics have noted in general but not analyzed in sufficient detail, the speed created by such crowding of events into small intervals of plot, narrative, and reading-time enhances comedy. Fielding's proliferation of events during the hours at Upton and in many other episodes contributes to our laughter. By deciding in favor of comedy, Fielding committed his narrative to acceleration as the prevailing tempo. Beyond this generic consideration, however, which by no means predetermined either the nature or the extent of his experiments with acceleration, Fielding's choices seem designed to stress what the Man of the Hill's exchange with Tom calls to explicit attention: that time flowing either too quickly or too sluggishly may be a sign of moral difficulties.

Jane Austen dramatized the point less overtly. Stuart Tave remarks, for example, that she usually chooses a crucial year as the appropriate time-interval for representation, implies the chronological relationship of its events to one another without specifying which year it is according to the calendar, and then shows that within the narrow confines of time and space depicted "there is much to be done and it must be done in the right time and in the right tempo." Tave also notes that time is not especially mysterious or oppressive in Jane Austen's view: for her characters "there come, again and again, times to make a judgment, times to make a moral choice, and there is a certain amount of time in which to make it, an amount appropriate to know what should be known, feel what should be felt, think what should be thought, do what should be done, neither too quickly nor too slowly for the occasion."[10] In *Tom Jones*, where time is more problematic for narrator, characters, and readers, things often happen at just the wrong time, usually to nice comic effect. At crucial moments there is seldom enough leisure: Fielding's villains and their accomplices are in too much of a hurry. Blifil does not even trouble to feign a leisurely courtship of Sophia. Squire Western's amusing impatience is a sign of his moral deficiencies. Allworthy banishes Tom too hastily. And it is Dowling who complained of "being hurried, and driven and torn out of his Life, and repeated many Times, that if he could divide himself into four Quarters, he knew how to dispose of every one" (p. 190). Just as the Man of the Hill stands for insufficient involvement with the pace of social time, Dowling is Fielding's opposite emblem for time that rolls on too quickly in the "silly Business of the World."

For its more worthwhile business, Fielding implies, there is time enough. The open-ended conclusion of *Tom Jones* implies as much by inviting readers to imagine Tom's marriage with Sophia continuing into a future limited only by what for them is a very distant mortality. Even Western slows down and "spends much of his Time in the Nursery, where he declares the tattling of his little Grand-Daughter, who is above a Year and a half old, is sweeter music than the finest Cry of Dogs in *England*" (p. 761). Fielding here contrasts an implied image of the hunt as an emblem of rapid motion with the picture of an old man and young child motionless together in a room. Neither is in a hurry;

nor have they any reason to be. Although even this final glimpse of Western has its grotesque overtones, it remains in mind at the novel's end as one symbol of the appropriately unhurried "pace of Time" created by Tom's marriage.

In describing the wedding-day, Fielding even includes an unobtrusive personification of time by referring to "that happy Hour which had surrendered the charming *Sophia* to the eager Arms of her enraptured *Jones*" (p. 759). The syntax which makes the hour an active agent giving Sophia to Tom is perfectly conventional. Fielding's choice of the phrase nevertheless suggests that the happy outcome is both a gift and triumph of time. Although this suggestion is more connotative than denotative, it is entirely in keeping with Fielding's other encouragements to read *Tom Jones* as a narrative which shows how wisdom and prudence are acquired by experience, and are in that sense, too, the gifts of time. Miller remarks that "Fielding's plot is a variant of the ancient theme, *veritas filia temporis*."[11] It is indeed to a degree which greatly enlarges the usual application of that idea. *Tom Jones* deserves fuller recognition as a major contribution to what is after all a very small body of western literature written in affirmation of time's power for good instead of in response to its destructiveness.

2

Before it is possible to pursue more fully such questions concerning relationships between time-concepts, temporal settings, themes, and tempo in Fielding and other novelists after Defoe, several issues require further theoretical study. The connections between tempo and spatial form, as well as the determinants of each, especially deserve a place on our agenda. Thus a more complete theory of subjective tempo than is now available would allow finer discrimination than I can provide between the usual attributes of Defoe's prose and those stylistic devices that control variation of pace. Shifts in what Genette calls modes of frequency are certainly crucial. So are such variables as the amount of repetition, the presence or absence of causal relationships between episodes, the extent to which readers are allowed to locate themselves along a clear time-line as they progress through a text, the manner of describing objects and events, the nature—whether comic or not—of what is described, the degree of allusiveness in any passage, the extent of moral or other complications introduced for the reader's consideration, and the placement of shifts to or from a metaphoric mode. Less clear, however, are the priorities.

Open-ended imagery and incomplete descriptions like those which play a role in slowing the pace throughout *A Journal of the Plague Year*, for example, do not themselves set that pace: they help to maintain it. Similar imagery and descriptions, which are characteristic of Defoe's prose style throughout his fiction, although not always so concentrated, do not in other contexts make such conspicuous contributions to the deceleration of pace. They may even help—or at least not impede—acceleration. Repetition, other aspects of frequency, and causal relationships (or the lack of them) between episodes determine the extent to which various stylistic devices are actuated to facilitate a shift in speed. But exactly how they do so, and in what order of precedence, are questions that my study of Defoe poses without answering.

Implications

Another is how spatial forms and related structures work to shape memories during and after reading any narrative. I have suggested how Defoe controls this process, where he does so most effectively, and why. But we have still to seek a complete grammar of spatial forms and their purposes, as well as a classification of all the different kinds of memory involved in reading. The invitations to paint miniatures of memory that abound in *Robinson Crusoe*, and to a lesser extent in *Moll Flanders* and *Roxana*, are mainly intended by Defoe to enforce explicit moral lessons that are central to those narratives and to proper judgments of Crusoe, Moll, and Roxana. The effect of these invitations is similar to the effect created for less emblematic purposes by some early illustrations to *Robinson Crusoe*, which show on the same plate events that took place at different times. Other varieties of spatial form in Defoe's fiction move toward the more purely aesthetic purpose of unifying narratives without coherent plots.

Uncertainties over what to make of *Colonel Jack* and *Captain Singleton*, for example, are partly caused by Defoe's avoidance in them of devices that maximize spatial form in order to sustain explicit moral judgments. The reader's memory is called into play very differently in *Colonel Jack*, for a retrospective "reading" that recalls the sequence of Jack's life in the same way that he finally sees it, and in *Captain Singleton*, mainly for the purpose of remembering moral issues raised but then forgotten by Singleton. In *A Journal of the Plague Year* the similarity of episodes and lack of causal relationships between most of them create a significant degree of spatial form. But that form differs in effect as well as purpose from the varieties of spatialization elsewhere in Defoe's fiction.

Events that were sequential in narrated time are not held

up to the mind's eye motionless for retrospective contemplation as sequences frozen along a clear time-line in *A Journal of the Plague Year*. Instead they are brought together in the reader's memory in ways that do not allow them to come to rest: there is something more akin to the kinetic stasis of Brownian motion as events not dated with respect to each other invite equally valid rearrangements in the reader's mind. H.F.'s associational ordering of his narrative encourages readers to remember it in the same way that he remembers the plague: their memories are no more able to follow the order of narrative sequence than H.F. is able to avoid mentioning incidents out of their chronological order. Even his final encouragement to recollect the entire narration does not subordinate the resulting memories to some one lesson as Defoe tries to do at the end of *Colonel Jack:*

> *A dreadful Plague in* London *was*
> *In the Year Sixty Five*
> *Which swept an Hundred Thousand Souls*
> *Away; yet I alive!*

Retrospective juxtaposition of H.F.'s anecdotes is encouraged by this poem and earlier passages, but it never settles into a clear order. Memories of *A Journal of the Plague Year* therefore contribute (by their resistance to ordering) to maintaining for readers the sense of a time that moved slowly. But there is no established category for this degree of kinetic spatialization that works retroactively to characterize tempo instead of enforcing theme.

Ingarden and, so far as I know, all other critics discount the possibility that tempo may be a significant aspect of aesthetic response when a work is remembered after it has been read. If the matter is considered at all, the assumption is simply that while objective tempo (as measured by the proportion of pages, and thus of narrating and reading time, to a given incident in plot time) may be analyzed, and in that way appreciated in retrospect, subjective tempo—the actual experience of time speeding up or slowing down— is only relevant during a reading. Afterward, in this view, there remains merely a "spatialized" schematic awareness of narrative sequence that may allow response to aspects of form not noticeable during a reading but at the expense of freezing the narrative in memory so that while it is considered as a whole the pace of its events cannot be felt. Remembering is thus denied its status as an activity with its own dynamics. Memories are assumed to be static. *A Journal of the Plague Year*, however, suggests otherwise.

As memories of its incidents return, their resistance to ordering along a clear time-line re-creates something like the slow pace of reading the book, which in turn imitates time's flow as experienced by those living through the plague year. However long readers spend thinking back over the narrative in response to H.F.'s poem, their experience of recollection will have the same quality of time which passes slowly; not primarily because of the unpleasantness of calling to mind incidents from "a dreadful Plague," but because consciously or unconsciously readers must choose among incidents competing on quite different grounds for recollection at each moment during the process of remembering. And once remembered, any incident, and especially any one of the many which are themselves repeated in H.F.'s narrative, has some claim to be remembered again in another connection. To be sure, every complex text invites reorderings in retrospect. Such reorderings are an important part of what critics do as they provide "readings." But not every text enforces such insistent reorderings by all readers, whether or not their concern is criticism, as *A Journal of the Plague Year* does in retrospect.

Nor is there always such correlation between the tempo of remembering and the tempo experienced while reading. Another question that deserves more attention from theorists is how novelists achieve correspondence or divergence between the tempo of reading and that of remembering a narrative. The purposes served by such relationships deserve consideration in practical criticism, if only to establish whether, for any text, there are significant correlations of this kind which contribute to its effects. The order of recollecting *Tom Jones*, for example, will tend to follow the order of narration by proceeding along a clear time-line of events from Tom's birth through his marriage, and it will proceed at a rapid pace. Incidents from the plot will be likely to come to mind in the order corresponding to that of both narrative and plot sequence instead of competing for priority of recollection as do incidents from *A Journal of the Plague Year*. Memories of Fielding's essays introducing each book may return in various sequences differing more readily from their order of presentation in the text but will not compete with each other for attention at any given moment to the extent that incidents from *A Journal of the Plague Year* do, because the essays take up distinct topics. They more readily stay compartmentalized and come to mind by association with different issues. That foreshortening by which details drop out of mind as any experience, including that of reading a book, is recollected serves for *Tom Jones* but not for *A Journal of the Plague Year* to encourage a rapid pace of recollection that corresponds to the brisk over-all pace of Fielding's narrative. Thus his experiments with acceleration are reinforced.

In remembering *Clarissa*, one realizes that foreshortening serves to clarify. Causal and other relationships that were difficult or impossible to perceive while the reader was immersed in the details which expand Richardson's portrayal of time and slow tempo for his readers finally become clear. The lessons enforced by his plot stand out more sharply in retrospect. The pace of remembering *Clarissa* is more rapid than the pace of reading it. The difference is not just in the clock-time involved—remembering always takes less time than reading—but in the quality of temporal experience. And the disparity is a distinctive aspect of *Clarissa*'s form. The effect is analogous to that induced on a much smaller scale by Hogarth's experiments with the adaptation of narrative techniques to visual works. In varying degrees *A Harlot's Progress*, *A Rake's Progress*, *Marriage à la Mode*, and *Industry and Idleness* each create an experience whose tempo during encounters with the plates one after another differs from the faster pace of recollecting the entire series.

In retrospect, lines of causation in the depicted events stand out more sharply than they do while one looks at any one plate; and the lessons, however ironic, of Hogarth's modern moral subjects also become more apparent. But there are differences in speed. Disparity between the slower tempo of encounter with each picture and the more rapid pace of recollecting it as one of a series is most apparent in *A Rake's Progress*. Poetic commentary at the bottom of each picture slows reader-viewers even more than the usual necessity of looking closely at details after grasping the main business of any Hogarthian plate. Each picture in *A Rake's Progress* creates a circular temporal structure: viewers will take in the action at a glance, perhaps pause to inspect details, then read the poem at the bottom, return to the picture with the words in mind, and perhaps return again to the text with more complete memories of the picture. This circular encounter can in principle be repeated any number of times, and it is therefore temporally open-ended, but in practice it is likely to involve only one complete circuit from picture to words to picture, and then on to the next plate. *A Harlot's Progress* and *Marriage à la Mode* do not have texts beneath each picture to slow their pace. The titles and biblical quotations which serve as ironic commentary on each plate of *Industry and Idleness* are more easily retained in memory than the poems included in *A Rake's Progress*. Hogarth thus keeps a circular structure of transition from words to pictures and vice versa for each plate but simplifies it to produce a faster tempo.

The over-all pace of *Industry and Idleness*, however, is slower than that of *A Harlot's Progress* and *Marriage à la Mode*. In them Hogarth avoids verbal commentary and also presents a more unified story-line which allows quicker movement from picture to picture, thereby intensifying the viewer's impression that events are speeding the protagonists to their fate. Even Hogarth's devices for achieving acceleration, however, operate within a framework that also enforces apprehension of the entire series. Ronald Paulson notes that "in looking at a Hogarth progress... you see one plate, then go in and explore all its inner relationships, and then, proceeding to the other plates, see it in relation to these, see indeed all six or eight of them arranged spatially on a wall. They are automatically read both diachronically and synchronically."[12] Here then is a narrative situation where it is possible to consider tempo in relationship to spatial form and where, moreover, the idea of spatial form might be taken literally. The plates really occupy space and can be seen together in a moment of time.

Or can they? By standing far enough away it is possible. Even then, however, awareness of the entire series is more a matter of memories than of seeing everything at once. It is difficult to avoid singling out one picture as the focal point of attention at any given instant while allowing other pictures in sight to fade away from notice at the periphery of vision. Reading each Hogarthian progress is a synchronic as well as a diachronic experience, not because several prints are in view at the same time. It is synchronic owing to devices by which Hogarth encourages viewers to remember previous pictures while looking at any one after the first and while looking at subsequent pictures as well when the plates are looked at again after going through an entire series. Hogarth's manipulation of such memories is largely responsible for setting the tempo of each progress. So, however, is the extent to which he creates memories of each plate while it is being looked at.

The memories do not involve the entire picture but its parts, whether words remembered while looking at visual images and vice versa, or, more significantly, one person or object remembered for purposes of comparison while the viewer focuses his attention elsewhere on the same plate. Hogarth usually crowds the visual field with details which invite comparison but which are too numerous or placed too far apart to grasp simultaneously. One result, as Paulson remarks, is that "Hogarth's is an art of multiple gestalts, one shifting into another as in a series of optical illusions. . . . His prints refuse to stand still, continuing to impose new gestalts and defeat expectations as long as we look at them."[13] For this reason, despite variations in over-all pace,

Hogarth's progresses are characterized no less than Fielding's narratives by achievement of a rapid tempo.

It is still not often enough granted, at least not by literary critics, that a single picture, or a series of them, may have a distinctive tempo contributing to realization of its formal effects—or for that matter that a single picture has any tempo at all. Yet surely this is another implication not only of recent studies of Hogarth but of new directions in criticism exemplified by Kermode's persuasive argument "in support of a revaluation of the element of temporal structure, memory, and expectation, as against the tendency to reduce our bibliocosms to merely spatial order." He grounds this argument on Gombrich's warning against making sharp distinctions between time and space even when looking at a painting because then, too, "there is a temporal element; one 'scans' the picture and could not do so without retinal persistence; one remembers what has passed and has expectations about what is to come."[14] Thus, even for single pictures, there is no such thing as a purely spatial experience. It follows that the tempo of cognition is a major dimension of visual no less than verbal art. It follows also that the degree to which memories are called into play during the apprehension of any picture may vary, and will always be a major (though not exclusive) determinant of its tempo. One result that may seem paradoxical is that a fast pace of the kind Hogarth achieves is only possible because of the way his progresses enforce an extended involvement taking up more clock-time than would be necessary for grasping pictures without so many details inviting comparison and dissolving into different configurations.

I mention this aspect of Hogarth's achievement in closing because it is the clearest eighteenth-century instance of temporal effects that deserve additional study because they are the converse of those achieved in *A Journal of the Plague Year:* Hogarth's devices for evoking memories to create synchronic temporal structures extend viewing time in a way that accelerates tempo. His progresses, moreover, are certainly the most important stage in the evolution of narrative techniques between Defoe's fiction and that of Richardson and Fielding. Hogarth's success in adapting many of the devices previously confined to prose narrations is recognized as especially relevant to Sterne's use of strategies borrowed in turn from the visual arts or worked out in reaction against their methods.[15] It is still too soon to write the history of fictional time in terms of influence, however. To do that even for the eighteenth century, we need a more comprehensive grammar of the effects created by shifts in tempo as well as by variations of spatial form.

Only then would it be possible to decide how far, and in what ways, Defoe's temporal structures were duplicated or extended by later writers. The impetus to investigate these matters has been lacking. The range—or even the fact of experimentation with variations in narrative tempo by Sterne's predecessors before Richardson and Fielding—has not been acknowledged, perhaps because until recent developments in cognitive psychology we have not had a vocabulary for doing so, perhaps because the issue only became explicit when Fielding called the tempo of *Tom Jones* to attention in a misleading way, perhaps simply because of our fascination with the other aspects of time brilliantly dramatized in *Tristram Shandy*. Whatever the reasons, it is now possible to appreciate the significance if not yet the entire role of Defoe's contribution to the articulation of modern time-consciousness in literature. His skillful use of temporal settings to convey meanings instead of enhancing verisimilitude, and his concern with the moral aspects of time, place him securely among the masters of an older tradition no longer viable between Fielding and the twentieth century but still traceable in *Tom Jones*. Defoe's experiments with forms that we now call spatial, and with the manipulation of tempo to enhance both representational and emotional power, associate him as securely with the newer provinces of writing. While Richardson and Sterne must be given credit for inventing the narrative modes that seem best suited to portray private duration, Defoe's account of the plague year is the first, and arguably still the best, portrayal of a public duration: a quality of passing time shared by an entire population during a crisis. In finding an appropriate form to convey that variety of temporal experience, Defoe deserves to be ranked among the most innovative of those early writers who explored the ways in which fictional time may shape the real time of reading.

Notes

Chapter 1
Fictional Time and Real Time

1. See Philip Stevick, "Fielding and the Meaning of History," *PMLA* 86 (1971):561–68.

2. For more thorough discussion of *Ada*, especially the background of Nabokov's time-reversal imagery, see Paul K. Alkon, "Historical Development of the Concept of Time," in *Biorhythms and Human Reproduction*, ed. Michel Ferin et al. (New York: John Wiley and Sons, 1974), pp. 3–22.

3. Alain Robbe-Grillet, "In The Labyrinth," *Two Novels by Robbe-Grillet*, trans. Richard Howard (New York: Grove Press, 1965), p. 140.

4. Wolfgang Iser, "The Reading Process: A Phenomenological Approach," *The Implied Reader: Patterns of Communication in Prose Fiction from Bunyan to Beckett* (Baltimore: Johns Hopkins University Press, 1974); Earl Miner, "The Objective Fallacy and the Real Existence of Literature," *PTL: A Journal for Descriptive Poetics and Theory of Literature* 1 (1976):11–31; Earl Miner, "That Literature Is a Kind of Knowledge," *Critical Inquiry* 2 (1976):487–518.

5. For some consequences of narrative sequence and a bibliography of the subject, see Earl Miner, "Time, Sequence, and Plot in Restoration Literature," in *Studies in Eighteenth-Century Culture*, ed. Ronald C. Rosbottom (Madison: University of Wisconsin Press, 1976), 5:67–85.

6. Roman Ingarden, *The Cognition of the Literary Work of Art*, trans. Ruth Ann Crowley and Kenneth R. Olson (Evanston: Northwestern University Press, 1973), pp. 94–145; subsequent references to this edition will appear parenthetically in my text.

7. A. A. Mendilow, *Time and the Novel* (1952; reprint ed., New York: Humanities Press, 1972), pp. 125–28.

8. J. Paul Hunter, *Occasional Form: Henry Fielding and the Chains of Circumstance* (Baltimore: Johns Hopkins University Press, 1975), pp. 142–65.

9. Henry Fielding, *Tom Jones*, ed. Sheridan Baker (New York: W. W. Norton and Co., 1973), pp. 58–59. Subsequent references to this edition will be given in the text by page number.

10. Paul K. Alkon, "Boswellian Time," *Studies in Burke and His Time* 14 (1973):239–56.

11. Ian Watt, *The Rise of the Novel: Studies in Defoe, Richardson, and Fielding* (Berkeley: University of California Press, 1957), p. 25.

12. Wayne C. Booth, *The Rhetoric of Fiction* (Chicago: University of Chicago Press, 1961), pp. 216–17.

13. Miner, "Time, Sequence, and Plot in Restoration Literature."

14. J. T. Fraser, ed., *The Voices of Time: A Cooperative Survey of Man's Views of Time as Expressed by the Sciences and by the Humanities* (New York: Braziller, 1966); Roland Fischer, ed., "Interdisciplinary Perspectives of Time," *Annals of the New York Academy of Sciences* 138, no. 2 (1967); Jiri Zeman, ed., *Time in Science and Philosophy: An International Study of Some Current Problems* (Amsterdam: Elsevier, 1971); J. T. Fraser, F. C. Haber, G. H. Muller, eds., *The Study of Time: Proceedings of the First Conference of the International Society For the Study of Time* (Berlin: Springer-Verlag, 1972); J. T. Fraser, N. Lawrence, eds., *The Study of Time II: Proceedings of the Second Conference of the International Society for the Study of Time* (New York: Springer-Verlag, 1975); Charles M. Sherover, ed., *The Human Experience of Time: The Development of Its Philosophic Meaning* (New York: New York University Press, 1975); C. A. Patrides, ed., *Aspects of Time* (Toronto: University of Toronto Press, 1976). See also Ricardo J. Quinones, *The Renaissance Discovery of Time* (Cambridge: Harvard University Press, 1972).

15. Homer O. Brown, "The Displaced Self in the Novels of Daniel Defoe," *ELH* 38 (1971):562–90; John J. Richetti, *Defoe's Narratives: Situations and Structures* (Oxford: Clarendon Press, 1975); Everett Zimmerman, *Defoe and the Novel* (Berkeley: University of California Press, 1975); see also Patricia Meyer Spacks, *Imagining a Self: Autobiography and Novel in Eighteenth-Century England* (Cambridge: Harvard University Press, 1976).

Chapter 2
Setting and Chronology

1. Daniel Defoe, *A General History of the Pyrates*, ed. Manuel Schonhorn (London: J. M. Dent and Sons, 1972), p. 68.
2. Patrick Pringle, *Jolly Roger* (London: Museum Press, 1953), pp. 123–24.
3. Defoe, *General History*, p. 234.
4. Ibid., pp. 392–93.
5. Manuel Schonhorn, "Defoe's *Captain Singleton*: A Reassessment with Observations," *Papers on Language and Literature* 7 (1971):38–51.
6. Ibid.
7. Woodes Rogers, *A Cruising Voyage Round the World* (London, 1712), p. 128.
8. Daniel Defoe, "The King of the Pirates," *Due Preparations for the Plague & The King of the Pirates*, ed. G. H. Maynadier (Boston: Dana Estes, 1904), pp. 29, 50.
9. G. A. Starr, "Defoe's Prose Style: 1. The Language of Interpretation," *Modern Philology* 71 (1974):277–94.
10. Defoe, *King of the Pirates*, pp. 30, 35.
11. Ibid., p. 39.
12. Everett Zimmerman, *Defoe and the Novel* (Berkeley: University of California Press, 1975), p. 57.
13. Manuel Schonhorn, "Defoe's *Journal of the Plague Year*: Topography and Intention," *Review of English Studies*, n.s. 19 (1968):391.
14. See David Hume, *A Treatise of Human Nature*, ed. Ernest C. Mossner (Baltimore: Penguin Books, 1969), esp. "Of the Probability of Causes," pp. 181–93.
15. Defoe, *Due Preparations*, pp. 47–48.
16. Ibid., p. 87.
17. Daniel Defoe, *The History of the Union of Great Britain* (Edinburgh, 1709), pp. 8, 11–12, 14.
18. Aristotle, *Rhetoric* 1417^b 12–15, trans. W. Rhys Roberts, in *Aristotle: Rhetoric and Poetics* (New York: Modern Library, 1954), p. 210. In another connection John Donne, "Sermon Number 2, Preached at Lincolns Inne," *The Sermons of John Donne*, ed. George R. Potter and Evelyn Simpson (Berkeley: University of California Press, 1953–62), 10 vols., 2:77, quotes the contemptuous description "*Chronica de futuro scribit*" and develops a met-

aphor based on warning against those who undertake "to write a Chronicle of things before they are done, which is an irregular, and a perverse way."

19. J. Paul Hunter, *The Reluctant Pilgrim: Defoe's Emblematic Method and Quest for Form in Robinson Crusoe* (Baltimore: Johns Hopkins Press, 1966). See also *Literary Uses of Typology from the Late Middle Ages to the Present*, ed. Earl Miner (Princeton: Princeton University Press, 1977).

20. G. A. Starr, introduction, *Moll Flanders* (London: Oxford University Press, 1971), p. xv.

21. Samuel Richardson, *Clarissa; or, The History of a Young Lady* (Oxford: Shakespeare Head Press, n.d.), 8 vols., 8:106.

22. Frank Kermode, *The Sense of an Ending* (London: Oxford University Press, 1967), p. 178.

23. Starr, Introduction, p. xv.

24. Samuel L. Macey, "Hogarth and the Iconography of Time," *Studies in Eighteenth-Century Culture*, ed. Ronald C. Rosbottom (Madison: University of Wisconsin Press, 1976), 5: pp. 41–53. See also Professor Macey's *Clocks and the Cosmos: Time in Western Life and Thought*.

25. Daniel Defoe, *The Political History of the Devil*, 4th ed. (London, 1739), p. 61.

26. Ibid., p. 62.

27. John Dryden, "The Dedication of the Aeneis," *The Poems of John Dryden*, ed. James Kinsley (Oxford: Clarendon Press, 1958), 3:1030–31.

28. Ibid.

29. Ibid.

30. Edward Phillips, *The New World of Words*, 3rd ed. (London, 1671).

31. *Cyclopaedia*, 7th ed. (London, 1751).

32. Sylvan Barnet, Morton Berman, William Burto, *A Dictionary of Literary Terms* (Boston: Little, Brown and Co., 1960); Karl Beckson and Arthur Ganz, *Literary Terms: A Dictionary* (New York: Farrar, Straus and Giroux, 1975).

33. Manuel Schonhorn, "Defoe's *Journal* . . . Topography and Intention," pp. 391, 393.

34. J. Paul Hunter, introduction, *Moll Flanders* (New York: Crowell, 1970), p. xxi.

35. David Leon Higdon, "The Chronology of *Moll Flanders*," *English Studies* 56 (1975):316–19. This discussion is also in-

cluded in David Leon Higdon, *Time and English Fiction* (London: Macmillan, 1977), pp. 56–62.

36. Samuel L. Macey, "The Time Scheme in 'Moll Flanders,'" *Notes and Queries* 214 (1969):336–37.

37. David Blewett, "'Roxana' and the Masquerades," *Modern Language Review*, 65 (1970):499–502.

38. Rodney M. Baine, "Roxana's Georgian Setting," *Studies in English Literature* 15 (1975):459–71.

39. A. A. Mendilow, *Time and the Novel* (1952; reprint ed., New York: Humanities Press, 1972), p. 94.

40. Ibid.

41. Samuel Johnson, "Preface to Shakespeare," *Johnson on Shakespeare*, ed. Arthur Sherbo. Yale Edition of the Works of Samuel Johnson (New Haven: Yale University Press, 1968), 7:78.

42. G. A. Starr, *Defoe and Casuistry* (Princeton: Princeton University Press, 1971). See also G. A. Starr, "Sympathy v. Judgement in Roxana's First Liaison," in *The Augustan Milieu: Essays Presented to Louis A. Landa*, ed. Henry Knight Miller, Eric Rothstein, and G. S. Rousseau (Oxford: Clarendon Press, 1970), pp. 59–76.

43. Samuel Johnson, *A Journey to the Western Islands of Scotland*, ed. Mary Lascelles, Yale Edition of the Works of Samuel Johnson (New Haven: Yale University Press, 1971), 9:9.

44. Ibid.

45. Samuel Holt Monk, introduction, *Colonel Jack* (London: Oxford University Press, 1965), pp. xxi–xxii.

46. Maximillian E. Novak, "Defoe's Theory of Fiction," *Studies in Philology* 61 (1964):656.

47. Monk, p. xxii.

48. Charles Gildon, *Robinson Crusoe Examin'd and Criticis'd*, ed. Paul Dottin (London: J. M. Dent and Sons, 1923); Dewey Ganzel, "Chronology in *Robinson Crusoe*," *Philological Quarterly* 40 (1961):495–512.

49. *Doctor Faustus*, I. 3. 315–20, *The Complete Works of Christopher Marlowe*, ed. Fredson Bowers (Cambridge: At the University Press, 1973), p. 171.

50. Samuel Johnson, *The Rambler*, ed. W. J. Bate and Albrecht B. Strauss, Yale Edition of the Works of Samuel Johnson (New Haven: Yale University Press, 1969), 5:37–38.

51. *Cyclopaedia*.

52. William Bowman Piper, "*Moll Flanders* as a Structure of Topics," *Studies in English Literature* 9 (1969):497.

53. Ibid.

54. Additional connections between novelistic form and Defoe's attention to biological time in *Moll Flanders* and *Colonel Jack* are suggested in two recent articles: Miriam Leranbaum, "Moll Flanders: 'A Woman on Her Own Account,'" in *The Authority of Experience: Essays in Feminist Criticism*, ed. Arlyn Diamond and Lee R. Edwards (Amherst: University of Massachusetts Press, 1977), pp. 101–17; G. A. Starr, "'Only a Boy': Notes on Sentimental Novels," *Genre* 10 (1977), 501–27.

Chapter 3
Time-Consciousness

1. Frank Kermode, *The Sense of an Ending* (London: Oxford University Press, 1967), p. 178.

2. For discussion of some generic issues involved in Defoe's choice of forms that resemble authentic biographies, see Ralph W. Rader, "Defoe, Richardson, Joyce, and the Concept of Form in the Novel," in *Autobiography, Biography, and the Novel: Papers Read at a Clark Library Seminar, May 13, 1972*, by William Matthews and Ralph W. Rader (Los Angeles: William Andrews Clark Memorial Library, University of California, 1973), pp. 31–72; Tyna T. Orren, "True and False Accounts by Defoe" (Ph.D. diss., University of Minnesota, 1976).

3. Daniel Defoe, *Robinson Crusoe*, ed. Angus Ross (Harmondsworth: Penguin Books, 1965), p. 313.

4. Samuel Johnson, *The Rambler*, ed. W. J. Bate and Albrecht B. Strauss, Yale Edition of the Works of Samuel Johnson (New Haven: Yale University Press, 1969), 3:223; St. Augustine, *Confessions*, bk. 10.

5. Johnson, ibid., p. 22.

6. G. A. Starr, *Defoe and Casuistry* (Princeton: Princeton University Press, 1971), p. x.

7. G. A. Starr, *Defoe and Spiritual Autobiography* (Princeton: Princeton University Press, 1965).

8. J. Paul Hunter, *The Reluctant Pilgrim: Defoe's Emblematic Method and Quest for Form in Robinson Crusoe* (Baltimore: Johns Hopkins Press, 1966), p. 151.

9. John Preston, "Plot as Irony: The Reader's Role in *Tom Jones*," *ELH* 35 (1968):365–80.

10. Henry Fielding, *Tom Jones*, ed. Sheridan Baker (New York: W. W. Norton and Co., 1973), p. 88.

11. Defoe's avoidance of predictive structures is discussed in Paul K. Alkon, "The Odds Against Friday: Defoe, Bayes, and Inverse Probability," *Probability, Time and Space in Eighteenth-Century Literature*, ed. Paula R. Backscheider (New York: AMS Press, forthcoming).

12. Quotations from "Eternity" are taken from Daniel Defoe, *Serious Reflections During the Life and Surprising Adventures of Robinson Crusoe: with his Vision of the Angelick World* (London, 1720), pp. 187–90.

13. For distinctions between the Augustinian tradition and the concept of eternity suggested by St. Anselm, which is less often reflected in English literature preceding Defoe, see Richard Douglas Jordan, *The Temple of Eternity: Thomas Traherne's Philosophy of Time* (Port Washington: Kennikat Press, 1972), pp. 12–30.

14. Daniel Defoe, *The Political History of the Devil*, 4th ed. (London, 1739), p. 74.

15. Maximillian E. Novak, *Defoe and the Nature of Man* (London: Oxford University Press, 1965), p. 12.

16. Everett Zimmerman, *Defoe and the Novel* (Berkeley: University of California Press, 1975), p. 145.

17. Starr, *Defoe and Spiritual Autobiography*, p. 183.

18. William H. McBurney, "*Colonel Jacque:* Defoe's Definition of the Complete Gentleman," *Studies in English Literature* 2 (1962):336, n. 37.

19. Zimmerman, pp. 145, 147.

20. Daniel Sennert, Nicholas Culpeper, and Abdiah Cole, *Two Treatises, The First of the Venereal Pocks ... The Second Treatise of the Gout* (London, 1660); Walter Harris, *Pharmacologia antiempirica ... Together with Some Remarks on the Causes and Cure of the Gout* (London, 1683); George Cheyne, *An Essay of the True Nature and Due Method of Treating the Gout* (London, 1722); Sir Richard Blackmore, *Discourses on the Gout, a Rhematism and the King's Evil* (London, 1726).

21. Hunter, pp. 165–66; see also the chapter on repentance, pp. 148–67.

22. Burton Pike, "Time in Autobiography," *Comparative Literature* 28 (1976):326–42.

23. W. J. Harvey, *Character and the Novel* (Ithaca: Cornell University Press, 1965), p. 100.

Chapter 4
The Reader's Memory

1. John J. Richetti, *Defoe's Narratives: Situations and Structures* (Oxford: Clarendon Press, 1975), p. 122.

2. Hans Robert Jauss, "Literary History as a Challenge to Literary Theory," *New Literary History* 2 (1970):7–37.

3. Frederic C. Bartlett, *Remembering: A Study in Experimental and Social Psychology* (1932; reprint ed. Cambridge: At the University Press, 1967); Donald A. Norman, *Memory and Attention* (New York: John Wiley and Sons, 1969); Michael J. A. Howe, *Introduction to Human Memory* (New York: Harper and Row, 1970); J. R. Anderson and G. H. Bower, *Human Associative Memory* (Washington: Halsted Press, 1973); Roberta L. Klatzky, *Human Memory: Structures and Processes* (San Francisco: W. H. Freeman, 1975); Jack A. Adams, *Learning and Memory: An Introduction* (Homewood: Dorsey Press, 1976); Norman Malcolm, *Memory and Mind* (Ithaca: Cornell University Press, 1977).

4. Northrop Frye, "Literary Criticism," in *The Aims and Methods of Scholarship in Modern Languages and Literatures*, ed. James Thorpe, 2nd ed. (New York: Modern Language Association of America, 1970), p. 69.

5. Stanley E. Fish, "Literature in the Reader: Affective Stylistics," *New Literary History* 2 (1970):123–61. For comments on how memories are impeded at one point in *Pilgrim's Progress* and for a reprinting of "Literature in the Reader," see Stanley E. Fish, *Self-Consuming Artifacts: The Experience of Seventeenth-Century Literature* (Berkeley: University of California Press, 1972), pp. 258, 383–427.

6. Ian Watt, "The Recent Critical Fortunes of *Moll Flanders*," *Eighteenth-Century Studies* 1 (1967):109–26.

7. G. A. Starr, *Defoe and Spiritual Autobiography* (Princeton: Princeton University Press, 1965), p. 161.

8. Watt, p. 119.

9. Ian Watt, *The Rise of the Novel* (Berkeley: University of California Press, 1957), p. 100.

10. Ibid.

11. Starr, p. 183.

12. Watt, *The Rise of the Novel*, p. 100.

13. On the distortions that may occur in remembering narra-

tives, especially in connection with the fact that memories are part of the cognitive search for meaning, see Bartlett.

14. Philip Stevick, *The Chapter in Fiction: Theories of Narrative Division* (Syracuse: Syracuse University Press, 1970), p. 23.

15. For experimental studies of the relationship between memory-storage and experienced duration, see Robert E. Ornstein, *On the Experience of Time* (Harmondsworth: Penguin Books, 1969).

16. Stevick, p. 18.

17. Maximillian E. Novak, "Defoe's 'Indifferent Monitor': The Complexity of *Moll Flanders,*" *Eighteenth-Century Studies* 3 (1970):364.

18. Ibid., p. 362.

19. C. S. Lewis, "On Stories," *Of Other Worlds: Essays and Stories,* ed. Walter Hooper (London: Geoffrey Bles, 1966), pp. 17–18.

20. W. J. Harvey, *Character and the Novel* (Ithaca: Cornell Univ. Press, 1965), p. 109. Perceptive comments on the relationship of ordinary memories to memories elicited while reading are included in Harvey's excellent chapter on "Time and Identity," pp. 100–129.

21. Joseph Frank, *The Widening Gyre: Crisis and Mastery in Modern Literature* (New Brunswick: Rutgers University Press, 1963), p. 9; italics mine. For the original essay, see Joseph Frank, "Spatial Form in Modern Literature," *Sewanee Review* 53 (1945): 221–40, 433–56, 643–53. For the argument which led Frank to revise, see Walter Sutton, "The Literary Image and the Reader," *Journal of Aesthetics and Art Criticism* 16 (1957–58):112–23. For controversies over the sociological implications of myth considered as an outcome of spatial form (which does not concern me in this chapter), see Philip Rahv, "The Myth and the Powerhouse," *Literature and the Sixth Sense* (Boston: Houghton Mifflin, 1970), pp. 202–15, and Frank Kermode, *The Sense of an Ending* (London: Oxford University Press, 1967). For an application of Frank's theory to Milton's poetry, see Jackson I. Cope, *The Metaphoric Structure of Paradise Lost* (Baltimore: Johns Hopkins Press, 1962). Other questions concerning the concept of spatial form are addressed in three valuable articles: Joseph Frank, "Spatial Form: An Answer to Critics," *Critical Inquiry* 4 (1977):231–52; Eric S. Rabkin, "Spatial Form and Plot," *Critical Inquiry* 4 (1977):253–70; William Holtz, "Spatial Form in Modern Literature, a Reconsideration," *Critical Inquiry* 4 (1977):271–84.

22. David Leon Higdon, "The Critical Fortunes and Misfortunes of Defoe's *Roxana*," *Bucknell Review* 20 (1972):77.

23. In the second edition of *Moll Flanders*, "know" is changed to "knew," which is more consistent with the entire sentence, referring as it does to Moll's comrades as executed. But this kind of slip into present tense is characteristic of Moll (and Defoe) elsewhere. For documentation of the revision, which does not alter expectations created by the sentence, see *Moll Flanders*, ed. G. A. Starr (London: Oxford University Press, 1971), p. 344.

24. John Locke, *An Essay Concerning Human Understanding*, ed. A. C. Fraser (1894; reprint ed., New York: Dover, 1959), 1:200.

25. Ephraim Chambers, *Cyclopaedia*, 7th ed. (London, 1752).

26. In "Here shall the pencil bid its colours flow / And make a *miniature* creation grow."

27. Henry Fielding, *Tom Jones*, ed. George Sherburn (New York: Modern Library, 1950), pp. 299, 475.

28. Sheldon Sacks, *Fiction and the Shape of Belief* (Berkeley: University of California Press, 1964), pp. 193–229.

29. Fielding, *Tom Jones*, pp. 466–67.

30. Samuel Richardson, *Clarissa* (Oxford: Shakespeare Head Press, n.d.), 2:347, 3:29.

31. Richardson, 1:xvi.

32. Ornstein, pp. 37–52, suggests why the process may alter retrospective estimates of duration. The relevance of his experiments to the experience of literary structures deserves more consideration.

33. Richardson, 1:xvii.

34. James Boswell, *The Life of Samuel Johnson, LL.D.*, 6 vols., ed. G. B. Hill, rev. L. F. Powell (Oxford: Clarendon Press, 1934–64), 2:175.

35. See, however, Sheldon Sacks, "Novelists as Storytellers," *Modern Philology* 73, no. 4, pt. 2 (May 1976), S97–S109.

36. Richardson, 1:x.

37. J. Donald Crowley, "Textual Notes," *RC*, p. 308, gives the revision as from ". . . th of . . ." to "1st of *Sept* 1659." Michael Shinagel, ed., *Robinson Crusoe: An Authoritative Text, Background and Sources, Criticism* (New York: W. W. Norton, 1975), p. 34, gives the revision as to "the first of *September*, 1659."

38. Homer O. Brown, "The Displaced Self in the Novels of Daniel Defoe," *ELH* 38 (1971):562–90.

39. Ibid., p. 586.

40. For an account of Puritan views about the difficulty of understanding events until they are recorded in a journal and then considered in retrospect, see J. Paul Hunter, *The Reluctant Pilgrim: Defoe's Emblematic Method and Quest for Form in Robinson Crusoe* (Baltimore: Johns Hopkins Press, 1966), pp. 82–86.

Chapter 5
Tempo

1. Quoted from Defoe's text as printed in Maximillian E. Novak, " 'Simon Forecastle's Weekly Journal': Some Notes on Defoe's Conscious Artistry," *Texas Studies in Literature and Language* 6 (1965):433–40.

2. Samuel Richardson, *Clarissa* (Oxford: Shakespeare Head Press, n.d.), 1:xiv.

3. See Marie Bonaparte, "Time and the Unconscious," *International Journal of Psychoanalysis* 21 (1940):427–68.

4. For what remains the standard general theory of tempo, and an excellent one so far as it goes, see A. A. Mendilow, *Time and the Novel* (1952; reprint ed., New York: Humanities Press, 1972), pp. 125–28.

5. Edmund Burke, *A Philosophical Enquiry into the Origin of our Ideas of the Sublime and Beautiful*, ed. J. T. Boulton (London: Routledge and Kegan Paul, 1958), p. 73.

6. G. A. Starr, "Defoe's Prose Style: 1. The Language of Interpretation," *Modern Philology* 71 (1974):293.

7. Tyna T. Orren, "True and False Accounts by Defoe" (Ph.D. diss., University of Minnesota, 1976).

8. Starr, pp. 278–79.

9. James Thorpe, *Principles of Textual Criticism* (San Marino: Huntington Library, 1972), pp. 3–49.

10. See Francis A. Yates, *The Art of Memory* (Chicago: University of Chicago Press, 1966).

11. Fielding's explanation of how he controls tempo by adjusting the ratio of reading-time to read-about time appears at the outset of book 2 in *Tom Jones*, where he rejects the journalistic method of newspapers that give the same number of words to each day's events. A classic modern discussion of distinctions between reading and read-about time is Gunther Müller, "Erzählzeit und erzählte Zeit," in *Festschrift für P. Kluckhorn* (Tübigen, 1948).

12. Walter J. Ong, S.J., *The Presence of the Word* (New Haven: Yale University Press, 1967), pp. 12, 69. See also p. 188, where Ong remarks that "there has perhaps never been an asceticism, and certainly never a Christian asceticism, which has not made much of silence as a way of life and a mode of communication and presence."

13. George Sherburn, "The Restoration and Eighteenth Century," in *A Literary History of England*, ed. Albert C. Baugh (New York: Appleton-Century-Crofts, 1948), 855.

14. Maximillian E. Novak, "The Extended Moment: Time, Dream, History, and Perspective in Eighteenth-Century Fiction," in *Probability, Time, and Space in Eighteenth-Century Literature*, ed. Paula R. Backscheider (New York: AMS Press, forthcoming).

15. Joseph Conrad, preface to *The Nigger of the "Narcissus," The Portable Conrad*, ed. Morton Dauwen Zabel (New York: Viking Press, 1947), p. 708.

16. Ong, p. 50. For a discussion of transitions from verbal to visual emphasis in English fiction from Richardson through Sterne, see Ronald Paulson, *Emblem and Expression: Meaning in English Art of the Eighteenth Century* (Cambridge: Harvard University Press, 1975), ch. 4.

17. Novak, "The Extended Moment," p. 11.

18. Aristotle, *Rhetoric*, 1413^b 15–25, trans. W. Rhys Roberts, *Aristotle: Rhetoric and Poetics* (New York: Modern Library, 1954), p. 197. John J. Richetti, *Defoe's Narratives* (Oxford: Clarendon Press, 1975), p. 237, comments on the "clumsy underlinings" of H. F.'s observation that it was "indeed *very, very, very* dreadful."

19. Henry Home, Lord Kames, *Elements of Criticism*, 6th ed. (1785; reprint ed., New York: Garland, 1972), 2:94–95.

20. Starr, "Defoe's Prose Style," p. 281.

21. Ibid., p. 287.

22. Gérard Genette, *Figures III* (Paris: Éditions du Seuil, 1972), pp. 145–82.

23. Orren, p. 210.

24. Orren, pp. 226–27. See also my discussion of Robbe-Grillet in "Historical Development of the Concept of Time," in *Biorhythms and Human Reproduction*, ed. Michel Ferin et. al. (New York: John Wiley & Sons, 1974), pp. 3–22.

25. F. Bastian, "Defoe's *Journal of the Plague Year* Reconsidered," *Review of English Studies*, n.s. 16 (1965), 151–73. A sim-

ilar view is taken by James Sutherland, *Daniel Defoe: A Critical Study* (Cambridge: Harvard University Press, 1971), pp. 170–71.

26. [Daniel Defoe], *The Storm* (London, 1704), p. 71.

27. Kames, 1:97.

Chapter 6
Implications

1. J. Paul Hunter, *Occasional Form: Henry Fielding and the Chains of Circumstance* (Baltimore: Johns Hopkins University Press, 1975), p. 223.

2. Frank Kermode, *The Sense of an Ending* (London: Oxford University Press, 1967), p. 19.

3. Henry Fielding, *Tom Jones*, ed. Sheridan Baker (New York: W. W. Norton, 1973), p. 27. Subsequent references to this edition will be given in the text by page number.

4. Thomas Cleary, "Jacobitism in *Tom Jones:* The Basis for an Hypothesis," *Philological Quarterly* 52 (1973):239–51.

5. Ibid., p. 251.

6. Henry Knight Miller, *Henry Fielding's Tom Jones and the Romance Tradition*, English Literary Studies Monograph Series No. 6 (Victoria B.C.: University of Victoria, 1976), pp. 44–45.

7. Ibid., p. 45.

8. Philip Stevick, "Fielding and the Meaning of History," *PMLA* 86 (1971):561–68.

9. Cleary, p. 245.

10. Stuart M. Tave, *Some Words of Jane Austen* (Chicago: University of Chicago Press, 1973), pp. 9, 6, 14.

11. Miller, p. 45.

12. Ronald Palson, *Emblem and Expression: Meaning in English Art of the Eighteenth Century* (Cambridge: Harvard University Press, 1975), pp. 46–47.

13. Ibid., p. 56.

14. Kermode, pp. 53–54. See also E. H. Gombrich, *Art and Illusion: A Study in the Psychology of Pictorial Representation* (Princton: Princeton University Press, 1960).

15. See especially William V. Holtz, *Image and Immortality: A Study of Tristram Shandy* (Providence: Brown University Press, 1970), and Paulson, pp. 48–57.

Index

Addison, Joseph, 202
Ages of man, 74
Allegory, 55
Anachronism, 40–58, 237–39
Anselm, St., 91
Apologues, 151
Aristotle, 39, 153, 204–5
Arthurian legends, 3
Augustine, St., 3, 6, 84, 91, 103
Austen, Jane, 87, 120, 243–44
Autobiography, 103. *See also* Spiritual autobiography

Bailey, Nathan, 47, 48, 71, 74, 79, 83, 134, 149, 160, 170, 198, 203, 210
Baine, Rodney M., 53
Bastian, F., 224–25
Blewett, David, 52, 54, 57, 63
Book as object, 20, 186
Booth, Wayne C., 20
Boswell, James, 17, 18
Brown, Homer O., 160, 162
Burke, Edmund, 175

Cabell, James Branch: *Jurgen*, 55
Calamy, Benjamin, 97
Calendar-time. *See* Time
Captain Singleton, 1, 123, 214, 247; pirate flags in, 23, 26, 27; modification of sources in, 26–27; chronology, 29, 33–36; symbolism in, 30, 176; spatial (not temporal) verisimilitude in, 31; tale of Knox's captivity in, 33; double temporal setting in, 57; ending of, 136; Singleton's name, 142; style of, 171–72; tempo in, 171–72, 174–79, 180–82; narrator's time-locus, 181; implied emotion in, 182
Causality, 194, 233–34, 240, 246
Chambers, Ephraim, 48, 74, 149
Chapters, 114–15, 200, 222
Character, 89, 90
Characterization, 123
Chaucer, Geoffrey, 30, 59
Chronology, 8, 74. *See also* Defoe
Cibber, Colley, 16
Clayton, Sir Robert, 53
Cleary, Thomas, 237, 241
Cognition, 10. *See also* Memory
Colonel Jack, 111, 114, 214, 247; chronology, 59–73 passim; private and public time in, 62; emblematic time-references in, 69, 71–72; biological and psychological time in, 74–76, 80, 262 (n. 54); memory as theme in, 94–102 passim; repentance, 94, 96–97; temporal structure of, 95, 133–35; gout, 96–97; ending of, 133–35, 155; beginning of, 135; parable of the prodigal son as narrative model of, 135; Jack's name, 142
Comedy: and difficulty of remembering *Tristram Shandy*, 106–7; and tempo of *Robinson Crusoe*, 196–99, 200–201; and tempo of *A Journal of the Plague Year*, 219–20; and tempo of *Tom Jones*, 243, 244
Concrete universals, 68
Conrad, Joseph, 201–2
Criticism, 9, 107–8

Dampier, William, 27
Defoe, Daniel. See individual works
Donne, John, 259 (n. 18)
Dryden, John: on anachronism, 45–47; *Absalom and Achitophel*, 54, 56, 57
Due Preparations for the Plague, 1, 37, 39, 225
Duration: of reading as aspect of form, 17, 82–84; portrayal of in *A Journal of the Plague Year*, 220–31. See also individual works by Defoe

Eliade, Mircea, 239
Emblem books, 145, 188
Esquemelin, Alexander Olivier, 27
Eternity, 6, 86–94
Eternity (Defoe), 91–94
Every, Henry, 35

Fielding, Henry, 42, 111, 154, 232, 255, 256; *Joseph Andrews*, 15, 241; *Tom Jones*: Fielding's comments on variation of tempo in, 15–17; remarks on reading-time in, 18–19; spatial form in, 20–21; 1745 rebellion in, 42, 236–38; temporal structure of, 87–88; conservation of character in, 89; Man of the Hill episode, 150–51, 241–42; allusions to previous episodes in, 150–52; tempo of, 152, 243, 244, 250; biological time in, 235–36; temporal setting of, 235–42; anachronism in, 237–39; theme of man's relationship to time in, 238–45; causality in, 240; only date in, 240; theme of the pace of time in, 242–45; ending of, 244–45; affirmation of time's power for good in, 245; theme of *veritas filia temporis* in, 245; how remembered, 250
Fish, Stanley E., 107–8
Frank, Joseph, 12, 132–33

Frequency, 213–17, 229, 246
Freud, Sigmund, 170
Frye, Northrop, 107, 111

Ganzel, Dewey, 69
Gardner, Martin, 5
General History of the Pyrates, A, 1, 23, 25
Genette, Gérard, 213, 215, 246
Gildon, Charles, 69
Gombrich, E. H., 254

Harvey, W. J., 104, 132
Hearing, as symbol of understanding, 194–96
Hemingway, Ernest, 30
Higdon, David Leon, 50, 140
History, 37, 40, 42, 64. See also individual works by Defoe
History of the Union of Great Britain, The, 38–39, 184, 222
Hogarth, William, 251–55
Holtz, William V., 265 (n. 21), 269 (n. 15)
Hourglass, 24
Hume, David, 234
Hunter, J. Paul, 15, 40, 50, 86, 97, 232–33

Ingarden, Roman, 10–15, 248
Irony, and reader's memory in *Moll Flanders*, 126–27
Italics, effects of in Defoe's texts, 185–86

James, Henry, 55, 56
Jauss, Hans Robert, 106
Johnson, Samuel, 56, 58, 80, 93, 149, 155, 169, 203; *Rasselas*, 41; definition of anachronism, 48; on biological effects of time, 73–74; on memory and novels, 84–85
Jolly Roger, 23–24
Journal of the Plague Year, A, 13, 17, 47, 167, 214, 246; allusions to memoranda in, 34; topicality of, 36–37; chronology, 39, 40; temporal setting, 49–50; narrative sequence of, 95, 168, 183–84,

222–24; ending of, 136, 248; tempo of, 171, 179, 208–23, 248–50; onomatopoeia in, 172–73; description of sounds in, 173–74, 203–4, 207–10, 213, 216–19; narrator's time-locus, 181–82, 226; and historical narratives, 184, 222; implied duration in, 216; burial pit episode, 217–19; narrative frequency in, 214, 215–17; portrayal of public duration in, 220–31, 249–50; tempo of the plague, 220–23, 226, 230–31; absence of chapters in, 222; reader's memories of, 223–24, 249–50; and spatial form, 223–24, 248; unity of time in, 226
Joyce, James, 55, 132; *Ulysses*, 55

Kames, Henry Home, Lord, 205–6, 229
Kermode, Frank, 42, 233, 234, 254
King of the Pirates, The, 1, 36, 61; pirate flag in, 26; temporal verisimilitude in, 31–33; chronology, 34, 39, 73

Landa, Louis, 171
Leranbaum, Miriam, 262 (n. 54)
Lewis, C. S., 120
Locke, John, 148–49

McBurney, William H., 96
Macey, Samuel L., 51
Marlowe, Christopher: *Dr. Faustus*, 72
Martel, John, 23, 24, 27
Mendilow, A. A., 15, 54, 55
Memoir, Defoe's understanding of, 63–64
Memoirs of a Cavalier, 40, 47, 64, 82
Memory: and chronology of plot-time, 8; role in cognition of literary works, 10–15; conscious and unconscious, 11; and forgetting of what has been read, 13, 111, 112; as theme in *Colonel Jack*, 94–102; and consolidation of related episodes, 113, 114, 127–29; and absence of chapters in Defoe's fiction, 114–15; used to define the reader's expectations, 117; of narrative future, 120–21; and Defoe's style, 122; and rhythms of similar events in Defoe's fiction, 123; and Defoe's use of puns, 127; and narrative point of view, 127; and irony, 127; and tempo, 129, 149–50, 248–49; and linear narrative sequences, 133; and verisimilitude, 167; and spatial form, 247; dynamics of, 249; and tempo of Hogarth's pictures, 253–54. *See also* Time; *individual works by Defoe*
Miller, Henry Knight, 238, 239, 245
Milton, John: *Paradise Lost* criticized by Defoe, 44–45
Moll Flanders, 35, 114, 119, 123, 214, 247; and calendar-time, 41, 43, 60; double temporal setting in, 50–52; anachronism in, 51–52; purpose of only date mentioned in, 51–52; emblematic time-references in, 73; biological time in, 76–80; portrayal of Moll's disordered time-perception, 77; time-locus of narrator, 93; critical controversy over coherence of, 109–10; control of reader's memories through episodes in, 110–32; ending of, 136; Moll's name, 141–43; spatial form and coherence of, 142–43
Monk, Samuel H., 60, 65, 67
Morley, Christopher: *Thunder on the Left*, 55
Myth, 20, 41, 105

Nabokov, Vladimir: *Ada*, 2–3, 4–5

New Voyage Round the World, A, 133
Novak, Maximillian E., 63, 94, 115, 119, 201, 202

Ong, Walter J. (S.J.), 194–95, 202
Orren, Tyna T., 184, 222, 223
Orwell, George, 62; *Nineteen Eighty-Four,* 6

Pace. *See* Tempo; *individual works by Defoe*
Paulson, Ronald, 252, 253
Picaresque narrative structures, 133, 234
Pike, Burton, 103
Piper, William Bowman, 78, 79
Plumb, J. H., 207
Political History of the Devil, 44–45, 92
Preston, John, 87
Proust, Marcel, 170, 213, 215
Puns, 127

Quelch, John, 23, 27

Repentance, 94, 96–97
Retrodiction, 88, 263 (n. 11)
Retrospective narratives, 169–70. *See also individual works by Defoe*
Rhythm: of similar events in Defoe's fiction, 123, 132; verbal, 174, 196; of conversation, 186–87; of speaking and writing contrasted, 191; of the plague portrayed in *A Journal of the Plague Year,* 220–23, 226, 230–31. *See also* Tempo
Richardson, Samuel, 1, 111, 130, 232, 235, 255, 256; *Clarissa:* mentioned, 15, 16, 17, 18; and calendar-time, 41–42; legal time in, 74; memory and narrative method of, 152–56; role of table of contents in, 153–54; and effects of retrospective narration, 154–55; and journalistic forms, 169, 170; causality and garden-elopement scene in, 233–34; how remembered, 251; *Pamela,* 16
Richetti, John J., 105, 141
Robbe-Grillet, Alain, 234; *In the Labyrinth,* 7–9
Roberts, Bartholomew, 24–25, 27
Robinson Crusoe, 95, 105, 123, 214, 247; Crusoe's calendar, 28–29; date of Crusoe's birth, 33, 35; Crusoe's journal, 34, 160–66; as myth, 41, 43; Crusoe's lost day, 60–61; chronology, 64, 69, 158–59; biological time in, 75–76; reading-time and moral effect of, 82–83; ending of, 137; spatial form in, 143–50, 224; alternative pasts and futures in, 145; time-levels in, 146; cumulative method of narration in, 156–67; naming of Friday, 159; subjective duration portrayed in, 165; power of self-confirming narrative in, 166; discovery of footprint, 179; writing and speaking in, 187–88; word-picture in, 188–90; sound and tempo in, 190–94, 196–99; symbolism of sound and silence in, 195–96; implied duration in, 197; narrative frequency in, 214
Rogers, Woodes, 29
Ross, Angus, 83
Roxana, 111, 123, 214, 247; anachronism in, 48–49, 52–54; double temporal setting in, 53–58; chronology, 63, 72; theme of memory compared with that in *Colonel Jack,* 100–101; biological and psychological time in, 101; rhythms of similar incidents in, 132; ending of, 136, 227; spatial form in, 137–39; repetition in, 140; Roxana's name, 140–41, 142; imitation of speaking voice in, 185–87

Index

Sartre, Jean-Paul: *Nausea*, 160
Schonhorn, Manuel, 26, 27, 36–37, 49
Science fiction, 6
Selkirk, Alexander, 29, 30
Sentence-length, 178
Serious Reflections, 86–94
Settings, 7, 9, 231, 234. See also individual works by Defoe
Shaw, George Bernard; *Saint Joan*, 44, 56
Sherburn, George, 200
Sidney, Sir Philip, 6
Silence, 190–91, 193
Simon Forecastle's Weekly Journal, 168–69, 214
Simultaneity: and printing, 194
Sound, 190–95. See also individual works by Defoe
Spacks, Patricia M., 258 (n. 15)
Spatial form, 12, 42, 107–8, 167, 194, 246; in *Tristram Shandy*, 20; defined, 132, 139–40; and coherence of Defoe's fiction, 143; and emblematic method in *Robinson Crusoe*, 145; and apologues, 151; and emotional force of narratives, 229; and memory, 247; discussions of, 265 (n. 21). See also indiivdual works by Defoe
Speed. See Tempo
Spenser, Edmund: *The Faerie Queene*, 55
Spiritual autobiography, 85–86, 163, 184
Starr, George A., 40, 41, 43, 57, 85, 94, 109, 180, 182, 185, 207
Sterne, Laurence, 1, 106, 170, 255, 256; *Tristram Shandy:* mentioned, 4, 13, 19, 195, 242; and spatial form, 20; and memory, 106–7
Stevick, Philip, 114, 240
Storm, The, 184, 185, 225, 226–29
Swift, Jonathan: *Gulliver's Travels*, 6; *A Tale of a Tub*, 83

Tave, Stuart, 243–44
Tempo: measuring of objective, 16; subjective and objective, 17–18; and representational power, 18; and suspense, 121; and symbolism, 176; and metaphors, 176–77; and clock-time, 178–79; and switches from narration to dialogue, 179; and meaning, 180; and imitation of speaking voice, 185–87; and aural imagination, 202–3; and reading aloud, 202–3, 205; and repetition, 204, 215; and incomplete description, 207, 210–13; and frequency, 213–17; of plague portrayed in *A Journal of the Plague Year*, 220–23, 226, 230–31; determinants of, 246; of remembering texts, 248–49; of cognition, 250. See also Comedy; Fielding; Hogarth; individual works by Defoe
Thorpe, James, 186
Time: mythic, 6, 20, 41; of reading, 8, 9, 17–20; calendar, 20, 28–29, 33–36, 39–43 passim, 49–73 passim, 158–59, 235–42; symbolic, 28–29, 59, 61, 70–73; biological, 73–80; ideas about and literary form, 81–82, 102–3; Defoe's view of man's relationship to, 86–94; extent of Defoe's concern with, 103–4; and the unconscious mind, 170. See also Fielding; Johnson; Richardson; individual works by Defoe
Time-travellers, 55, 56
Tolstoy, Count Leo: *Anna Karenina*, 5
Typography, 200
Typology, 40

Verisimilitude: of Boswell's *Life of Johnson*, 18; spatial, 31–33; temporal, 31–33, 153, 197; and dates, 59, 69, 72, 73;

and moral effects as measure of book's value, 83; and memories of previous parts of text, 166–67

Watt, Ian, 109, 110, 111, 112, 115, 130

Woolf, Virginia: *Orlando*, 55
Word: religious tradition of, 194–95
Wordsworth, William, 211
Wynne, Emmanuel, 23, 27

Zimmerman, Everett, 34, 94, 96